Canto is a paperback imprint which offers a broad range of
titles, both classic and more recent, representing some of the
best and most enjoyable of Cambridge publishing.

The seeds of speech
Language origin and
evolution

JEAN AITCHISON

Rupert Murdoch Professor of Language and Communication,
University of Oxford

CAMBRIDGE
UNIVERSITY PRESS

PUBLISHED BY THE PRESS SYNDICATE OF THE UNIVERSITY OF CAMBRIDGE
The Pitt Building, Trumpington Street, Cambridge, United Kingdom

CAMBRIDGE UNIVERSITY PRESS
The Edinburgh Building, Cambridge CB2 2RU, UK   www.cup.cam.ac.uk
40 West 20th Street, New York NY 10011–4211, USA   www.cup.org
10 Stamford Road, Oakleigh, Melbourne 3166, Australia
Ruiz de Alarcón 13, 28014 Madrid, Spain

First published 1996
Canto edition 2000

Printed in the United Kingdom at the University Press, Cambridge

Typeset in Photina 10/12pt [VN]

A catalogue record for this book is available from the British Library

Library of Congress cataloguing in publication data

Aitchison, Jean, 1938–
    The seeds of speech: language origin and evolution / Jean Aitchison.
    p.   cm. – (Cambridge approaches to lingusitics)
Includes bibliographical references and index.
ISBN 0 521 78571 5 (paperback)
1. Language and languages – Origin.   2. Language acquisition.
3. Linguistic change.   I. Title.   II. Series.
P116.A38   1996
401–dc20   95–47738   CIP

ISBN 0 521 78571 5 paperback

Cover illustration: Linda Combi

Contents

Foreword

'The origin of human language is truly secret and marvellous'
wrote Jacob Grimm in 1851.[1] And unravelling the beginnings of
speech is at first sight as daunting today as in Grimm's time: 'the
echoes of time are lost and its lips are dumb' as R. L. Garner
commented around a century ago.[2] Inevitably, no records of
sounds or writing remain from the early beginnings of language.
The fragments of evidence are all indirect: prehistoric bones, the
behaviour of our ape relatives, linguistic theory, and various other
sources all provide clues (chapter 1). Yet in recent years, huge steps
forward have been taken, as this book will explain.

The topic exerts a perennial fascination: almost all cultures have
legends about how speech began. In China, a demigod gave names
to plants and animals, in India articulate speech was attributed to
the god Indra, and in Greece, to the god Hermes.[3] In the western
Christian tradition, God, after forming 'every beast of the field, and
every fowl of the air',[4] brought them to Adam, the first man, to see
what he would call them. But where did Adam get his inspiration?
The answer is unknown. Either he gave plants and creatures the
names which were 'their own' in some sense, or he invented
arbitrary ones.

Yet in spite of the unsatisfactory nature of the biblical account,
many respectable scholars in the past were unwilling to go against
it (chapter 1). Only in the twentieth century has religious dogmatism
declined sufficiently to allow serious work on the topic to proceed
unhampered.

However, the restraining effect of religion never truly damped
down the numerous bizarre speculations which sprouted up like

weeds. The biblical story itself spawned a variety of odd beliefs, the most pervasive being that Hebrew was the original human language. In the seventeenth century, Francis Mercury van Helmont, for example, argued that the tongue naturally forms sounds which were identical to those uttered by Adam in the Garden of Eden, and that natural Hebrew was older even than Adam, having been used by God for summoning creatures into existence.[5]

The cascade of weird, wild and woolly ideas perturbed the linguistic establishment. They dismissed the whole topic as a playground for cranks, and declared it a 'no-go' area (chapter 1): in 1866, the Linguistic Society of Paris, the foremost language society of its time, banned papers about language origin. And this disapproval continued for over a century, in line with the linguist William Dwight Whitney's comment: 'The greater part of what is said and written on it is mere windy talk.'[6]

All this changed in 1990, when Steven Pinker and Paul Bloom published an influential paper entitled 'Natural language and natural selection' alongside a commentary by over thirty peers in the respected journal Behavioral and Brain Sciences. This paper 'demolished some intellectual roadblocks in progress in understanding the relation between evolution and language'.[7] Pinker and Bloom emphasized that language evolved by normal evolutionary mechanisms, and commented that 'there is a wealth of respectable new scientific information relevant to the evolution of language that has never been properly synthesized'.[8]

This book attempts to provide such a synthesis in a form accessible to the non-specialist: no prior knowledge of language or evolution is required. The book could also be regarded as an informal, readable introduction to linguistics. It summarizes the basic underpinnings of language: the human mouth, ears, brain, and so on. Then it discusses how single words might have arisen, and eventually strung together. As the chapters proceed, more information is added, following as far as possible the path taken by our ancestors as they elaborated language over the millennia.

Of course, advances in our understanding of the nature of language over the past half-century have helped us to look in the right directions. The linguist Noam Chomsky has directed attention to the fact that language is preordained in modern humans, and a recent book *The language instinct* (1994) by Steven Pinker has made arguments for linguistic innateness available to a wide audience.

But the biologist Eric Lenneberg was perhaps the most important linguistic pioneer. In 1967, his ground-breaking book, *The biological foundations of language*, was published. Previously, fierce arguments about whether language was due to 'nature' (biological programming) or to 'nurture' (teaching and learning) had raged in the field of language acquisition. Lenneberg showed that the answer lay somewhere between the two: language had all the hallmarks of behaviour controlled by maturation – that is, like walking, or sexual behaviour, it develops 'naturally' at a preordained time in an individual's life, provided that an adequate, 'nurturing' environment is present. Viewed in this light, the nature versus nurture controversy fades away. In short, language is now known to be 'innately guided behaviour'. Humans are naturally guided to pay attention to certain aspects of language, then they fill in the gaps via learning. They operate much as bees do with flowers (chapter 3). Bees were surely not born with an encyclopaedia of flower types in their minds, yet they unerringly fly to flowers rather than bus-stops or coloured umbrellas. Bees, it transpires, are naturally guided by scent above all, but also by colour and shape. They instinctively fly to flowers due to a combination of these factors which they 'naturally' notice and prioritize, but they have to learn the details of the particular plants in their environment. Humans behave similarly with language.

Of course, holes still remain in our knowledge: in particular, at what stage did language leap from being something new which humans discovered to being something which every newborn human is scheduled to acquire? This is still a puzzle.

But convergence may provide answers. That is, in evolution a bound forward sometimes occurs which is more than the sum of the seemingly small steps which contribute to it. In language, mental developments coincided with physical ones.

Mentally, humans knew how to 'put themselves into another person's shoes', possibly as an offshoot of their ability to deceive one another (chapter 6). This in turn led to an ability to refer to people and things which were out of sight or even non-existent.

They also started to use vocal sounds as grooming devices, the forerunner of the 'hello, how are you?' type of social talk which humans indulge in today.

Physically, a deprived physical environment led to more meat-eating and, as a result, a bigger brain. The enlarged brain led to the premature birth of humans, and in consequence a protracted childhood, during which mothers cooed and crooned to their offspring. An upright stance altered the shape of the mouth and vocal tract, allowing a range of coherent sounds to be uttered (chapter 7).

Together, the mental and physical developments paved the way for language as we know it – though many details still need to be clarified.

Advances in knowledge are like clear patches in a fog, as pointed out by the writer J. G. Farrell in his novel *The siege of Krishnapur*:[9]

> The advance of science is not . . . like a man crossing a river from one stepping-stone to another. It is much more like someone trying to grope his way forward through a London fog. Just occasionally, in a slight lifting of the fog, you can glimpse the truth, establish the location not only of where you are standing but also perhaps of the streets round about . . . The wise scientist deliberately searches for such liftings of the fog because they allow him to fill in the map of his knowledge . . .

The fog surrounding language origin is gradually lifting. In this book I have tried to explain clearly what we already know. Future generations will, I hope, pick up from here and fill in the gaps.

Jean Aitchison
September 1999

Preface

This book deals with human language: how and why it began, how it evolved, and what holds all languages together. This is an enormous topic, which has in the past attracted people with a wide range of interests. This perhaps accounts for the scattered nature of the evidence. This book tries to present an overview of our current knowledge. In some ways, it's several books woven into one, since the angles from which the topic can be approached are multiple.

Many books on language start with an outline of what language involves, its key characteristics, and so on. This book takes a different path. A minimum about language is discussed in the early chapters, just enough to highlight some of its puzzling features. This sets the scene for an exploration of its origin and evolution. As the book progresses, more information about language is added, following as far as possible the elaboration which our ancestors built in to language as it evolved over the millennia.

Inevitably, some decisions had to be taken as to what to include, and what to omit. I have tried not to repeat material from other books I have written: *The articulate mammal* (4th edition 1998), *Language change* (2nd edition 1991), *Words in the mind* (2nd edition 1994). Occasional overlaps were unavoidable, but I have kept them to a minimum.

I am very grateful to the numerous people who sent me offprints, made interesting suggestions, or were willing to engage in stimulating conversations about the topic.

I would like to thank warmly those who read either the whole draft manuscript or large chunks of it. Their helpful and often detailed comments have undoubtedly improved the final text.

These are (in alphabetical order) Judith Ayling (Cambridge University Press), John Ayto (University of Sussex), Roger Goodwin (University of Sussex), Patricia Ingham (University of Oxford), Diana Lewis (University of Oxford), and Paul Meara (University of Swansea). Of these, my thanks go above all to Diana Lewis, my research assistant, who patiently and cheerfully helped to track down obscure references, to keep the bibliography organized, and to prepare the final manuscript. Without her help, it would all have taken a good deal longer.

Oxford   Jean Aitchison

Part 1
Puzzles

1 A natural curiosity:
How did language begin?

'Actually,' says Liz, 'what I *do* suffer from is curiosity. I want to know *what really happened.*'
'When?'
'At the beginning. When human nature began. At the beginning of human time. And I know I'll never know. But I can't stop looking. It's very frustrating. When occasionally it comes over me that I'll never know, I can't quite believe it. Surely, one day, I will find out?'

Margaret Drabble, *A natural curiosity*

We humans have evolved into quite strange beings. Whatever happens in the future is unlikely to be any odder than what has already happened in the past. We differ from other animals in that we cook our food and wear clothes. Other unusual characteristics are a tendency to kill each other, and a mild preference for making love face to face. But perhaps the most important distinguishing feature is human language. This extraordinary system allows us to communicate about anything whatsoever, whether it is present, absent, or even non-existent:

In the Land of the Bumbley Boo
You can buy Lemon pie at the Zoo;
They give away Foxes
In little Pink Boxes
And Bottles of Dandylion Stew.[1]

Nobody has ever encountered the bizarre delights of this fictional land. Yet we have no difficulty in understanding these lines written by the comic writer Spike Milligan. This is quite strange, compared with the communication systems of other animals, which are mostly confined to messages about everyday events, such as food, danger, mating and territorial rights.

Humans are the odd ones out. We are a zoological curiosity, as bizarre in our own way as the hoatzin, a South American bird with a bright blue face, big red eyes and orange crest, which inhabits the Amazon rain forest. Alone among birds, the hoatzin has developed a digestive system similar to that of a cow.[2] We humans are equally strange, because language with its fast and precise sounds has more in common with birdsong than with the vocal signals of our ape relatives.

Lunatic lovers

So how did it all begin, this powerful, weird communication system of ours? Frustratingly, we do not know. The origin of language is criss-crossed with controversy and befogged in mystery. Our earliest written records are around 5,000 years old, though most are more recent. By comparing different early languages, we can reconstruct what some languages may have been like up to 10,000 years ago, according to the standard view.[3] Yet language must have evolved at least 50,000 years ago, and most researchers propose a date around 100,000 years ago. Until recently, how it all began was an unfashionable question, a playground for cranks.

Curious theories abounded. Take the Noah's Ark view, that Chinese was possibly the primitive language of humankind. It was spoken by Noah and his family in the Ark, and so survived the flood. At least, this was the opinion of the seventeenth-century writer, John Webb, in 'An historical essay endeavouring the probability that the language of the Empire of China is the Primitive Language'.[4] He is a typical 'lunatic lover of language', a name given to the crazy fringe who promote private and peculiar ideas about speech and its origins.[5]

Or consider the views of James Burnett Lord Monboddo, a Scottish lawyer, who in 1773 published a book in six volumes on *The origin and progress of language*. He maintained that humans learned how to spin and weave from spiders, how to construct dams from beavers, and how to sing and speak from birds. The cuckoo, the raven and the parrot, he noted, produced almost alphabetical sounds. Therefore in his view human articulation was the result of imitating such birds. 'Lord Monboddo gives the impression of being an English gentleman accustomed to having even his most eccentric and fanciful ideas listened to with deference', an Italian researcher aptly commented.[6]

Or take the Abbé O'Donnelly, a Frenchman who claimed in the mid nineteenth century to have deciphered the hieroglyphs on an obelisk brought to Paris from Luxor in Egypt. He boasted of his 'new and prodigious discovery of the original universal language', asserting that he had shed light on the 'form of words at the birth of speech'. His translation 'was sufficient to open the eyes of a mole', he noted – though he lamented that his discoveries had not yet been acknowledged, with his 'words and results being blown away by the wind'.[7]

As absurd claims sprouted like puffballs, the question of language origin was shunned by serious scholars. In 1866, a ban on the topic was incorporated into the founding statutes of the Linguistic Society of Paris, perhaps the foremost academic linguistic institution of the time: 'The Society does not accept papers on either the origin of language or the invention of a universal language.'[8]

Inquiry into language origin was considered a waste of time. The American linguist William Dwight Whitney noted in 1893:

No theme in linguistic science is more often and more voluminously treated than this . . . nor any . . . with less profitable result in proportion to the labour expended; the greater part of what is said and written upon it is mere windy talk, the assertion of subjective views which commend themselves to no mind save the one that produces them, and which are apt to be offered with a confidence, and defended with a tenacity, that is in inverse ratio to their acceptableness. This has given the whole question a bad repute among sober-minded philologists.[9]

Yet scholarly disapproval did not stop speculation. In 1977, one researcher counted twenty-three 'principal theories' of language origin.[10] Another acidly commented: 'The very fact . . . that human animals are ready to engage in a great "garrulity" over the merits and demerits of essentially unprovable hypotheses, is an exciting testimony to the gap between humans and other animals.'[11]

It's like a juicy fruit dangling just out of reach. Humans have a natural curiosity about it seemingly built into their minds: 'Few questions in the study of human language have attracted so much attention, provoked as much controversy, or resisted so resolutely their answers as that of the origin of language', noted a recent writer.[12]

So what has changed now? The origin and evolution of language has suddenly become a respectable topic. In the past few years, there has been an explosion of papers in reputable journals, as well as several books. A cynical view is that academic areas of interest swing in and out of fashion like clothes. But there is a more realistic, twofold explanation.

First, religious dogmatism has declined. At one time, respectable scholars were often unwilling to contradict the view found at the beginning of the Bible, that God formed all living things, and then assigned the naming of them to Adam, the first man: 'And out of the ground the Lord God formed every beast of the field, and every fowl of the air; and brought them unto Adam to see what he would call them: and whatsoever Adam called every living creature, that was the name thereof. And Adam gave names to all cattle, and to the fowl of the air, and to every beast of the field.'[13] The eighteenth-century philosopher Jean Jacques Rousseau had to argue for the double invention of language to counter this problem: 'Adam spoke, Noah spoke; but it is known that Adam was taught by God himself. In scattering, the children of Noah abandoned agriculture, and the first common tongue perished with the first society.'[14]

Second, and more importantly, sufficient progress has been made in the study of humans and their place in the animal world to be able to approach the topic in a useful way. All primates, the animal 'order' to which humans belong, have some overlap in their sound-producing and hearing abilities. But the vocal output of our primate relatives is less illuminating than was once hoped: 'Quite simply, the normal state of affairs is not to find unequivocal correlations between the sound and its behavioral context. Instead, the same sound often occurs in apparently different situations, and a variety of sounds can be found to occur in a given situation.'[15] In addition, classification of the sounds is difficult: 'Boundaries are blurred by intermediate or transitional acoustic forms'.[16] In the circumstances, a straight comparison between, say, chimp and human vocalizations is limited in what it can reveal.

More informative, perhaps, is a comparison with the animal

communication system which has most in common with human
language. As mentioned earlier (p. 4), this may be birdsong. Let us
consider the matter further.

A bird-like skill

'I happen to be acquainted with an anti-social African gray
parrot in England named Toto, whose owner brings him out
now and then in the evening to show him off to guests', wrote a
New Yorker journalist. 'After a few minutes of bad-tempered
staring at the company, the bird usually says, "Toto go bye-byes
now," and his owner carries him back to the proper room and
puts him in his cage, safe and private under a tea towel. Is Toto
really talking?'[17]

Toto is talking, but he does not have 'language' as humans
understand it. Yet Toto, like humans, has an ability to make
distinctive sounds that is rare in the animal world – even though
the method Toto uses to produce them is rather different from that
used by humans.[18] But this is not the only similarity between birds
and humans. There are several others.[19]

Many birds emit two types of sounds: calls, such as a danger call
or a congregation call, which are mostly innate, and songs, which
often involve learning. Humans also have inbuilt 'calls', the cries
uttered by babies, at least two of which are distinguishable
worldwide: a pain cry and a hunger cry.[20] But language itself
requires learning, and it exists alongside this old 'call' system. Birds
and humans therefore share a double-barrelled system, with one
part in place at birth, and the other acquired later.

In birdsong, each individual note is meaningless: the sequence
of notes is all-important. Similarly, in humans, a single segment of
sound such as *b* or *l* does not normally have a meaning. The output
makes sense only when sounds are strung together. So this
double-layering – known as duality or double articulation – provides
a further parallel. And in both birds and humans, sound segments
are fitted into an overall rhythm and intonation pattern.

As with humans, the song of a single species of bird may have
different but related 'dialects'. The white-crowned sparrow, a
Californian resident, has dialects so different, even within the San

Francisco area, that 'someone with a cultivated ear would be able to tell where he or she was in California, blindfolded, simply by listening to their songs'.[21] And both birdsong and human language are normally controlled by the left side of the brain, even though the mechanisms by which this control is exercised are quite different. Young birds have a period of sub-song, a type of twittering which emerges before the development of full song. This is like the 'babbling' of human infants who experimentally produce repetitive *bababa*, *mamama* type sequences when they are a few months old. Many birds have to acquire their song during a shortish 'critical period' when they are young, otherwise they never learn to sing normally. Similarly, humans acquire language best during a 'sensitive period' in the first few years of life.[22]

In short, both birds and humans produce fluent complex sounds, they both have a double-barrelled, double-layered system involving tunes and dialects, which is controlled by the left half of the brain. Youngsters have a type of sub-language en route to the full thing, and are especially good at acquiring the system in the early years of their lives.

But some very real differences also exist. Mostly, only male birds sing. Females remain songless, unless they are injected with the male hormone testosterone.[23] And considerable variation is found between the songs of different birds, more than between different languages.[24] In addition, bird communication is a fairly long-distance affair, compared with the intimacy of human language. Sometimes, the effect can travel over several kilometres, as with the New Zealand kakapo, a flightless parrot which makes spectacular sonic booms, somewhat like the note produced by blowing across the top of a bottle, in its efforts to procure a mate.[25] These kakapo booms can go on all night, and leave the kakapo in such a state of arousal that it has attempted to copulate even with the feet of the ornithologists studying it.

As the kakapo's behaviour suggests, the purposes for which birds vocalize are somewhat narrower than those of humans. Birds sing in order to attract a mate, or to repel trespassers.[26]

A link between language origin and mating, and between language and song has sometimes been proposed: 'Language was born in the courting days of mankind – the first utterances of speech I fancy to myself like something between the nightly love-lyrics of puss upon the tiles and the melodious love-songs of the nightingale', suggested the Danish linguist Otto Jespersen,[27] though this theory has been damned by others: 'If our hominid ancestors used song in sexual advertisement and courtship, more recent selective forces have made such a habit much rarer', was one response to Jespersen's ideas.[28] Or as another noted: 'As for courtship, if we are to judge from the habits of the bulk of mankind, it has always been a singularly silent occupation.'[29] At the most, perhaps, language was an additional aid: courtship was not its primary role.

In short, humans use language for many more purposes than birds use song. Birds do not, for example, serenade the beauties of nature, as poets such as Christopher Marlowe sometimes assumed:

> By shallow Rivers, to whose falls,
> Melodious byrds sing Madrigalls.[30]

The similarities between birdsong and human language show that parallel systems can emerge independently in quite different species. Certain features have apparently proved useful for sophisticated sound systems. Yet this observation raises as many problems as it solves. Let us now consider how we might explore the origins of our extraordinary communication system.

The pieces of the puzzle

The origin of language is like a vast prehistoric jigsaw puzzle, in which numerous fragments of evidence must be painstakingly assembled, somewhat in the manner of Agatha Christie's fictional detective Hercule Poirot:

> Mrs. Gardener was wrestling with a jigsaw ... 'But about detecting, I would so like to know your methods...'
> Hercule Poirot said 'It is a little like your puzzle, Madame. One assembles the pieces. It is like a mosaic – many colours and patterns – and every strange-shaped little piece must be fitted into its own place.'
> Poirot went on: 'And sometimes it is like that piece of your puzzle just now. One arranges very methodically the pieces of the puzzle – one sorts the colours – and then perhaps a piece of one colour that should fit in with – say, the fur rug, fits in instead in a black cat's tail.'[31]

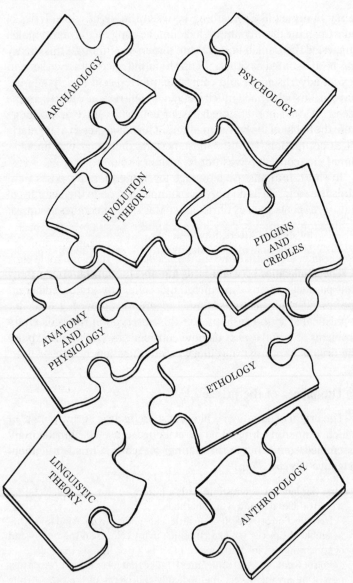

Figure 1.1 The pieces of the puzzle

The pieces of the language puzzle are of two main types, external (non-linguistic), and internal (linguistic), that is clues from outside human language on the one hand, and information gleaned from languages on the other (see Fig 1.1).

External evidence comes from at least half a dozen different areas of knowledge: origin of species (evolution theory), digging up remains (archaeology), how bodies work (anatomy and physiology), animal behaviour (ethology), human minds (psychology) and human societies (anthropology).

Linguistics, the study of language, provides the internal evidence. Among its multiple branches, pidgins and creoles are particularly valuable sources of information.

Pidgins are subsidiary language systems, spoken by people with no common language. They have a small vocabulary: a few basic words are stretched to cover a wide range. For example, in Tok Pisin, spoken in Papua New Guinea, *pik man* 'pig man' is a male pig, *pik meri* 'pig woman' is a sow, and *pikinini pik* 'child pig' is a piglet. *Pul bilong kanu* 'pull of canoe' is a canoe paddle, *pul bilong pisin* 'pull of bird' is a bird's wing, and *pul bilong pis* 'pull of fish' is a fin. The grammar is simple: word endings are few, so the order of words is important. *Yu mas pul strong* 'you must pull strong' means 'You must paddle (your canoe) energetically', *Mi go painim pis* 'I go find fish' means 'I'm going fishing'.

Creoles are pidgins which have become someone's first language – usually when speakers of different languages have married, and communicated via a pidgin, which has been learned by their children as a first language. At this point, the creole expands dramatically, and is eventually indistinguishable from any other language.

Pidgins and creoles are in one way unlike early language in humans, as they are based on one or more existing languages. But they are in other ways illuminating, because they are similar the world over. They may show how humans 'naturally' devise and elaborate a simple system.

The Greek historian Thucydides, writing in the fifth century BC, hoped that his words 'would be judged useful by those who want to understand clearly the events which happened in the past, and which, human nature being what it is, will at some time or other be repeated in the future in much the same way'.[32] This book is taking the reverse path over pidgins and creoles, in assuming that recent developments can provide information about what might have happened in the much earlier past.

External and internal fragments of evidence overlap and interweave, and the external versus internal distinction is not always clearcut: the comparison between human language and birdsong contained a mixture of both. But the overall message is clear: evidence has to be assembled from both outside language, and inside it, much as a detective in a murder enquiry must not only hunt widely for clues, but must also examine the corpse with care. This leaves a problem. How is all the evidence to be woven together?

'Science is built up with facts, as a house is with stones. But a collection of facts is no more a science than a heap of stones is a house', said the French scientist Jules Poincaré.[33] In house-building, it's essential to have an overall plan, and not just heap up stones randomly. Similarly, in research, it's important to have a theory, a framework into which to place the pieces. If they do not fit, the old theory has to be abandoned, and a new one proposed. But how can the stones be structured, when it's unclear what kind of a building is under construction?

Sometimes, an intermediate stage is needed, before a full plan is possible. An architect starts by asking basic simple questions, such as: 'What is the building for?' An answer such as: 'To provide shelter from the weather' leads to other questions, such as: 'What kind of weather, hot or cold?', 'How many people must it shelter?', and so on. Similarly, preliminary questions on the nature of language can be asked, which will lead onwards. At the same time, key questions can be identified, some of which have been asked for decades. Let us consider some of these.

The amoeba question

> An amoeba named Sam, and his brother
> Were having a drink with each other
>   In the midst of their quaffing,
>   They split themselves laughing,
> And each of them now is a mother.[34]

Did language evolve like an amoeba, as a simple outline which gradually became elaborated? Or was it a sprawling mish-mash which slowly neatened itself up into a coherent system? The best-known nineteenth-century theories about language origin took the amoeba viewpoint. The so-called 'pooh-pooh' theory traced language back to instinctive cries of pain or joy, perhaps 'Ooh!', 'Ee!', 'Ah!' The 'bow-wow' theory assumed that the noises of animals were all-important, as ancient hunters imitated the growls and squeaks of a beast they planned to track down. The 'yo-he-ho' theory suggested that words such as 'Heave!' came first, originating in the involuntary grunts which occur in heaving and hauling.[35]

But language need not have started with single words, it could have begun with whole melodies: 'For moving a young heart, or repelling an unjust agressor, nature dictates accents, cries, lamentations...', Rousseau proposed, 'and that is why the first languages were singable and passionate before they became simple and methodical.'[36] This idea was taken up by Otto Jespersen with his 'puss upon the tiles' scenario (pp. 8–9): 'The speech of uncivilized and primitive men was more passionately agitated than ours, more like music or song.'[37]

More recently, the amoeba question has arisen again, though in a more sophisticated guise. According to one view, proposed by the linguist Derek Bickerton, an innate 'bioprogram' caused simple basic distinctions to leap into place, both in the development of language in the species, and in creoles.[38] This bioprogram is supposedly part of the human mind-set.

But according to an alternative, 'spaghetti junctions' view, various possibilities were tried out, like a car with numerous possible exits on a motorway: 'Spaghetti Junction' is the nickname given to a particularly complicated British motorway intersection (cloverleaf). Maybe different routes were chosen on different journeys. In the long run, several factors converged to make speakers more likely to choose some options rather than others.[39] But the final route selected was not automatic. It may have taken generations to become firm, and was probable rather than inevitable.[40]

The rabbit-out-of-a-hat problem

The rabbit-out-of-a-hat problem links in with the amoeba question. According to one view, language emerged fairly suddenly, like a rabbit pulled out of a hat. Reasons for this viewpoint differ. Some propose a remarkable mutation in the early hominid gene pool, others suggest that an already enlarged brain found itself an extra use: 'Such a conception of language emergence is reminiscent of the Roman myth, where Minerva sprang forth from the head of Jupiter, fully armed and wonderfully wise', it has been suggested.[41]

In contrast, others assume that language evolved slowly and piecemeal, over multiple millennia, like a mosaic being painstakingly assembled out of various bits and pieces.[42]

This debate has been rumbling on for over a century, as when Whitney disagreed in 1872 with Heymann Steinthal, a professor at the University of Berlin:

> We think our appreciation of the wondrous character of language a vastly higher one than Professor Steinthal; for while he holds that any two or three human beings, putting their heads together, in any age and under any circumstances not only can, but of necessity must, produce it in all its essential features, we think it a possible result only of the accumulated labor of a series of generations, working on step by step, making every acquired item the means of a new acquisition.'[43]

But the amoeba question and the rabbit-out-of-a-hat problem cannot be solved in isolation. Considerably more background information is needed about the nature of language before they can be unravelled.

In the remaining chapters in part 1, 'Puzzles', three puzzling but important questions about language will be considered. First, what is language for (chapter 2)? Second, why do languages differ so much (chapter 3)? Third, does language depend on general intelligence, or is it an independent skill (chapter 4)?

These issues will prepare the way for part 2, 'Origin', which will in turn lead to part 3, 'Evolution'. Finally, part 4, 'Diffusion', will consider how language diffused around the world, and what holds all languages together, in spite of their geographical dispersal.

Summary

The origin of language has long been a disreputable study – but recently there has been a new upsurge of interest. Numerous pieces of evidence, both linguistic and non-linguistic, must be pieced together as if in a gigantic jigsaw puzzle.

Human language is bizarre: it can cope with any topic, even imaginary ones, and has more in common with bird communication than with the calls of our ape cousins. The similarities of language and birdsong suggest that sophisticated sound systems may independently acquire similar features.

The amoeba question is a key issue: whether language started out simple and then became elaborated, or whether it was intrinsically messy and then got neatened. This ties in with the question of speed, as to whether language emerged fast, like a rabbit out of a hat, or slowly over millennia. This and other questions of language origin need to be discussed against further background information about language.

2 A peculiar habit:
What is language for?

> It is worth repeating at this point the theories that Ford had
> come up with, on his first encounter with human beings, to
> account for their peculiar habit of continually stating and
> restating the very, very obvious, as in 'It's a nice day', or 'You're
> very tall', or 'So this is it, we're going to die.'
> His first theory was that if humans didn't keep exercising their
> lips, their mouths probably seized up.
> After a few months' of observation, he had come up with a
> second theory, which was this – 'If human beings don't keep
> exercising their lips, their brains start working.'
>
> Douglas Adams, *The restaurant at the end of the universe*

What exactly is language FOR? To many people, the answer seems
obvious. It's for the transfer of useful facts, such as 'Dinner will be
served at eight o'clock', 'Peter's uncle has twisted his ankle', and
'Kangaroos live in Australia'. The belief that 'information talking'[1]
is the primary role of language dates back at least to the
seventeenth century, when the English philosopher John Locke
argued in his influential *Essay concerning human understanding*
(1690) that language is 'the great conduit, whereby men convey
their discoveries, reasoning, and knowledge to one another'.[2]

But language does not necessarily involve the transfer of
information, often it is just polite chatter, as satirized by Douglas
Adams in the quotation at the top of the chapter.

Even when information is apparently transferred, its reliability
is not guaranteed. The speaker might have been lying, or even
misunderstood: 'We are now at take-off', said the pilot of a Boeing
747. He meant: 'We are now in the process of taking off.' The
air-traffic controller assumed he meant: 'We are waiting at the
take-off point.' In consequence, 583 people died as two aeroplanes
collided on a runway in Tenerife.[3]

Weaker claims about the purpose of language seem superficially plausible: 'Language... was invented by man as a means of communicating his thoughts, when mere looks and gestures proved insufficient', proposed the nineteenth-century scholar Max Müller.[4] Yet the notion of 'thought' is vague, and could cover the intention behind just about every possible utterance, from commands to apologies to poems.

This chapter will therefore consider the purpose problem, and discuss how it relates to the origin of language.

Multiple purposes

The question 'What is language for?' can be divided into two: 'For what purpose did language develop?' and 'For what purpose is language used nowadays?' The answers to these two questions may not coincide. A poet today might answer: 'To write poetry', yet this may not have been an early use.

Language today is used for so many purposes, that the basic one is hard to perceive. Introductory books usually list a range, typically:[5]

(1) providing information:
The train at platform five is the London–York Express
(2) giving commands:
Don't shout!
(3) expressing feelings:
Oh what a beautiful morning!
(4) social talking:
Hi, how are you doing?
(5) word play and poetry:
The apple made cider inside her inside.
(6) talking about language:
Donking isn't a word!

And more could be added, such as asking questions, getting rid of superfluous nervous energy, and so on (see Fig. 2.1).

The original role of language is therefore unclear. But this needs to be identified in order to understand why language developed. One way forward is to look at what language today is good at, and what it finds difficult to express. This may provide clues about its early functions.

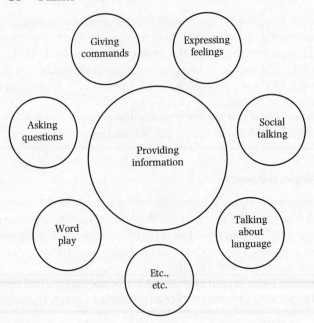

Figure 2.1 Traditional view of language functions

A conveyer of information?

Language is moderately good at conveying simple pieces of factual information, such as 'Bob is Petronella's cousin', providing the speaker is telling the truth. Such information talking is usually assumed to be at the core of language, as mentioned above. Yet its efficiency in this role depends on the type of information being conveyed.

Language is bad at handling spatial information, whether for tying knots, following routes or learning about the circulation of the blood. The English writer Hilaire Belloc once said: 'If you can describe clearly without a diagram the proper way of making this or that knot, then you are a master of the English tongue.'[6] Perhaps he should have said: 'Even if you are a master of the English language, you will have considerable difficulty describing a knot.' Consider the instructions for doing one of the simplest knots, a figure of eight:

1. Pass the end of the rope over the standing part.
2. Take the end under the standing part away from the loop.
3. Bring the end of the rope back up over itself towards the loop.
4. Pass the end down through the loop.
5. Pull tight.[7]

Without its accompanying diagram, this description is difficult to follow, although accurate. In this case, a picture is truly 'worth a thousand words'.

Or take the following information from a widely used guidebook to Brazil:

> The hike begins...where a paved jogging track runs for 1200 metres...At the end of the track pick up the trail on the other side of the cement tank in the tall grass. Follow this trail (always taking the uphill forks) for 100 metres. At the old foundations, some 30 metres above the water, the trail ascends steeply for 60 metres until levelling off on the narrow ridge...The trail to follow is up the far left-hand side ridge. At the base of the rock the trail deviates slightly to the right.[8]

These instructions are possibly as clear as language allows – but a map would have made things clearer.

Language is also poor at conveying information about sensation or emotion. 'There is no language for pain. Except bad language. Except swearing. There's no language for it. Ouch, ow, oof, gah. Jesus. Pain is its own language', says Martin Amis in his novel *London Fields*.[9] 'The paucity of language we have to describe emotional life can constrain our capacity to communicate the range and subtlety of our emotional responses', commented the journalist Susie Orbach.[10] And the poet Byron aptly expresses the failure of language to capture deep feelings when he talks of his pleasure in pathless woods and the lonely shore,[11] where he can:

> mingle with the Universe, and feel
> What I can ne'er express.

Language is therefore poor at conveying spatial information and information about feelings. And there are other problems too, as will be discussed below.

A propensity for lying

> Matilda told such Dreadful Lies,
> It made one Gasp and Stretch one's Eyes;
> Her Aunt, who, from her Earliest Youth,
> Had kept a Strict Regard for Truth,
> Attempted to Believe Matilda;
> The effort very nearly killed her.[12]

Officially, lying is often discouraged, as in Hilaire Belloc's *Cautionary tales for children*, where Matilda who told lies ends up burned to death.

Yet 'little white lies' – trivial untruths told for social reasons – are common, especially in cultures where politeness requires a reply: 'How far is it to the top of the mountain?' asked a visitor to Greece, at wooded Mount Pelion. 'About an hour's walk' was the answer she received from a villager at the foot of the mountain, from a shepherd half-way up, and from a goatherd two-thirds of the way to the summit.

Even in cultures where lying is officially discouraged, people are still 'economical with the truth' – a phrase coined by a government official to deny he was lying. Fanciful elaboration is also common: Pooh-Bah, a character in the light opera *The Mikado*, speaks of adding 'corroborative detail, intended to give artistic verisimilitude to an otherwise bald and unconvincing narrative'.[13] Lying is so common, a whole anthology of real-life lies was recently published.[14] And some fibbers even take pleasure in their skill, according to the English writer Rudyard Kipling in his poem 'The Lie'.

> There is pleasure in the wet, wet clay,
> When the artist's hand is potting it.
> There is pleasure in the wet, wet lay,
> When the poet's hand is blotting it ...
> But the pleasure felt in these is as chalk to Cheddar cheese
> When it comes to a well-made Lie. –
> To a quite unwreckable Lie,
> To a most impeccable Lie!
> To a water-tight, fire-proof, angle-iron, sunk-hinge, time-lock,
> steel-faced Lie![15]

In short, 'the human race is greatly given to lying', as the journalist Katherine Whitehorn commented.[16] Indeed the ultimate goal of language learning may be the skill of lying, the ability to talk convincingly about something entirely fictitious, with no back-up circumstantial evidence, since, according to one view, 'real lying . . . is the deliberate use of language as a tool . . . with the content of the message unsupported by context to mislead the listener'.[17] This is quite odd, compared with the communication systems of other animals, which are mostly confined to fixed messages about everyday events, such as food, danger, mating and territorial rights.

Yet the skill of lying is a valuable one, since it involves displacement – reference to absent or non-existent events. This is an important characteristic of language. A tabby cat cannnot relay information about past happenings: 'It's a disgrace: that drunken lout threw a bowl of water over me yesterday', nor warn another of a future danger: 'Be careful, my dear, that snotty child likes pulling cats' tails.' Displacement is especially useful for talking about negative information: 'Sorry there's no milk: it hasn't arrived yet.'

A human could do all this and more. Furthermore, narrating stories is deeply ingrained in all human cultures: most of literature is based on the ability to make non-existent events plausible. So an ability to talk about non-reality is a useful skill, which may be used for good or evil purposes. It is crucial to language, and its origin will be discussed in chapter 6.

But, to conclude, even when language contains information, this may be false or misleading. 'Information talking', therefore, may not be the main or original role of language – even though it is nowadays an important one. Let us now turn to what language is good at.

Talking for the sake of talking

Language is particularly good at promoting interaction between people. It 'oils social wheels', even when nothing of substance is said, as pointed out by the anthropologist Bronislaw Malinowksi, who argued against 'the false conception of language as a means of transfusing ideas from the head of the speaker to that of the listener'.[18] He stressed the social importance of 'talking for the sake of talking', which he labelled 'phatic communion'.

It's easy to think up examples. Ritual words and gestures are exchanged when people meet: 'Good morning', 'Hi there!', 'Hello again!', and there are standard topics of conversation. In Britain this is traditionally the weather, as the eighteenth-century lexicographer Samuel Johnson noted: 'When two Englishmen meet, their first talk is of the weather.'[19] In other cultures, it may be the health of relatives, as in the following exchange between a villager and a city-bred young man who has just returned to his home village in Karnataka, South India:

> Young man: How are you?
> Villager: By the grace of God, all are fine. My son is employed now. Many people have come to offer their daughters to him already. My daughter attained puberty recently. She is sent to her husband's place. If that Lord Venkateshwara of Tirupathi opens his eyes, I will be a grandfather soon.[20]

Conversational interaction between friends often supplies a minimum of information, but a maximum of supportive chat. This often takes the form of repetition, both self-repetition and other-repetition, as in the following conversation:

> Marge: Can I have one of the Tabs?
> Do you want to split it?
> Do you want to split a Tab?
> Kate: Do you want to split MY Tab?
> Vivian: No.
> Marge: Kate, do you want to split my Tab?
> Kate: No, I don't want to split your Tab.[21]

Meaningless words, or even misunderstood words can keep a conversation going, a point often satirized by Alan Bennett in his plays:

> Les: He's had a stroke. What is a stroke?
> Marjorie: Why?
> Les: This old man had had one.
> Marjorie: What old man?
> Les: I'm telling you.
> Marjorie: Les.
> Les: What?
> Marjorie: You're still not thinking about the army.
> Les: No.

Marjorie: You've not been getting yourself vaccinated?
Les: No. I want to tell you about this couple. Listen to me about
       this couple. This husband and wife.
Marjorie: I'm not interested in husbands and wives.[22]

So 'solidarity talking', talking to maintain social contacts, is
widespread and important. It may be one of the major original roles
of language, as will be outlined in chapter 6.

Smooth tales

Language is a major tool in power struggles. Its persuasive force
in private and public life has been recognized throughout the ages:
'Every woman is infallibly to be gained by every sort of flattery, and
every man by one sort or another', said the Earl of Chesterfield in a
letter to his son (1752). A somewhat cynical heroine in Jane
Austen's *Pride and prejudice* comments to a honey-tongued suitor:
'It is happy for you that you possess the talent of flattering with
delicacy. May I ask whether these pleasing attentions proceed from
the impulse of the moment, or are the result of previous study?'[23]
Or consider the editor trying to fob off an investigative journalist in
Michael Dobbs's novel *House of cards*: 'His mind was charging
through his Thesaurus of flannel, words which were noncommittal
but which left their audience with an appropriately warm feeling of
encouragement. It was a well-thumbed volume.'[24]

In recent times, the power of persuasion is obvious in advertising:
'You can fool all the people all of the time if the advertising is right
and the budget is big enough', commented the American film
producer Joseph E. Levine.[25]

And political language, according to George Orwell, 'is designed
to make lies sound truthful and murder respectable, and to give an
appearance of solidity to pure wind'[26] – an assertion supported by
an extract from the official minutes of a meeting at the White
House (1969): 'You can say that this Administration will have the
first complete, far-reaching attack on the problem of hunger in
history. Use all the rhetoric, as long as it doesn't cost money',
American ex-president Richard Nixon is reported as saying.[27]

But it's not just flattery, advertising and political language which influence people. So can various other forms of language, as satirized by W. S. Gilbert in the light opera *Patience*:

> You must lie upon the daisies and discourse in novel phrases of
>   your complicated state of mind,
> The meaning doesn't matter if it's only idle chatter of a
>   transcendental kind.
> And everyone will say,
> As you walk your mystic way,
> If this young man expresses himself in terms too deep for me,
> Why what a very singularly deep young man this deep young
>   man must be![28]

To take a more recent example, academic gobbledegook is used to impress in a science-fiction story: 'Olgarkov had originated the fashionable saying "Silence is an epiphenomenon of organisation". No-one knew what it meant, but it sounded good at parties.'[29]

An important role of language, then, is to influence others: 'Language is an efficient way to change another's behavior', notes one researcher. 'By talking, we can change what someone does. Sometimes what gets done involves nonverbal consequences, as when we ask someone to move something or to bring something to us. Sometimes it involves verbal consequences, as when we change what someone else has to say about something.'[30]

In conclusion, language is particularly good at interaction and persuasion. The question of how other primates interact and persuade, and how this relates to the origin of language will be explored in chapter 6 (see Fig. 2.2).

But these observations raise an important question: if language is so good at handling these social aspects of our lives, is it just something humans have invented as a social device, a cultural artefact, similar to table manners? Or is language ability a special inbuilt skill? This question might be answered if another puzzle is considered. Why do languages differ so much? This will be the topic of the next chapter.

Summary

This chapter looked at the role of language. The uses of language are so numerous and complex in modern society, that its

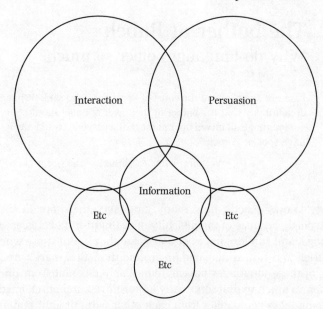

Figure 2.2 Realistic view of language functions

original role was considered by looking at what language is good at, and what it is bad at.

In spite of the widespread view that language is primarily for conveying information, language is not particularly good at this: it is poor at handling spatial information, and information about emotions. And even factual information may be false, as humans often lie. But lying reveals an important property of language, that of displacement – dealing with absent phenomena.

Language is particularly good in social roles, at maintaining social ties and influencing others.

The social roles of language lead to a crucial question: is language a cultural artefact, such as table manners, or is it a special inbuilt skill?

3 The bother at Babel:
Why do languages differ so much?

I am not like a lady at the court of Versailles, who said: 'What a dreadful pity that the bother at the tower of Babel should have got language all mixed up; but for that, everyone would always have spoken French.'

Voltaire, letter to Catherine the Great (1767)

Nobody knows exactly how many languages there are in the world, partly because of the difficulty of distinguishing between a language, and sub-languages or dialects within it. But those who have tried to count usually end up around the 5,000 mark.[1] And many of these languages appear remarkably different from one another, so much so that some early linguistic researchers claimed that 'languages could differ from each other without limit and in unpredictable ways'.[2]

For a start, consider two sentences from Mohawk, an American-Indian language once spoken around the Mohawk River in New York State:

Ieksá:'a   raksá:'a   wahonwá:ienhte'
girl   boy   hit
'The girl hit the boy'

Ieksá:'a   raksá:'a   wahshakó:ienhte'
girl   boy   hit
'The boy hit the girl'[3]

The immediate response of an English speaker is to ask how any Mohawk speaker knows who is doing what to who, since the words for 'boy' and 'girl' come in the same order in both sentences, and in exactly the same form. The answer is: 'Look inside the verb.' In the first sentence, the sequence -honwá- in the verb shows that a female did something to a male, and in the second the sequence -hshakó- indicates that a male did something to a female.

Or think about Mam, a language spoken in western Guatemala.

This language has no general word for *lie*, as in 'lie down', 'lie on the ground', 'lie in bed'. In Mam, there are numerous different words. A Mam speaker has to note not only who or what is lying – human, animal or thing – but also the position adopted, as in the following partial selection of terms for a human male:

mutsl	'he is lying on his stomach'
pak'l	'he is lying on his back'
tşaltš	'he is lying on his side'
qinl	'he is lying outstretched'
leql	'he is lying sprawled (probably intoxicated)'
kutşl	'he is lying alone in a house (probably sick)'[4]

And the same thing is true of standing: speakers need to observe whether the person was standing up without support, or was leaning forwards or backwards against anything, whether they were standing upright or with their head bent, whether they had their legs apart, or were standing on one leg. And so on. And further words are required for different types of sitting. As the writer of the article from which the above examples are taken noted: 'Why the speakers of Mam have an insatiable need for an ever finer elaboration of various visual impressions remains to me fascinating, but unexplained.'[5]

Or going further afield, consider the Guugu Yimidhirr language, spoken in the north-eastern tip of Australia.[6] Guugu Yimidhirr has a weird system for handling full nouns, by English standards. Look at the following sentences:

Billy-ngun	nganhi	nhaadhi
Billy	me	saw
'Billy saw me'		

Ngayu	Billy	nhaadhi
I	Billy	saw
'I saw Billy'		

Billy	dhadaa
Billy	going-to-go
'Billy is going to go'	

In Guugu Yimidhirr, the order of words is fairly variable. To distinguish between the person who saw and the one who was

seen an ending is added. This is unsurprising, even though Guugu
Yimidhirr adds the ending -*ngun* onto Billy, the person seeing,
rather than the person seen, as is more usual in European
languages.

But now consider the third sentence above. Billy is the person
going, but he does not have an ending. Why? There is no need for
any special ending on Billy, it transpires, *except* when Billy does
something which involves someone else, a so-called ergative system.[7]

These examples from Mohawk, Mam and Guugu Yimidhirr
provide a brief glimpse of some of the differences found between
human languages. This leads to a serious question: why do
languages differ so much?

The 'Tower of Babel' solution is possibly the oldest response.
This widespread myth claims that one primitive language existed
until some event destroyed this unity. In its best-known form,
found in the Bible, humans tried to build a tower which would
reach the sky. God, in anger at this presumptuousness, 'did there
confound the language of all the earth: and from thence did scatter
them abroad upon the face of all the earth'.[8] These days, this old
myth has relatively few supporters. It also mistakenly implies that
fixed systems are an advantage.

This chapter will first point out why rigid systems are a
disadvantage. It will then consider reasons why languages might
differ.

The blue-footed booby problem

'If it moves, salute it; if it doesn't move, paint it.' This rigid
rule-of-thumb is allegedly used by sailors on board ship.[9] A similar
type of rule is used by the blue-footed booby, a seabird which
inhabits the Galapagos islands.[10] Its 'nest' is a ring of guano
(birdshit) marked out on the ground. Here, booby parents work by
a strict application of the rule: 'If a chick is inside the ring, care for
it; if it is outside, ignore it.' A booby chick which has flopped or been
pushed outside will simply be ignored, no matter how much it
struggles and twitters, even if it is less than a metre away from its
parents.

As booby behaviour shows, owners of rigid systems face a

serious problem. They cannot handle new situations, and are obliged to choose between a fixed set of options. Consider the grasshopper which has to choose between six messages in its chirps:

(1) Isn't life good!
(2) I feel like making love
(3) You're trespassing on my territory
(4) She's mine
(5) Would you like to make love?
(6) How nice to have made love![11]

It's as if humans had to choose between 'Hallo', 'Goodbye', 'Please', 'Thankyou', 'I love you' and 'Hurrah!'

In human language, an obsessive desire for exactness is likely to be a sign of mental illness, as a bizarre case history shows.

Sixteen-year-old Alice 'keeps asking questions', her father informed the psychiatrist: 'Nothing we say seems right.'[12] For months, she asked about leaves, starting with 'Are the leaves green?' As her father described it:

> Of course I'd say 'Yes the leaves *are* green.' And then she'd ask 'Are they dark green or light green?' So I'd say 'Well some are dark green and others light.' But that doesn't satisfy her. She points to a particular tree and a particular leaf on it, and wants to know exactly what colour green that leaf is. When I can't answer just right, she gets upset and starts screaming.[13]

Alice found her mother as irritating as her father. 'Mum confuses me', Alice informed the psychiatrist, 'she can't make up her mind...I asked her if she thought Sue, my best friend was pretty...first she said Sue was quite pretty. Later I asked her again. She said she thought she was really pretty. Then again, that she was very pretty.'[14]

Alice was diagnosed as suffering from obsessive–compulsive disorder: she had to have an exactness and consistency in words that was impossible. Alice's decision-making problems over language might spread to everybody if a rigid system were imposed.

A rigid system would effectively stifle creative thought, as George Orwell realized in his futuristic novel *Nineteen eighty-four*. Syme, a philologist, was one of a team of experts compiling a dictionary of Newspeak, the official language:

'The Eleventh Edition is the definitive edition,' he said. 'We're getting the language into its final shape ... We're destroying words – scores of them, hundreds of them, every day. We're cutting the language down to the bone ...' His thin dark face had become animated, his eyes had lost their mocking expression and grown almost dreamy.

'It's a beautiful thing, the destruction of words ... Don't you see that the whole aim of Newspeak is to narrow the range of thought? In the end we shall make thoughtcrime literally impossible, because there will be no words in which to express it. Every concept that can ever be needed, will be expressed by exactly *one* word, with its meaning rigidly defined and all its subsidiary meanings rubbed out and forgotten.'[15]

The blue-footed booby, the grasshopper, Alice and Orwell's philologist all show that systems which allow some flexibility are better than rigid ones. The Babel myth was probably wrong in regarding language diversity as a bad thing, a divine punishment. Differences between and within languages are signs of a flexible, adjustable system.[16]

Swiss army knife or Auntie Maggie's remedy?

Differences between languages form the basis of a long-standing controversy. A 'Swiss army knife' view proposes a specialized linguistic system, which allows variation. An 'Auntie Maggie's remedy' viewpoint suggests that languages vary because they are a product of human general intelligence.

Swiss army knife supporters argue that the human mind resembles a gadget which incorporates numerous specialized devices, each of which has its own special task: a cork-screw uncorks bottles, a knife cuts, and a file smooths off rough edges, and so on.[17] According to this view, humans acquire language by utilizing a dedicated language-handling mechanism. Languages differ because a degree of flexibility is built into the system.

Auntie Maggie's remedy supporters, on the other hand, regard the human mind as a multi-purpose reasoning device which can handle numerous different tasks. It resembles the powerful cure-all which treats all ailments in the old music-hall song:

> It's my Auntie Maggie's home-made remedy,
> Guaranteed never to fail.

Rub your mental powers onto any problem, and it will be solved, just as Auntie Maggie's remedy cured any physical illness. According to this view, language is just one of the many different puzzles which children encounter. They use their all-purpose powerful minds to sort out how it works, just as they also discover how to build up bricks or multiply ten by five. Human languages therefore differ because they are the product of human general intelligence, which can solve puzzles in alternative ways.

A much discussed question, then, is whether language is 'hard-wired' or 'soft-wired' in humans. Hard-wired abilities are those that are *preprogrammed* to emerge, such as flying in pigeons. Soft-wired abilities are those that an animal is *capable* of acquiring via learning, as when pigeons can be trained to peck at letters of the alphabet to get food. A hard-wiring versus soft-wiring distinction is therefore a fashionable way of referring to a long-standing 'nature–nurture' debate over instinctive versus learned behaviour which has been going on for centuries.[18] (See Fig. 3.1.)

Hard versus soft wiring can sometimes be distinguished by the ease with which an animal acquires a particular type of behaviour. Hamsters quickly learn to scrabble or rear up in order to get a food reward, but they cannot be persuaded to wash their faces for this purpose.[19] Humans readily learn to be frightened of snakes, a fear which is thought to be innate, but they do not normally fear cars, even though cars are potentially more dangerous in modern cities.[20]

But this criterion is not easy to apply to language. Children learn language fast and easily from one viewpoint, in that it takes less than one tenth of a normal lifetime to learn to speak fluently. But they acquire it slowly and with difficulty from another. It takes around five years to get a basic knowledge of language, another five to grasp routine subtleties, and a further ten for a really useful vocabulary range. Mastery of most animal communication systems is achieved much faster, even allowing for the longer life-span of humans.

And in recent years, the 'Swiss army knife' (hard-wiring) versus 'Auntie Maggie's remedy' (soft-wiring) controversy has been on the verge of collapse. It turns out that there's a fuzzy border between hard (instinctive) and soft (learned) skills. For example, young pigeons hard-wired for flying have to spend time learning

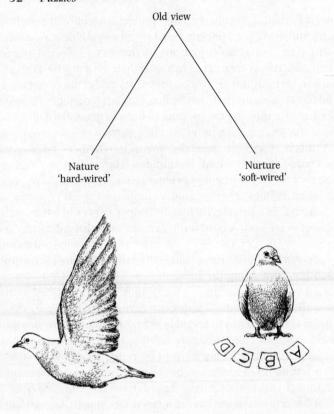

e.g. *pigeons fly*   e.g. *pigeons distinguish alphabet letters*

Figure 3.1 Old nature–nurture view

how to do this, and they acquire the soft-wired skill of distinguishing alphabet letters mainly because they have been hard-wired with acute eyesight.[21] The next section will outline some further examples which show how instinct and learning interact.

The birds and the bees

The notion of 'innately guided behaviour' largely sweeps aside the old nature–nurture, hard–soft, instinct–learning controversies.

Most behaviour requires some learning, which 'is often innately guided, that is, guided by information inherent in the genetic makeup of the animal. In other words, the process of learning itself is often controlled by instinct.'[22]

Bees and birds provide good examples of this. Their behaviour can shed light on the working of flexible systems which are partly hard-wired, and partly soft-wired.

The hardworking nature of bees appealed to the eighteenth-century moralist who wrote the following verse for children:[23]

> How doth the little busy bee
> Improve each shining hour,
> And gather honey all the day
> From every opening flower!

But he failed to point out the oddest fact about bees, that they can recognize flowers in the first place. 'Every opening flower' covers a huge range, from roses to marigolds to foxgloves to heather, which look different and smell different. But bees cannot possibly have an inbuilt encyclopaedia listing all possible plants. So what happens?

Apparently, bees have some generalized inbuilt information about flowers, but they have to fill in the details themselves. Bees spontaneously land on small, brightly coloured objects that, like flower petals, have a high proportion of edges to unbroken areas, and which, like flower middles, have centres which absorb ultra-violet light, and so appear dark to bees. But not all such objects contain nectar and pollen. So additional learning is required.

A bee's ability to remember different colours, patterns, shapes and odours was tested by checking how reliably bees returned to particular artificial 'flowers'.[24] The bees, it turned out, first learned about odour. Mostly, they had to smell a 'flower' only once to remember it, though not all odours were learned with equal ease. Next, bees learned about colour, though this took longer, about three visits, depending on the colour. Thirdly, bees learned about flower shapes, though this took them longer still, about five or six visits, and they preferred 'busy' patterns to simple ones.

The order of importance – odour, then colour, then shape – is probably based on cue reliability. The odour is fairly fixed, but the colour can fade or alter in different lighting conditions, and the

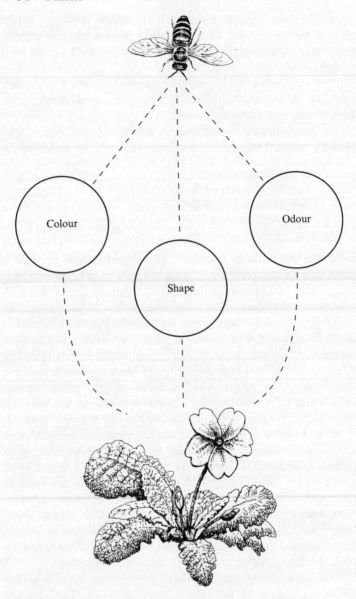

Figure 3.2 Innately guided behaviour

shape can change from the wind or the viewing angle. And bees also have to learn the time at which food is available from each flower.

Honey bees are therefore guided to particular targets by instinct, but they then have to memorize further details. They sort and remember this new information according to preordained principles (see Fig. 3.2).

The bird and nest-robber problem parallels the bee and flower problem. Most birds have an inbuilt alarm call, and some have a variant, a so-called 'mobbing call' which summons other birds to attack and mob a predatory bird such as a jay which is liable to steal eggs and nestlings. But birds need to distinguish nest-robbing owls, crows and jays from harmless birds such as robins. They cannot have a complete bird book in their minds, and they cannot afford to make too many mistakes. So how do they do this?

European blackbirds, it turns out, learn from one another, as was shown by an ingenious experiment. Two groups of blackbirds were each shown a stuffed bird. The blackbirds could see into each others' cages, but they could not see the bird being shown to the other blackbird group. At first, both groups were shown the same bird. When they were shown a stuffed owl, they all emitted the mobbing call, and tried to attack the owl. When they were shown a harmless bird, a stuffed Australian honeycreeper, they showed very little interest. Then the experiment changed. One group was shown the owl, while simultaneously the other was shown the honeycreeper. The group exposed to the owl became agitated, emitted the mobbing call, and tried to attack the owl. The blackbirds shown the honeycreeper stayed quiet – but only for a moment. When they heard and saw the frenzied behaviour in the other cage of birds, they too joined in. They emitted the mobbing call, and tried to attack the honeycreeper. Moreover, this behaviour did not disappear. On future occasions, they always tried to mob the harmless honeycreeper. And they passed this honeycreeper aversion to the next generation, who all mobbed honeycreepers.[25]

Both the birds and the bees, then, show how innately guided learning works: nature lays down the framework, and organizes the learning scheme, but experience fills in the details. Birds and bees reveal that 'much learning . . . is specialized for the learning of tasks the animal is likely to encounter. The animal is innately equipped to recognize when it should learn, what cues it should attend to, how to store the new information and how to refer to it in the future.'[26]

The birds and the bees provide lessons that can be applied to human language, as the authors of the study point out. Language also is an example of innately guided learning, learning guided by information which is an intrinsic part of human genetic make-up. The outline framework is ready-made, and so is the learning scheme. But the finer points are filled in by experience. This explains why languages differ.

This is perhaps not surprising: language is a type of biologically controlled behaviour, that is, behaviour which develops naturally providing that children are exposed to speech. This has been known since at least 1967, when Eric Lenneberg wrote a pioneeering book, entitled *Biological foundations of language*. He pointed out that such behaviour emerges before it is strictly needed for survival, that it is not the result of a conscious decision, and is not triggered by immediate external events. Direct teaching and intensive practice have relatively little effect, and a regular timetable of language 'milestones' is found among normal children.[27]

But these observations raise a further question. If humans are preprogrammed to develop language, at least in outline, can a 'language component' be identified in the mind? This will be the topic of the next chapter.

Summary

This chapter asked why languages differ so much. Flexibility and variation was pointed out to be an advantage in the animal world, and rigidity a disadvantage, so differences between languages are potentially useful.

Two long-standing views on differences between languages were considered. The Swiss army knife (hard-wired) view proposes that language is a special skill, but has variety preprogrammed into the system, The Auntie Maggie's remedy (soft-wired) view suggests that language is acquired via general intelligence, and that it presents problems which are solved differently by different languages. But hard versus soft wiring is now a largely outmoded controversy.

Many examples of animal behaviour are a mixture of nature and nurture. Bees recognizing flowers, birds learning about predators, and human language are examples of innately guided behaviour, in which the outline framework and learning mechanisms are provided by nature, and the details filled in by experience.

4 Distinct duties:
Is language an independent skill?

> The master manufacturer, by dividing the work to be executed into different processes, each requiring different degrees of skill and strength, can purchase exactly that precise quantity of both which is necessary for each process; whereas, if the whole were executed by one workman, that person must possess sufficient skill to perform the most difficult, and sufficient strength to execute the most laborious, of the various operations.
>
> Charles Babbage, *On the economy of machinery and manufacturers* (1832)

'The general law of organization . . . is that distinct duties entail distinct structures', said the nineteenth-century philosopher Herbert Spencer.[1] In its broad outlines, this is obvious. A car's electrical system does not work in the same way as its gears, nor does the human heart perform the same function as the liver.

Undoubtedly the human mind/brain works in a highly compartmentalized way, at least for some tasks: the human eye relays what it registers to a specific brain location, a portion at the far back.[2] And within that area, quite minute specialization is found: an artist who became colour-blind as the result of a car accident had suffered damage to 'bean sized areas' in his brain, for example.[3]

But the eye is a very old part of the brain and body, and it has had multiple millennia to evolve. Human language is very recent in evolutionary terms, 250,000 years ago being the earliest guess, 100,000 the average, and 50,000 the latest. It has pressed into service different peripheral organs (the mouth, the ear) and various brain regions, both in the outer brain (the cerebrum) and in deeper layers. So it may not have had time to evolve its own structure.

Language appears to be innately guided behaviour, in which inbuilt guidelines help the learner (chapter 3). But to recognize that there are innate furrows still leaves the independence question largely unanswered. To what extent is language an independent skill, and to what extent is it linked to other aspects of cognitive ability? On this issue, language is a key bone which academic dogs fight over.

As a next step, therefore, it's important to discover whether language can be separated from other human mental abilities. This appears to be so. Language can fail when other aspects of general intelligence remain unaffected. And, more interestingly, language can sometimes exist when other systems have failed. Let us consider these bizarre and rare phenomena.

The speechless monk

Take the case of Brother John, a monk who throughout the 1970s had had epileptic seizures. This fifty-year-old native speaker of French worked on the editorial staff of his order's pious periodical, reading and answering up to fifty-five letters to the editor a day. He had frequent epileptic episodes, which varied in severity. When a short 'spell' took place, lasting five minutes or less, he felt bizarre, kept very quiet, did not understand spoken language and did not talk.

More dramatic were his longer spells, which occurred a dozen or more times a year, and lasted several hours. During these, he remained conscious, unless he chose to sleep. He lost his ability to use language, and was aware of this, yet he was otherwise able to think and act normally, and kept a small transistor radio at hand in order to assess when his comprehension returned. On his spoken speech, he noted: 'I know that certain words I say are not correct, but I do not know which ones and I do not know how I pronounce them. Sometimes, instead of talking nonsense, I prefer not to talk at all.'[4]

When his spoken speech was tested during a spell, similar-sounding nonsense words tended to recur, often variants of the nonsense sequence *tuwari*. When shown a picture of a telephone, he immediately pointed to the telephone in his room and said (with the few real French words translated into English): 'That's it, there. The furi twar. No. Glarity tuware tuwa tuware ari tuware tuware tuwarere tu tuware tu'.[5] He was, however, fully capable of tape-recording his own deviant speech, as he had been requested to do. After a spell, he discussed his earlier inability to name a television: 'I knew what it was – this is why I could point at the TV set in my room – but I could not tell you the word since I could not tell it to myself.'[6] His reading and writing were also affected. He once had difficulty finding his way, and explained: 'I knew where to look for the names of the streets, I could see them but I could not read them.'[7]

Brother John's Swiss hotel episode possibly illustrates most clearly the narrow linguistic nature of his disabilities. Once, while travelling from Italy to Switzerland, he had a seizure. He managed to disembark from his train at the correct stop, together with his suitcases, and find a hotel. This first hotel turned him away, and he moved on to a second, which accepted him. He gave the receptionist his passport, indicating the page where she could find the information to fill in the registration form. He was then shown his room, and given his key. Later, still suffering from his spell, he felt hungry, and found the hotel restaurant. There he was able to order a meal by pointing to a section on the menu where he guessed main courses were listed. He was disappointed to discover he had ordered fish, which he disliked, but still ate potatoes and other vegetables. He then returned to his room, and slept the rest of his spell away. Hours later he woke up, with his speech restored. Feeling foolish, he apologized to the receptionist for his previous behaviour, and she was apparently sympathetic.

Brother John therefore shows that language can be detached from other mental skills. As the authors of this study note, the Swiss hotel event 'is strikingly demonstrative and ... compels assent as to the language specificity or near specificity of our patient's paroxysmal episodes as well as to his state of mind and mental capacities in the course of such episodes'.[8]

There are numerous similar cases in the literature of stroke victims and others whose language is damaged, while many aspects of their intelligence remain intact, or nearly so. Perhaps the best-known case is that of Genie, the Californian teenager who was kept isolated by her father until the age of almost fourteen.[9] She was found in 1970, thin, undernourished and speechless. She eventually learnt to speak in a rudimentary fashion, though what she wanted to say clearly outstripped her ability to say it, as in:

Ruth Smith have cat swallow needle
'Ruth Smith has a cat who swallowed a needle'
Father hit Genie cry long time ago
'My father hit me and made me cry a long time ago'
Water think swim think swim
'I'm thinking about taking a swim'

But even more remarkable than Brother John and Genie, perhaps, are cases of people who can talk fluently, but have other crippling mental problems.

The cocktail party syndrome

'She was thinking it's no regular school. It was just good old no buses.' This now-famous sentence was produced by Laura, an American teenager (earlier known as Marta). She is one of an increasing number of children who speak fluently, but whose intelligence is so low that they can't look after themselves, they can't sort objects, they can't handle money, and may not even know their age: 'I was 16 last year, and now I'm 19 this year', Laura once announced.

The phenomenon is known appropriately enough as 'the cocktail party syndrome' or the 'chatterbox syndrome', since the talkers seem to be talking for the sake of talking, sometimes without making sense, as in one of Laura's longer passages:

It was kind of stupid for dad, an' my mom got um three notes, one was a pants store, (of) this really good friend, an' it was kind of hard. An' the police pulled my mother out of (there) an' told the truth. I said, "I got two friends in there!" The police pulled my mother (and so I said) he would never remember them as long as we live! An' that was it! My mother was so mad![10]

But Laura is not just stringing together phrases she has heard other people produce, even though several ready-made sequences recur, such as 'this really good friend'. Original grammatical errors show that she is creating her utterances afresh, as in:

It was *gaven* by a friend
I don't know how I *catched* it
These are two classes I've *tooken*
Three tickets were *gave out by a police* last year

Laura is not the only child of this type, though she is perhaps the one we know most about. There are reports of two boys, Antony and Rick,[11] and a hydrocephalic girl, known as D. C.,[12] though D. C. is puzzling. Her utterances make superficial sense, even though she invents the stories she relates, as in:

> We go to this river to do canoeing and I fell in the river once ... that wasn't funny; that was frightening. I said I'd never go ... I said I'd never go canoeing again, and I still go canoeing now. And that's three years later that was. But my dad's got a canoe and we go canoeing. I threw my dad in once. Me and my brother threw him in together ... That was funny that was.[13]

The way these children use language suggests that there is a specialized linguistic circuit in the mind, which is partially separate from other circuits.

Some further bizarre cases support this view. Consider Christopher, a twenty-nine-year-old man, who is unable to look after himself, yet is obsessed by languages other than his own. Apart from English, which he learned as a child, he can cope with Danish, Dutch, French, German, Greek, Hindi, Norwegian, Polish, Portuguese, Russian, Spanish, Swedish and Welsh, as well as having a smattering of Finnish and Turkish.[14] Here is a translation by Christopher from Swedish, followed by an accurate version:

> (1) Christopher's version: 'Mia is sitting, crouched down in the kitchen sofa with her knees bent and her feet tied up in the lovely night-shirt. The cat spins in her knee.'
> (2) Accurate translation: 'Mia is curled up on the kitchen sofa with her knees drawn up and her feet tucked into her stripey nightie. The cat is purring in her lap.'

Christopher's main mistake is to use the word *spin* which resembles the Swedish word for 'purr' in place of the English word *purr*. Christopher's effort is pretty impressive for someone whose non-verbal IQ is around 60.

A further set of interesting children are those with a little-understood disorder known as 'Williams Syndrome'.[15] The sufferers are severely impaired in many cognitive tasks, especially those that involve spatial orientation, where they cannot integrate separate items into a coherent whole. For example, they are unable to organize the components of a bicycle into a picture of a whole bicycle, nor can they handle a test in which a triangle has to be formed by the arrangement of smaller circles. Yet their language is often elaborate and sophisticated, as in the following description of a brain-scan by a seventeen-year-old Williams Syndrome girl:

> There is a huge magnetic machine. It took a picture inside the brain. You could talk but not move your head because that would ruin the whole thing and they would have to start all over again. After it's all done they show you your brain on a computer and they see how large it is. And the machine on the other side of the room takes pictures from the computer. They can take pictures instantly. Oh, and it was very exciting.[16]

Williams Syndrome sufferers, like the other cases mentioned, indicate that language is a separate ability, which can be dissociated from other cognitive abilities.

The master manufacturer

All the cases outlined above suggest that the mind is like the master manufacturer, who divides the work to be executed into different processes. As the the Greek philosopher Plato suggested, it may be possible to 'carve the mind at its natural joints'.[17] The human mind contains a number of different components or 'modules', a term borrowed from computer terminology. Each of them has its own particular task. A dedicated language-handling mechanism appears to be one of them (see Fig. 4.1).

The term 'module' may imply a spurious rigidity. Perhaps the alternative phrase 'domain-specific specialization' is a better one: this suggests that the human mind has developed specialized circuits to handle particular 'domains'. Just as the heart handles the pumping of blood round the body, and the kidney filters out certain poisonous elements, similarly, in the mind, different mechanisms handle different problems.[18] Yet another possible phrase for this is 'functionally isolable subsystem'.[19]

Within a complex structure, there are several advantages of specialization.[20] One is that the breakdown of one component does not normally lead to a total collapse. A person who is blind is not

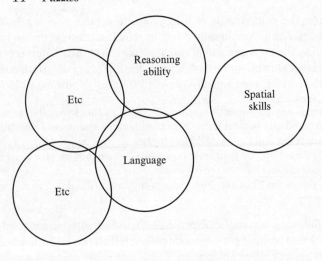

Figure 4.1 Modules in the mind

necessarily deaf. In a house, a telephone failure does not usually cause a collapse of the central heating system. In fact, all complex systems, from cars to Sydney Harbour bridge work on this 'components' system: breakdown in one portion does not lead to a general catastrophic failure of everything.

Another advantage is speed: just as a central heating system in a domestic house has a limit on the number of radiators it can effectively heat, so a response which has to travel round the whole system in a human would take too long: a human can often dodge swiftly out of the way of a hurled brick, but would probably be unable to respond this fast if the whole brain was involved.

A further advantage is efficiency: 'Do you want a machine which will clean all of your house reasonably well? Or do you care most about spotless carpets? If so, get a specialized carpet cleaner.' This type of advice is handed out in consumer magazines. But it is a fairly general rule: the more widespread the function, the less good a gadget is at particular tasks. The more specialized something is, the less easy it is to apply it across-the-board: a dedicated carpet cleaner will not be good at cleaning drains or polishing silver.

The language circuit

Faced with evidence such as that discussed in this chapter, many linguists believe, like the pioneering American linguist Noam Chomsky, that 'the principles [of language] do not generalize, that they are in crucial respects specific to the language faculty',[21] which has its own 'specific properties, structure, and organization'.[22] In short, they argue for a hard core of specialized linguistic knowledge. Chomksy claims that the mind is 'constituted of "mental organs" just as specialized and differentiated as those of the body',[23] and that language is one of these. Of course, just as the heart can be separated into different chambers, so language itself may be made up of distinct components: this question will be discussed later (chapter 16). The point here is that language is to a large extent separable from other cognitive abilities.

But it may be unrealistic to speak of a language 'organ', because language uses numerous different parts of the brain. So 'language circuits' might be more appropriate, as neurologists point out (chapter 7). Perhaps language should be regarded as a London sightseeing bus, which has its own specialized preordained routes: language in the brain is more like the blood which moves around the body than a static organ like the kidney or liver (see Fig. 4.2).

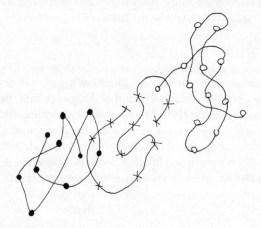

Figure 4.2 Modules as circuits

Language, then, either utilizes, or devises, its own special circuits. Some of these are pre-set, others probably develop in the course of life. As one researcher notes: 'In human development, a process of modularization can arise as a *result* of development, and not merely as part of the mind's innate specification.'[24] Habits and non-habits utilize different pathways within the brain.[25] The British physiologist, Henry Maudsley, once pointed out: 'If an act became no easier after being done several times, if the careful direction of consciousness were necessary to its accomplishment on each occasion, it is evident that the whole activity of a lifetime might be confined to one or two deeds.'[26] So practice can lay down new pathways.

Yet such pathways can be laid down only if they fit in with an animal's pre-set preferences, as shown by the hamsters which could not be trained to wash their faces, and the bees which were innately guided to learn about flowers (chapter 3).

But the special language circuits are not the whole story. Humans can use their huge intelligent brain to think about their linguistic skills. This is perhaps the difference between a child such as Laura and a normal speaker: 'Although the fluent-speaking retarded child probably has an intact linguistic module, the normal child also has the potential to become a grammarian.'[27]

If the mind has its own language circuit, then the next question is to ask how this evolved. This will be the topic of the next section.

Summary

This chapter considered the question of language independence. A number of case studies have shown that language can be separated from general intelligence. Brother John and Genie could think clearly even when they were unable to speak their thoughts. Laura, Christopher and others can talk fluently, even though they are severely mentally handicapped in other respects. This suggests that language has its own specialized circuit within the mind/brain.

Part 2
Origin

5 The family tree:
The evolutionary background

Some folks'll boast about their family trees,
And there's some trees they ought to lop;
But our family tree, believe me, goes right back,
You can see monkeys sitting on top!

R. P. Weston and Bert Lee, 'St. George and the Dragon'

Evolution is often thought of as a ladder. Yet this may be misleading. Ladders allow only a single-file ascent. So the ladder-image can lead to the wrong assumption that humans 'grew' out of monkeys or apes, who are 'below' us on the rungs: 'Descended from the apes? My dear, we will hope it is not true. But if it is, let us pray that it may not become generally known' is a remark supposedly made by the wife of a canon of Worcester Cathedral.

A well-known novel, *Tarzan of the apes* (1912), promoted this fallacy in a stirring fictional account of Tarzan, a human brought up by apes, which implies that apes are part-way towards being real people:

Many travellers have seen the drums of the great apes, but Tarzan . . . is, doubtless, the only human being who ever joined in the fierce, mad, intoxicating revel of the Dum-Dum. From this primitive function has arisen, unquestionably, all the forms and ceremonials of modern church and state, for through all the countless ages, back beyond the uttermost ramparts of a dawning humanity our fierce, hairy forebears danced out the rites of the Dum-Dum to the sound of their earthen drums, beneath the bright light of a tropical moon in the depth of a mighty jungle which stands unchanged.[1]

But today's great apes are not so much our ancestors, as our relatives: cousins from whom we diverged 6 or more million years ago – and monkeys are even further removed. A better image is one of a bush with multiple branches.[2] The only surprise, perhaps, is that humans are the only ones on the primate bush who talk. Let

49

us begin by considering who else inhabits our bush, and how long ago they diverged from us.

The biological bush

Our biological bush is that of primates, the animal 'order' to which we humans belong, a subdivision of the class of mammals (breast-feeders). As a group, primates have good eyesight with forward-directed eyes, acute hearing, flexible hands and feet, nails rather than claws, and relatively large brains. Different primate families inhabit the bush: hominids (human-like creatures), panids (chimpanzees), and pongids (gorillas) are perhaps the best-known, of whom the chimps are our closest relatives (see Fig. 5.1).

The apparently huge gap between chimps and hominids set off a hunt in the last century for a 'missing link' between the two, but no definitive intermediary has yet emerged. Until recently, the earliest known hominid was 'Lucy', *Australopithecus afarensis* (southern ape of Afar), who lived in Africa around 4 million years ago. Unlike the apes, she walked on two feet. She is usually regarded as a direct ancestor of humans, though she may have been a cousin.[3]

But some recently unearthed bones in Ethiopia are even earlier. Bone fragments first found in 1993 dating from almost 4½ million years ago are the earliest hominid remains. They belong to an animal about the size of a bonobo (pygmy chimp). The first bones found were all from above the waist, and it is still not clear if this small creature, named *Australopithecus ramidus*, could walk upright or not.[4] Additional findings from the area, including hip joints, are still being checked, assembled and argued over.[5]

Our own genus *Homo* (Man) is a subdivision of the hominid family, and probably split away from the australopithecines (southern apes) around 3 million years ago (see Fig. 5.2).

Around 2 million years ago, a tool-using *Homo* emerged, known as *Homo habilis* (handy Man), an odd-looking person by today's standards: 'Put him on the subway and people would probably move to the other end of the car.'[6] About 1½ million years ago came *Homo erectus* (upright Man), who used fire, and looked fairly ordinary: 'Put him on the subway and people would probably take a suspicious look at him.'[7]

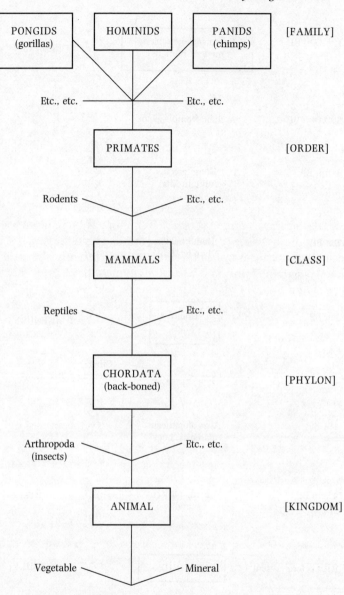

Figure 5.1 The primate bush

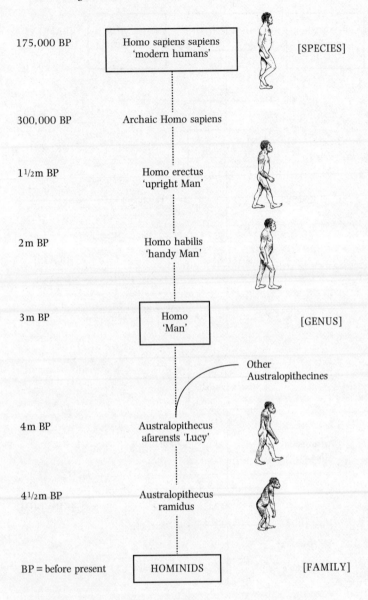

175,000 BP   Homo sapiens sapiens   [SPECIES]
                  'modern humans'

300,000 BP   Archaic Homo sapiens

1½m BP   Homo erectus
                  'upright Man'

2m BP   Homo habilis
                  'handy Man'

3m BP   Homo   [GENUS]
                  'Man'

                                Other
                                Australopithecines

4m BP   Australopithecus
                  afarensis 'Lucy'

4½m BP   Australopithecus
                  ramidus

BP = before present   HOMINIDS   [FAMILY]

Figure 5.2 The genus *Homo*

About 300,000 BP (before present), *Archaic Homo sapiens* (archaic wise Man) arrived on the scene, and around 200,000– 150,000 BP modern humans, *Homo sapiens sapiens*, emerged. The development of language was somewhere between 250,000 BP and 50,000 BP, with the average estimate being around 100,000 years ago,[8] all recent dates in evolutionary terms. Language may have been the trigger which activated a dramatic and widespread advance in technology and culture from around 50,000 BP.[9] Humans began to use not just stone, but also other raw materials such as antler, bone and clay. Paintings were made on cave walls, and living sites increased in size.

This explosion of language and culture is at first sight mysterious. But ever since the pioneering work of Darwin, the process of evolution has gradually become clearer.

The book that shook the world

The 'book that shook the world'[10] was Charles Darwin's *On the origin of species*, published in 1859. Darwin demonstrated that humans were the products of evolution, not individual creation. 'The worldview formed by any thinking person in the Western world after 1859 . . . was by necessity quite different from a worldview formed prior to 1859', it has been claimed.[11] Darwin was not the first to propose evolution, but was probably the first to fully propound it.

Darwin in 1859 spoke of his theory as the principle of Natural Selection:

> Any variation, however slight and from whatever cause proceeding, if it be in any degree profitable to an individual of any species . . . will tend to the preservation of that individual, and will generally be inherited by its offspring. The offspring, also, will have a better chance of surviving . . . I have called this principle, by which each slight variation, if useful, is preserved, by the term Natural Selection.[12]

According to Darwin, evolution happened very slowly: 'As natural selection acts solely by accumulating slight, successive, favourable variations, it can produce no great or sudden modification; it can act only by very short and slow steps.'[13] This slow progress made it unobservable, he assumed: 'We see nothing of these slow changes in progress, until the hand of time has marked the long lapses of ages, and then so imperfect is our view into long past geological ages, that we only see that the forms of life are now different from what they formerly were.'[14]

This mystifying process has been argued about for decades.[15] But Darwin was wrong. It IS possible to see changes in progress. Evolution is not, after all, unobservable: it is a case of knowing where to look. And a number of studies have demonstrated natural selection in action.

The beaks of Darwin's finches provide a showcase for evolution. These birds were named after Darwin, though detailed study of their behaviour has taken place only in the last quarter-century.[16] Thirteen species of finches live on the Galapagos islands, all of which are assumed to have evolved from a common ancestor. The birds are darkly coloured, are of similar shape, and vary in length between about three and six inches. They vary also in their diet and habitat – often reflected in their common names, tree finch, ground finch, cactus finch, mangrove finch, and so on. More importantly, the shape of their bills differs, some deep, large and hooked, others narrow and slender.

Darwin himself suggested that climate was a major factor in evolution, and this proposal is strongly borne out by these finches. Their home islands are sometimes drenched by rains, sometimes parched by drought, and this has had massive effects on their survival rate. On one of the small islands, Daphne Major, only two finch species reside, one being the medium ground finch. Just about every ground finch was briefly caught and banded with highly visible leg-bands by two researchers: Peter Grant, a professor of zoology at Princeton University, and his wife Rosemary.

In 1977 and again in 1982, there was a drought, and many birds disappeared – only 15 per cent of the ground finches remained. The most conspicuous feature of the survivors was their large beak size. During normal wet seasons, grasses and herbs produce an abundance of small seeds. But in dry seasons, the small seeds get eaten fast, and birds with bigger, deeper beaks are better equipped to crack open the large seeds which remain. If droughts continue, the cumulative effects of selection in the direction of deep beaks could lead to an alteration in the appearance of a species – though intervening wet years, with an abundance of easily available small seeds, might favour smaller, shallower beaks, resulting in long-term oscillation.

The finches show how weather conditions strongly favoured certain birds – and if one particular type of weather had persisted, then those with suitable beaks for surviving would predominate, and the others possibly die out. The beak variation is partly genetic, partly environmental: birds inherited beak size from their parents, but in the case of the large beaks, adequate nourishment was a contributory factor.

Bird-beaks might seem a long way from humans and language. But a similar event – a radical change in climate – is now thought by many to be the trigger behind language. Let us consider this scenario.

East Side story

Evolution is often thought of as descent down different branches of an upside-down tree. But descent down different sides of a mountain might be a more useful way of envisaging human development. In the distant past, a group of ape-like creatures were perched metaphorically on the top of a mountain. They decided to come down, and split into two groups, each group choosing a different side of the mountain. Once descent had started, then the routes turned out to differ substantially. There was no turning back, and the differing terrain forced quite different life styles onto each group.

This 'different routes down' scenario is not so far-fetched. Something very similar may have happened when we split from our cousins the apes, according to one increasingly influential view. We were all living together in Africa, until a catastrophic event occurred, probably a series of major earthquakes or a 'tectonic crisis', as it is sometimes referred to.[17] This created the Great Rift Valley, which separates the wet forests of west Africa from the relatively dry grasslands of east Africa. The Rift Valley itself sank, but a line of peaks formed on the western rim of the valley, splitting Africa's inhabitants into two major groups (see Fig. 5.3).

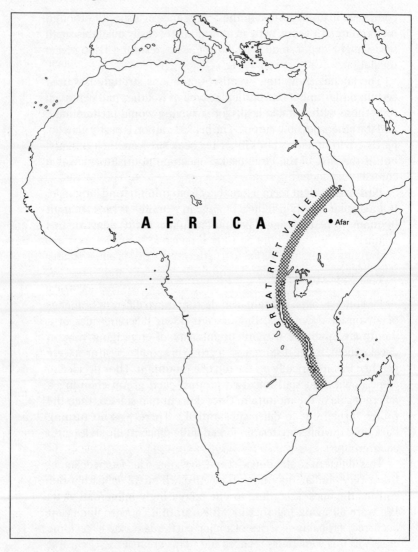

Figure 5.3 The Great Rift Valley

'As for humans, we are unquestionably a pure product of a certain aridity', it has been claimed.[18] After the catastrophe, our ape cousins were left in the lush and pleasant tree-terrain of the humid west. Our own ancestors were stranded in a relatively treeless savannah in the increasingly dry east, where they were forced to adapt – or die. An unfavourable climate forced a deprived species to live on its wits and, in the long run, develop language.

'East Side story' is the apt name given to this Rift Valley hypothesis. It is supported both by climatologists, and by the archaeological evidence: chimpanzees are found only to the west of the Rift Valley, and hominid fossils are found only to the east.

A transition to an even drier climate may have been the triggering factor in the divergence of the australopithecines (southern apes) and the genus *Homo* (Man). The australopithecines remained vegetarian. Our ancestors possibly broadened their diet, perhaps scavenging for meat. This led to a better-nourished brain, a greater degree of social organization, and an increase in brain size.[19] A long-term trend towards drier, harsher weather required increasing adaptation from the surviving hominids. And one of these adaptations was language.

This East Side story supports the claim that humans came 'out of Africa'. This is backed up by further evidence. Let us consider some of this.

Genetic blueprints

Fire burn and cauldron bubble: bubbling vats of human cells, recombinant DNA, surging and swelling, pulsing and heaving, multiplying by the million, the more the merrier; all the better, the more efficiently for biologists and computers to work upon the structure of the living cell, the blueprints of our lives, decoding the DNA which is our inheritance. A snip here, a section there, excise this, insert that, slice and shuffle, find a marker, see what happens.[20]

DNA, short for deoxyribonucleic acid, is responsible for the transmission of genetic information. A small proportion of human DNA slices and shuffles itself relatively fast. It can provide vital information on the movements of early humans.

Each of a human's multi-million cells has a nucleus, and most of an individual's 100,000 or so genes are located on DNA molecules in this nucleus, to which males and females contribute equally. This nuclear DNA is highly stable, and individuals from different sides of the planet barely differ.

But a handful of genes – a mere thirty-seven according to one count[21] – are found elsewhere, on the mitochondria. These are specialized structures attached to the cell, whose purpose is to provide cells with energy. Their DNA carries information primarily about their own manufacture. Mitochondrial DNA derives only from the female, and so can reveal an individual's maternal ancestry. Its sequences mutate relatively rapidly, and it has therefore been referred to as a 'fast ticking clock'.[22]

Arguably, evolution can be measured by concentrating on these fast-mutating genes. Measuring is possible on the assumption that the rate of change is fairly uniform – though this is sometimes queried.[23]

A tree of early human relationships can therefore be established, by examining samples of mitochondrial DNA from around the world. The general pattern seems clear, though details are disputed. Humans originated in Africa.[24]

The Africa conclusion is supported by another piece of evidence: the homogeneity of the human data compared with that of chimpanzees, which show as much as ten times the genetic variation of humans. 'That fact alone suggests that all of modern humanity sprang from a relatively small stock of common ancestors.'[25]

The DNA evidence ties in with that from blood. All humans have one of a limited number of blood groups. In addition, they are either 'positive' or 'negative' for the so-called 'rhesus factor' (Rh), a blood antigen – an antigen being something which stimulates the production of an antibody. Relatively good worldwide information is available about this, for practical reasons. A pregnant Rh-negative woman carrying a Rh-positive fetus needs to be identified so that treatment can be carried out immediately after delivery, otherwise the baby will die.

The proportion of Rh-negative individuals differs from population to population. It's very low in Australia and the Far East (0–1% of the population). It's quite high in northern Africa and Europe

(9-25%). It's somewhere between these two extremes in most of Africa and the Middle East (1-9%). Africa, then, is most probably the base from which the other levels developed.[26]

But this scenario still leaves a number of how and why questions unanswered. Let us consider these.

A language bonfire

Did language emerge suddenly like a rabbit out of a hat? Or slowly like a snail creeping up a wall?

The rabbit-out-of-a-hat view suggests that there was a sudden evolutionary leap, in which language emerged as if pulled by a conjurer out of a hat. This proposal is particularly associated with the linguist Noam Chomsky. Humans are endowed with an innate language faculty, claims Chomsky, and he argues that this 'poses a problem for the biologist, since, if true, it is an example of true "emergence" – the appearance of a qualitatively different phenomenon at a specific stage of complexity of organization'.[27]

Chomsky is not the only rabbit-out-of-a-hat proponent. The abrupt origin of language is sometimes supported for a quite different reason: that a large brain could have suddenly invented an extra use for itself. This brain-first or language-first controversy will be discussed in the next chapter.

'What use is half a wing for flying?' is the question asked by those who believe in leaps in evolution. But just as half a wing is probably helpful as a parachute, enabling a future bird to jump off a high branch and come down slowly, similarly, half a language probably had its uses. Something as complex as language is unlikely to have suddenly popped out of the evolutionary hat.

The opposing view is that language developed very very slowly, creeping upwards in complexity over millennia, like a snail making its way slowly slowly up a very high wall. On a graph, this would appear as a slow upward slant, as language capacity gradually increased among hominids. But this smooth upward movement does not tie in with our general understanding of how evolution works, in which progress tends to be more uneven.

A fits-and-starts view comes somewhere in between these two extremes – periods of relative stagnation alternating with periods of fast growth. This scenario is consistent with the notion of 'punctuated equilibria', put forward in a now-famous paper by the evolutionists Niles Eldredge and Stephen Jay Gould.[28] They argue that in evolution there were periods of rapid development, interspersed with long periods of little or no evolutionary change, which they label *stasis*. Yet stopping and starting like an old-fashioned elevator is a somewhat unlikely scenario for language. Once it started to evolve, it probably kept going, as its usefulness became apparent.

The rabbit-out-of-a-hat, snail-up-a-wall, and fits-and-starts viewpoints therefore all present problems. But there is a solution, which combines all three scenarios – that of a language bonfire.

A language bonfire is a compromise solution, but it is also the most likely. Probably, some sparks of language had been flickering for a very long time, like a bonfire in which just a few twigs catch alight at first. Suddenly, a flame leaps between the twigs, and ignites the whole mass of heaped-up wood. Then the fire slows down and stabilizes, and glows red-hot and powerful.

This slow-quick-quick-slow scenario, with its gradual beginning – explosive growth – eventual slowing down and stabilizing, is represented on a graph as an 'S-curve', an upward swing in the shape of a letter S. It underlies many world happenings, such as tides rising and falling. As a tide runs out, at first just a few gallons of water seep out. Then the vast majority of water surges seaward. Then the remaining few gallons eddy out slowly (see Fig. 5.4).

For the language blaze to take hold, the foundations must have been laid, but probably not fully exploited. In human discoveries, the basic insights have sometimes been around for decades or more, but their possibilities not realized. Stationary steam engines, for example, had existed for around a century, used at first to pump water out of mines, before Richard Trevithick set one on wheels and ran it along rails at the beginning of the nineteenth century.[29]

Probably, a simplified type of language began to emerge at least as early as 250,000 BP.[30] Piece by piece, the foundations were slowly put in place. Somewhere between 100,000 and 75,000 BP perhaps, language reached a critical stage of sophistication. Ignition point arrived, and there was a massive blaze, during which language developed fast and dramatically. By around

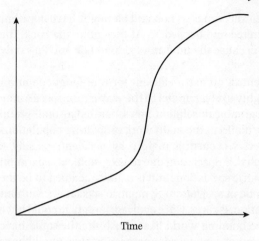

Time

Figure 5.4 S-curve

50,000 BP it was slowing down and stabilizing as a steady long-term glow. This would tie in with the sudden flowering of culture from around this time (chapter 13).

The bush fire

But there's a distinction between language emergence (the bonfire) and its diffusion – the spread to other humans (a bush fire). In language change, there's usually a ripple effect. A change spreads out like ripples on a pond. In the early stages of language, before 'take off' point, progressive waves of embryo languages might have rippled through the hominid population, who became accustomed to a simplified type of verbal exchange.

A small isolated band of individuals might then have formed the core of a new group of super-efficient talkers. It's a scenario found in William Golding's novel *The inheritors*: an earlier race with a limited form of language is eventually eliminated by a new group with superior language skills. The old group use language sparsely: 'Wait. Ha there. Fa there. Nil too. Lok!'[31] Later, Lok and Fa, survivors from the old group, watch the new people, 'the inheritors', whose language is more developed: 'They did not gesticulate much nor dance out their meanings as Lok and Fa might have done but their thin lips puttered and flapped.'³² At the end of the book, the old group die out because the inheritors kidnap Lok and Fa's only surviving infant.

The development of an extra-efficient form of language in an isolated area is highly likely, parallel to the way a new species may emerge when geographical isolation has separated a small group from the main population, 'the main work of splitting populations into incipient species occurring mainly by accident, usually a caprice of geography'.³³ Speciation due to geographical separation is known as allopatric speciation, and is usually claimed to be the most common mode of speciation. Sympatric speciation, without geographical isolation, is rarer. Once evolved, language could have swept through the hominid world like a bush fire. It would have given its speakers an enormous advantage, and they would have been able to impose their will on others, who might then learn the language.³⁴

Inspired selection

There's one final question. How did humans hit on something as bizarre as language, a type of communication that has more in common with birdsong than with the grunts of other primates (chapter 1)?

Nature is over-prolific in providing possible pathways along which animals may travel. Most species are over-endowed with possible courses of action, according to recent research. Waiting in the wings, as it were, are a range of behaviours which could be triggered, given the right set of circumstances.

This insight started in biology, especially in work on immune systems.³⁵ Species are endowed with many more possible antibodies than they can ever expect to use to combat diseases. Indeed, if a new disease came along, and antibodies did not already exist, then the species would be wiped out before any started to develop. Successful evolution may be a case of inspired or even accidental selection. An animal chooses, sometimes by forced choice, to go along one route, rather than another.

Humans are exploratory animals with initiative – maybe partly because only hardy and creative individuals survived in the testing East Side. Out of the numerous routes available, these early humans took an innovative one, which paid dividends:

> Two roads diverged in a wood, and I –
> I took the one less traveled by,
> And that has made all the difference.

This was a comment by the poet Robert Frost on his life,[36] but it applies equally to humankind and language.

Once a path is chosen, then this constrains future choices. An animal which selects to give birth to live animals, could not go back to producing eggs, just as a tree which started to drop its leaves could not go back to keeping them all the year round. Once humans came down from the trees and started walking and talking, they were obliged to continue.

But just how did humans happen to have available the basic abilities which allowed them to choose language as an option? This will be the topic of the next chapter.

Summary

Humans are cousins of apes, not descended from them. Humans split off from the apes maybe more than 6 million years ago. Modern humans evolved around 200,000 years ago, and modern language possibly emerged even later, perhaps around 100,000 years ago.

Humans may have separated from apes when the Great Rift Valley split Africa. Apes remained happily swinging in trees. Hominids in their harsher landscape were forced to adapt, scavenge and live on their wits. At some point, they developed language. The 'out of Africa' hypothesis for humans is supported by evidence from mitochondrial DNA and blood groups.

Over language origin, neither the fast development (rabbit-out-of-a-hat) supporters nor the slow haul (snail-up-a-wall) proponents are likely to be entirely right. The emergence of language may have been like a bonfire: slow beginning (from around 250,000 BP), fast development (from around 100,000 BP), then gradual slowing down into a long-term steady glow.

Many groups of speakers might have had an embryo language, but full language may have developed among a small group whose language had evolved further than those of others. This could have enabled them to outwit existing groups, to whom they may have taught their language.

6 A devious mind:
The basic requirements

My mother ... predicted that
Future rulers would conquer and control
Not by strength, nor by violence,
But by cunning.

Aeschylus, *Prometheus bound* (fifth century BC)

'No truth appears to me more evident, than that beasts are endow'd with thought and reason as well as men',[1] commented the eighteenth-century Scottish philosopher David Hume. The words 'thought' and 'reason' are wide-ranging. But increasingly, we humans are found to share with our ape relatives some basic aspects of thought and behaviour, including some that are crucial to language.

Humans, like other primates, are often called 'social animals'. But this vague term applies equally well to herds of cows. The quality of the links is what counts. Primate social structure is characterized by strong family ties, active interaction at the group level, and a well-defined ranking or 'pecking order'. To promote these, two types of behaviour have emerged: a predisposition to groom one another, and, among the more intelligent species, an ability to make guesses about the mental state of others. This ability to 'put oneself into another person's shoes' can be used to aid others or to deceive them.

These key properties may underlie the development of language. They tie in with the two things language is especially good at: aiding interaction with others, and influencing them (chapter 2).

This chapter will explore the matter further. It will then assess an oldish theory, but one which still surfaces at intervals – that gesture was the missing link between primate communication and human language. Finally, it will discuss a brain-first versus language-first controversy: was a big brain a prerequisite for language? Or did language cause the large human brain?

Gossip not grooming?

The people of Bartledan were remarkably like human beings to look at, but when you said 'Good evening' to one, he would tend to look around with a slight sense of surprise, sniff the air and say that, yes, he supposed that it probably was a goodish evening.

Humans love yakking to one another, even when they have nothing of importance to say (chapter 1), as satirized above in Douglas Adams's science-fiction novel *Mostly harmless*.[2]

'Do gossip and lack of grooming make us human?' is a question asked by some researchers.[3] Social chit-chat may be the human equivalent of the friendly grooming found in other primate groups. It's even been called 'grooming talking'.[4] 'You can stroke people with words', comments the novelist F. Scott Fitzgerald.[5] 'Tina knows how to stroke', said the former deputy of magazine editor Tina Brown.[6]

Widespread grooming may be feasible only when groups are small, and substitute procedures may have to be found when they get large. A group size of 150 led to its abandonment, it has been claimed.[7] A more sophisticated social structure could have led to increased brain size. This larger brain made language possible, and also desirable, given the need to find a grooming substitute.

The grooming theory fits in with the observation that language is an intimate type of interaction, better at close quarters than across vast spaces (chapters 1–2). But group size alone may not be particularly important, and bands of 150 may have occurred earlier, with no language development.[8] The quality of the interactions matters more than overall numbers: the bleating of sheep might turn into language if herd-size alone was crucial.

Gossip rather than grooming might have been promoted by several factors. Humans are 'naked apes' with little hair for grooming. Spoken language leaves the hands free for other activities, perhaps important in open savannah where humans possibly lived at one time (chapter 5). Sounds can be heard in the dark, and messages can be transmitted rapidly.

Parent and baby contact may also have played a part. Mothers and fathers probably smiled and cooed at their infants even before language evolved. 'It would have made excellent biological sense for any new communicative displays to "piggy back" onto this open channel – to take advantage of a long-standing commitment to maternal–infant attachment by embedding new information in the same stream of clues ... I have speculated that this is what our ancestors did when they invented spoken language', suggests one researcher.[9]

Quite how humans hit on language is still unclear in its details, but chimp pant-hoots give a clue. They show that expressions of solidarity via vocalization come easily to primates. These deep huhh-uhh huhh-uhh in–out pants are uttered primarily by male chimpanzees. At one time, they were thought to be a simple cohesion call, but this turned out not to be the case. So primatologists were left with a problem: 'Males seemed to be communicating something to each other, but just what it was nobody quite understood.'[10] Some recent research may have solved the question.[11] Males pant-hoot most often when they are close to other males with whom they have some type of alliance. This indicates that the pant-hoots are connected with male–male bonds. They also differ slightly from group to group, suggesting that group membership is reinforced by hearing them. Some human male sporting teams appear to be carrying on the tradition.

Man of many wiles

Tell me, O muse, of the man of many wiles...

said the Greek epic-writer Homer, introducing the devious hero Odysseus, the man who, by living on his wits, finally arrived unscathed at his home island of Ithaca after a ten-year voyage.[12] Odysseus is a successful human, in that he achieved his goal of reaching home. He was a winner, not a loser. And he sometimes deceived others to achieve his ends.

The ability to deceive may be an important prerequisite for language. But it's not confined to humans, in spite of popular sentiment. In the last century, animals were often assumed to be straightforward, and humans to be dishonest self-seekers. Take the nineteenth-century biologist T. H. Huxley:

A man has no reason to be ashamed of having an ape for his grandfather. If there were an ancestor whom I should feel shame in recalling it would rather be a *man*...who...plunges into scientific questions with which he has no real acquaintance, only to obscure them by an aimless rhetoric, and distract the attention of his hearers from the real point at issue by eloquent digressions and skilled appeals to religious prejudice.[13]

The extent of animal deception is only now becoming clear. Stick insects, for example, have a natural camouflage which makes them hard to spot among twigs. But some animals can intentionally deceive: they can knowingly alternate their behaviour between the misleading and the straightforward.

A wide variety of animals deceive intermittently: 'There is no doubt that clever dogs can dissemble up to a certain point', noted the famous ethologist Konrad Lorenz.[14] His dog Stasi had an inflamed front paw. If Lorenz bicycled in a direction which was uncongenial to her, she limped pitifully. But the pain appeared to disappear if he turned in a direction she liked. Old dog Bully had failing eyesight, and sometimes inadvertently barked at homecoming members of the family. After realizing his mistake, he would push past Lorenz, and bark furiously at a neighbour's gate, as though he had been addressing an enemy in that garden from the beginning. Such anecdotes led to the realization that intentional deceit was not confined to humans.

But the deceit of dogs is not well-planned. True deceit involves 'tactical deception': 'Acts from the normal repertoire of the agent, deployed such that another individual is likely to misinterpret what the acts signify, to the advantage of the agent.'[15] Such intentional deceptive behaviour can properly be called 'lying'.[16] Most primates can do it. Humans are very good at it (chapter 1), and can even reason about it, as in Ruth Rendell's novel *The crocodile bird*:

> Liza listened outside the door. She heard Eve tell Jonathan it was half-term. Perhaps it was. In that case what she said wasn't really untrue. Of course, that depended on what you meant by a lie. It was a lie if by lying you meant intending to deceive. Eve certainly intended to deceive Jonathan in thinking Liza went to school.[17]

The *ability* to deceive is not necessarily a bad thing. In order to hoodwink intentionally, it is essential to understand someone else's point of view. This is a powerful skill, which may be used selfishly or unselfishly. To exercise it, it's necessary to mentally 'put oneself into another person's shoes'. Humans can do this: they can imagine alternative possible worlds, and treat others as if they had 'mental states'.

Those who can represent the minds of others in their own minds are said to have a 'theory of mind', something possessed by all normal humans.[18] A few unfortunates suffer from a puzzling deficit, an inability to understand another's point of view. This condition is sometimes referred to as 'mindblindness', and it is a major symptom of autism.[19] To 'mindblind' humans, the world is a confusing place which they never 'get the hang of'. Some can talk, but they have great difficulty in fully understanding other people.

Animals who possess a theory of mind are good at social manipulation. A recent survey carried out by researchers at the University of St Andrews has assessed which primates, alongside humans, are particularly good at hoodwinking one another.[20] Successful deceit often involves secrecy, so the task was a difficult one. But the results were surprisingly clearcut. Intentional deception was found among most primate species, but some are much better at it than others. Monkeys are fairly poor at it. Baboons and great apes are good at it. Among the great apes, chimps, our nearest relatives, turn out to be exceptionally skilled deceivers. And it starts young. An infant chimp may scream as if it is being attacked in order to persuade its mother to comfort and feed it. An older chimp may lead others away from hidden food, then double back and scoff the lot itself while the others are elsewhere.

Great apes engage in complex social manipulations which show remarkable cunning, the researchers concluded. The manipulations are always selfish, at least in non-humans. This ability to deceive has been labelled 'Machiavellian intelligence',[21] after the fifteenth-century Italian Niccolo Machiavelli who wrote a guide showing ways in which a future ruler could manipulate others.[22]

Open-country living may have aided this aptitude for deception, since both chimps and baboons who are good deceivers are less tree-oriented than monkeys who are poor deceivers.[23] Away from the trees, more social organization among large groups might be needed, with more opportunities for deception. The use of cunning perhaps helped to cause an enlarged brain, which in turn made it possible to use this large brain for developing a superb manipulative device: language.

Possibly only one primate branch, the great apes, has a true theory of mind, the ability to attribute intentions to others. Among them, only the *Homo* line made the final step to language. But we are not so far away, perhaps, from our ape cousins: 'Modern great apes may completely lack the formalizing systems of language, but they do not appear to lack understanding of what this kind of communication is about.'[24]

Arguably, humans may not be as self-seeking as other primates. Our enlarged brain allowed a greater awareness of others, and the brain's use for unselfish, as well as selfish, purposes. Almost certainly, a theory of mind is a desirable acquisition, even if it can be used for deceit: it allows human language to discuss people and events removed in time and place. This property of displacement is one of language's most valuable characteristics.[25]

The search for the missing link

But there's a missing link. Exactly HOW did language get started? According to one controversial view, sign language provided a stepping-stone. Humans with their pliable, tool-making hands devised a system of gestures before the human vocal tract could handle a full range of sounds. At a later date, the signs were transferred to vocal noises.[26]

The gesture theory is an old one. The eighteenth-century French thinker Abbé Etienne Bonot de Condillac suggested that early humans might instinctively point at something they wanted.[27] The gesture became conventionalized, as 'little by little they succeeded in doing deliberately what at first they had done only by instinct'.[28] These gestures were sometimes accompanied by sounds, he surmised: 'One, for example, who saw a place where he had been frightened, would imitate the cries and actions which were the signs of fright in order to warn the other not to expose himself to the same danger'.[29] The original preference for gesture, Condillac suggested, was because primitive humans did not suspect that the human voice could be far more variously modulated and articulated than those few natural cries. Consequently they opted for 'action language' which was, he assumed, easier and more natural than phonetic language. In the long run, the sounds became more important than the gestures – though Condillac does not fully explain this mysterious process.

Modern supporters of the gestural theory emphasize four points. First, language is not inevitably spoken. Second, gestures are universal and obvious (a mistaken belief). Third, signs are easier to acquire than 'full' languages. Fourth, language and gesture may be linked in the brain. Let us consider these.

'Language is independent of speech, and does not presuppose its prior existence' notes the linguist John Lyons,[30] pointing out that language is 'a multi-layered or multi-stranded phenomenon, each of whose layers or strands may be of different antiquity and of different origin'.[31] He proposes a gestural origin of speech, though he accepts that evidence in favour of it is 'admittedly, not very strong'.[32] Certainly, the observation that language need not be spoken provides very little support for the idea: alternative media, such as sign, writing and touch (braille) are found only partially around the world, compared with spoken language which is everywhere. The existence of sign language, now firmly recognized as a 'full' language, simply emphasizes that language is biologically inbuilt in modern humans: the urge for it to emerge is so strong that it can be transferred to different modalities.

The idea that gestures are the same the world over has a wide appeal. A couple of centuries ago, the sign language of the deaf was heralded as a universal language: 'The universal language that your scholars have sought for in vain of which they have despaired, is here; it is right before your eyes, it is the mimicry of the impoverished deaf. Because you do not know it, you hold it in contempt, yet it alone will provide you with the key to all languages', claimed the eighteenth-century writer Abbé de l'Epée.[33]

The apparent naturalness of gestures such as pointing gives the hypothesis a superficial plausibility. In the words of the nineteenth-century writer Franz Grillparzer: 'The only signs that are intelligible prior to all convention are gestures, and so the first language will have been a gesture-language. This comes so naturally to man that even today we accompany our speech with gestures.'[34]

Similar arguments are still put forward: 'In some respects it is more natural to communicate with the hands than with the voice . . . Even today, of course, we resort to gesture when we wish to communicate with those who speak a different tongue', claims a modern researcher.[35]

Yet this view is a mirage. Apart from a few gestures such as pointing, the remainder are not particularly obvious. Reportedly, some English students who had hired a rowing-boat were arrested off the coast of Greece as they unknowingly approached a military installation: locals had tried to warn them, but the students had interpreted the local 'go away' gesture as a 'come hither' one. As for sign languages, there are hundreds of them, and more than fifty are described in detail in a recent encyclopaedia.[36]

Gestures, then, are neither obvious nor universal. But the 'signs as stepping stones' supporters defend the supposed 'naturalness' of signing in another way: signs can be 'picked up' more easily than speech, it is sometimes claimed, judging by the relative ease with which primates such as the famous signing chimp Washoe and others have acquired a language-like system based on American sign language.[37] Some mentally handicapped children have also found signs easier to grasp than ordinary language.[38] But humans have never automatically taken the easiest way forwards, especially if it is inefficient: signs cannot be seen in the dark, and they occupy the hands.

Deaf children have been brought into this argument: children born without hearing spontaneously produce sign-like gestures at a time when hearing babies go through a vocal 'babbling' phase, the production of *bababa, mamama* type sequences, it has been claimed. Sign 'babbling' therefore apparently replaces sound babbling.[39] But the study of these deaf infants is inconclusive: the authors observed the phenomenon in only two nine-month-old children, both of whom had signing parents, whom they might have been imitating.

Brain structure is another factor used by supporters of a sign-language origin for language. The left hemisphere of the human brain is specialized both for right-handedness and for language, suggesting a neurological connection, especially as hand movements tend to occur during speech.[40] In addition, babies between nine and twelve months old sometimes gesture towards an object as they attempt to pronounce some type of word, though not necessarily a real word. This involves an area at the front of the brain which in monkeys plays a role in the visual guidance of reaching. It's a brain area activated also when people mentally look up the meaning of isolated words. But it plays a relatively small role in complex language processing.[41]

Let us therefore summarize. Gestures are regarded by some as a 'missing link', adopted before humans were capable of making a wide range of vocal sounds. Supporters of this view point out that language is not inevitably spoken, that signs are easily learnable, that humans are skilled with their hands, and that words in isolation activate a brain area used in reaching and pointing. Some mistakenly argue that sign language is universal and obvious.

But these are fairly flimsy arguments. They show only that language is often supported by visual aids, such as winks, hand-waving, and shrugged shoulders, as well as tactile aids, such as pushes, pats and kisses. These gestures presumably aided vocal communication millions of years ago, the same as they do today. But they were probably not elaborated into a complex system.

But perhaps some people cling to the gestural theory because it allows them to think of themselves as industrious and conscientious tool-users, who used their hands as extensions of their tools, and their voices as extensions of their hands. It provides a happier self-image than the probable truth, that we are a race of manipulative persuaders, albeit friendly ones.

The pop hypothesis

'Our brain is three times as large as we would expect for a primate of our build', according to one researcher.[42] But there's a crucial chicken-and-egg question. Is our big brain the cause of language? Or did language cause our big brain? This is a major controversy.

The brain-causes-language supporters suggest that language is a by-product, an afterthought which made use of an existing powerful mental apparatus. Recently, it's become known as the 'pop hypothesis', following on from a discussion on an electronic bulletin board, when one contributor asked: 'But how do we know that human language didn't just "pop" into being after the mind crossed a certain threshold for other reasons?'[43] It's a view supported by the prominent evolutionist Stephen Jay Gould.[44]

According to Gould, anyone who believes in the purposeful evolution of language is putting forward a topsy-turvy argument, and saying in effect: 'Our brains were made to carry language, so we have language.' He and a colleague label their opponents' ideas 'Panglossian', from Dr Pangloss, a character created by the eighteenth-century French satirical writer Voltaire. Dr Pangloss argued that 'Our noses were made to carry spectacles, so we have spectacles.' What we should be saying, they claim, is: 'We have this amazing brain, so we might as well use it for language.'[45]

'Exaptation' is the key to language, they believe: the adaptation of an existing structure for a new purpose. The spandrels in the San Marco cathedral in Venice are used to demonstrate this point. Spandrels are the inevitable by-product of mounting a dome on rounded arches which are placed at right angles to one another: they are the tapering triangular spaces formed between the arches. In the cathedral, these have been adorned with eye-catching and delightful paintings: one, for example, depicts a seated evangelist above a slender water-pourer. So stunning are these murals, that they are often the first thing noted by a visitor, who might as a first impression assume that the pillars and dome were designed purely as a mounting for the paintings. On second thoughts, however, it becomes clear that the spandrels were a by-product of the cathedral's basic design, and the murals must have been a lucky afterthought (see Fig. 6.1).

So according to the 'language is a spandrel' view, language is an ingenious afterthought, something which simply made use of a pre-existing powerful brain. Perhaps this happened when walking upright freed the hands to carry food and tools: 'What were the hominids to do with their mouths rendered thus relatively idle except when they were eating? The answer is: they chattered.'[46]

But this by-product view is highly unlikely, as language is too complex. Exaptation – a re-use of an existing structure – is un-

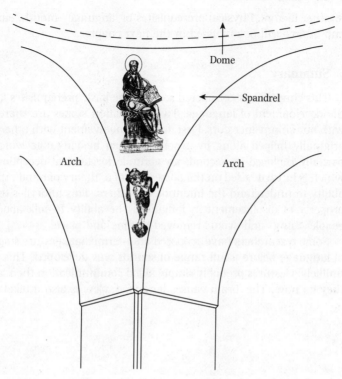

Figure 6.1 A spandrel, based on a spandrel in the San Marco cathedral in Venice

doubtedly a powerful force in evolution. But in all documented cases, complex structures are used for simple purposes, and not vice versa. A type of wading bird uses its wings as a sunshade: there is no evidence of any bird using what was originally a sunshade as wings. You can use a television as a paperweight, but you cannot use a paperweight as a television.[47] The complexity of language, and the interwoven adaptations of the mouth, larynx and brain make it unlikely that language could have developed as an accidental by-product.

The brain-first vs language-first controversy may be an artificial one. Language and the human big brain may have emerged simultaneously,[48] though the initial enlargement was possibly due to other factors. Physical prerequisites of language – mouth, ears and brain – will be discussed in the next chapter.

Summary

This chapter has considered some of the basic prerequisites for the development of language. Two foundation stones are shared with our chimp ancestors. First, friendly involvement with others, originally helped along by grooming, then by language which partially replaced it. Second, an aptitude for tactical deception, which is in turn based on the possession of a 'theory of mind', the ability to understand the intentions of others. This underlies the property of displacement in language, the ability to talk about people, things and events removed in time and place.

Some researchers have proposed an intermediate gesture stage of language before a full range of sounds was developed. This is unlikely. Gestures probably simply aided communication then, as they do now. The 'brain causes language' view is also unlikely.

7 Broken air:
Inherited ingredients

Soune is noght but eyre ybroken
And every spech that ys yspoken,
Lowde or pryvee, foule or faire,
In his substance ys but aire;
For as flaumbe ys but lyghted smoke,
Ryght too soune ys aire y-broke.

Geoffrey Chaucer, *The house of fame* (*c*.1375)

Chaucer, writing in the fourteenth century, was wrong to regard flame as lighted smoke, but right to regard speech as broken air.[1] But the broken air of speech is highly complex, and requires a range of physical structures for handling it. Speech is 'a thing of shreds and patches',[2] a hotch-potch whose ingredients probably evolved at different times in human prehistory.

At least four interlinked parts are needed. For outgoing sounds (production), there must be an organizer which decides what sounds are needed, and a sound-producing device to make them. For incoming sounds (reception), there must be a device to receive them, and another to interpret them. The organizer and interpreter are the key to the whole operation. But to be effective, they must be attached to the sound-producer and the sound-receiver – or some efficient substitute (see Fig. 7.1).

All these ingredients are partially present in our chimp cousins, some of them in a highly developed state. Our hearing mechanisms seem to be more similar to theirs than dissimilar. Our mouth and larynx (voice-box) are streamlined versions of those of other primates. Our large brain is similar in structure to theirs, but much bigger, and with more voluntary control over vocal output. The size may be partly the result of humans 'getting it all together' – acquiring the networks which link up the various language components.[3]

This chapter will consider the various bits and pieces, starting

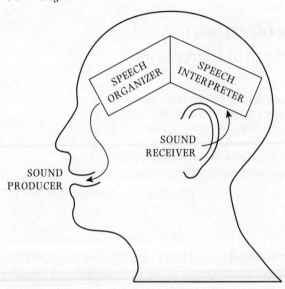

Figure 7.1 Basic ingredients for speech

with the probable oldest, those which appear to be most strongly shared with other primates.

Telling noise from signal

The man I work with – Gunther – started to go deaf fairly recently. The doctors couldn't explain why but his hearing problems became so bad that he was obliged to be fitted with a hearing aid. He told me that, initially, he found the amplified sound in his head alarmingly hard to cope with. Everything came at him in a rush, he said, trying to explain the effect, sounds were suddenly unfamiliar and new. 'You see, Hope,' he said a little plaintively, 'the problem was that I couldn't tell what was irrelevant and what was important . . . I couldn't tell noise from signal.'[4]

Humans are 'tuned in' to the sounds of their own species. Manufacturers of hearing aids have not succeeded in capturing something which our ears do naturally: pick out human voices from other noises, as shown by the above extract from William Boyd's novel *Brazzaville beach*. Just as bullfrogs respond to bullfrogs,[5] and macaque monkeys tune in to other macaques,[6] human babies are able to recognize human voices with ease, twelve hours after birth, according to one report.[7] In general, animals tune in to sounds which they themselves are capable of making, and, in particular, to those of their own species.

But there's an imbalance. Ability to recognize calls is often far in advance of an ability to produce them. Sometimes also juvenile calls differ from adult ones. This is fairly clear in human children, but it's also found in other primates. Baby squirrel monkeys emit a call, when separated from their mother, which disappears as the animal gets older.[8] And young vervet monkeys learn to distinguish vervet calls before they can properly produce them, a skill which takes at least two years to acquire.[9]

Reception and production skills are therefore separate. Many mammals learn to discriminate between sounds they can never make, as Charles Darwin noted in 1871: 'That which distinguishes man from the lower animals is not the understanding of articulate sounds, for, as every one knows, dogs understand many words and sentences.'[10] And even though primates cannot produce the sounds of human language, they may be able to hear them.

Basic properties of the ear are common to humans and other primates. In a now-famous experiment, human infants between one and four months old were able to hear the difference between [p] and [b] quite easily, but were unable to distinguish between different types of [b], when in physical measurements the [b] differences were quite substantial. And similar results were later obtained with [b] versus [d] versus [g], which the infants also distinguished from one another. This phenomenon has been called 'categorical perception', because the babies appeared naturally to place certain speech sounds into one category or another.[11]

A few years after this experiment came a surprise finding. Other primates, in this case rhesus and chinchilla monkeys, were able to do the same thing.[12] Both children and monkeys were given pacifiers to suck, each of which was wired to a pre-set sound.[13] At first this was one sound, say [p], so as the subjects sucked, they heard [pah-pah-pah]. They gradually got bored and sucked more slowly. Then the [p] was changed to [b]. An increase in the sucking rate showed they had noticed the difference. This demonstrates the highly sensitive nature of primate ears, and their similarity across species.[14]

The humans and monkeys may not have heard the sounds in exactly the same way.[15] Humans listening to the calls of Japanese macaque monkeys pay attention to different aspects of the sound signal: humans notice the duration of the sounds, but this does not seem to be so important for the macaques.[16] But one thing is clear: the primate ear is highly sensitive, and can normally discriminate far more sounds than the animal is able to produce.[17]

Quite why primates developed such acute hearing is unclear. But the pitch frequencies needed for recognizing consonants may correspond to the range found in the breaking sounds of dry branches and leaves. So our sensitive ears perhaps reveal our tree-top origins.[18]

Speech reception involves more than simply distinguishing between different sounds. Humans can tell who is speaking, and also the mood of speakers – whether they are angry, sad, and so on. But so, it appears, can other primates.[19] These different abilities – voice recognition and understanding emotional effect – are apparently handled by different brain areas.[20]

The hearing prerequisites for language were therefore mostly in place before humans split from chimps. Perhaps only integration of the various parts and fine-tuning were necessary in order for sounds to be fully discriminated.

Making noises

Speech mostly uses exhaled air, so lungs are required to puff out wind (the respiratory component). A voice-box is needed to transform the air into noise (the phonatory component). A muscular tongue, even-sized teeth and powerful lips are necessary for a wide range of sounds (the articulatory component).[21]

Lungs are of very great antiquity. According to Charles Darwin, lungs developed from swim bladders, inflated sacs which allow fish to float. But swim bladders arose from lungs, judging from recent research. A few fish even retain the connection of the swim bladder with their windpipe, and can inflate the bladder by gulping air at the surface.[22]

The voice-box or larynx is another antique feature. It contains the vocal folds (or chords), thin strips of membrane deep in the throat. Humming sounds are made when these folds just touch one other and vibrate as air is pushed through them. The vibration can be felt if a finger is placed on the Adam's apple while saying *hmm* or *bzz*. The vocal folds were probably in origin a valve which closed off the lung/swim bladder in water, so preventing flooding.[23] In primates, this valve evolved into a membrane used for closing off the lungs in order to make the rib-cage rigid when extra effort was needed. It's still used today by any human swinging from a beam, but also in more mundane activities such as lifting a suitcase and defecation, as well as in speech.

The human larynx is more streamlined than that of other primates, in that it contains fewer appendages.[24] It is also lower in the throat, though why this happened is unclear. Walking on two feet may have been the trigger that set in motion a cascade of anatomical changes, including a lowered larynx.[25] Other researchers, however, dispute the link with bipedalism.[26] According to one theory, primates developed hand–eye co-ordination for food gathering, leading to sophisticated sight, but weaker smelling capacities. Consequently, primate muzzles became shorter, which in turn reduced the size of the upper jaw, but not of the tongue. As this became thicker and more muscular in humans, it may have pushed the larynx down in the neck.[27] (See Fig. 7.2.)

The lowered larynx was an advantage for speech, but at a price. Unlike other primates, humans can choke to death, since we cannot close our lungs off when we eat. This was noted even by Darwin, who commented on 'the strange fact that any particle of food and drink which we swallow has to pass over the orifice of the trachea (windpipe), with some risk of falling into the lungs'.[28]

Nobody knows when the larynx reached its current low position, and the archaeological evidence is disputed. A modern-shaped hyoid bone, a bone normally located at the top of the human windpipe, has been found recently on a skull which may or may not be human dating from around 100,000 years ago.[29] But it's unclear whether the bone was located in the same position as in modern humans.

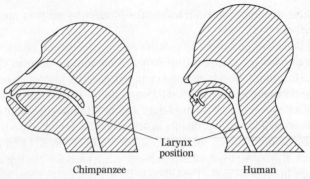

Chimpanzee   Human

Figure 7.2 Chimp vs human vocal tract

In the long run, the lowered larynx led to our modern-day human vocal tract – the section shaped like an upside-down letter L which runs from the top of the larynx to the mouth. This L-shape increased the number of sounds which could be pronounced, and also their clarity, as will be explained in the next section.

Vowels and consonants

The hoots of chimps are embryo syllables, which provide the basic frame for speech sounds. The core of a syllable is the vowel, and primitive vowels are found in numerous animals as well as primates. Vowels have been described as 'simple', in that 'some of the sounds that very simple animals like bullfrogs make are really short, isolated vowels . . . the acoustic properties and physiology of human sustained vowels and bullfrog mating calls are similar'.[30] Chimps also can produce vowel-like sounds, but not very distinct ones.[31]

Vowels are made by altering the flow of air from the lungs via different tongue shapes. In this, humans have at least two important advantages over chimps. First, humans have a chunky muscular tongue, over which they have good control. Second, they can produce vowels via the mouth, rather than the nose. The L-shape caused by the lowered larynx allows humans to seal off the nasal cavity by raising the 'soft palate', the back of the roof of the mouth. Before this happened, nasalized sounds only would have been possible, in which the air is expelled partially through the nose: these nasal sounds are more difficult to recognize than non-nasal ones.[32]

These advantages allow humans to produce three fairly extreme vowels: [i], [a], [u]. These are stabler than others, in that they vary relatively little. They provide 'anchor points' for identification.[33] The vowel [i] is particularly important. It is produced with the tongue pushed forward with the front part raised, a so-called high front vowel. The result is somewhat like the sound sometimes used to imitate mouse squeaks, conventionally spelled 'ee-ee' or 'eek-eek'. It is counterbalanced by [u], a high back vowel, in which the tongue is pulled back, with the back part raised, as in the 'ooh!' of surprise or appreciation. The third of the trio, [a] is produced with the mouth fairly open, and the tongue low and fairly central, somewhat like the 'ah!' of realization or recognition. Relatively few words would have been easily distinguishable without these key vowels, and only humans can articulate them (see Fig. 7.3).

Before the key vowels were possible, clear words were unlikely, and the situation might have been similar to that described by

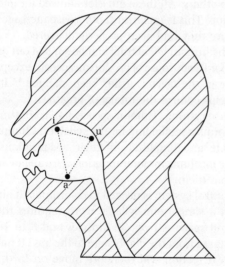

Figure 7.3 Vowel triangle

Edgar Rice Burroughs, in his fanciful novel *Tarzan of the apes* (1912): 'The language of the apes had so few words that they could talk but little of what they had seen in the cabin, having no words to accurately describe the strange people or their belongings.'[34]

As for consonants, primate lip-smacks use essentially the same mechanism as humans do for [p], [b] and [m] – and these are among the first sounds reliably produced by human infants. Less reliably, primates can move the tip of the tongue up against the teeth and roof of the mouth to produce sounds such as [d], [s], [t].[35] But only humans can produce [k] and [g], which even now are relatively unstable sounds in that they tend to change.[36]

Modern humans have even-sized teeth, a thick, muscular tongue, and interlaced facial muscles, all used in making precise speech sounds. It's unclear how much these features owe to language, because they are also useful in other ways. Even-sized teeth are helpful for grinding up grains and roots so they can be easily digested. Tongue musculature aids in gathering together fragments of food in the mouth. Face and lip muscles are required for social interaction, allowing a wider range of facial expressions, especially smiling. Probably, the effect was cumulative, each function helped develop others. All these muscles allowed a rapid rate of delivery to develop. This is important, otherwise messages might be forgotten before they had been properly delivered.

Overall, nothing in the human vocal tract can be singled out as being specialized solely for the purpose of producing speech, except perhaps for one muscle in the larynx, it has been claimed.[37] In animals, this muscle helps control the intake of breath.

But sounds are not everything. Human speech has a rhythm and intonation which forms a scaffolding for the syllables. Chimps can vary the pitch, rate and amplitude of their vocalizations, suggesting that the basic mechanisms for intonation were available before humans split from them.[38]

Finally, an overall control system is needed to co-ordinate it all: 'The utterance of even a simple one-syllable word requires the coordination in time and space of over 70 muscles and 8 to 10 different body parts, ranging from the diaphragm to the lips', it has been claimed.[39] The next section will therefore move on to the brain, where this co-ordination happens.

The proper brain

'Without the proper brain to run it . . . a new mouth was of no help.'[40] The new mouth, relocated larynx, and fairly old ears, needed to be co-ordinated by the most important component, a developed brain.

'Why does everybody call me bighead?' runs a popular song, and with reason. We modern humans have a brain around three times the size of that of the average chimp, twice as large as that of *Homo habilis*, a third as big again as that of *Homo erectus*.[41] (See Fig. 7.4.)

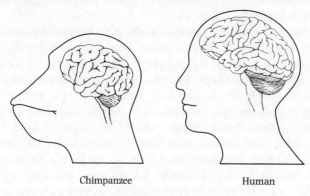

Chimpanzee   Human

Figure 7.4 Chimp vs human brain

The relationship between brain size and language is unclear (chapter 6). Possibly, increased social interaction combined with tactical deception gave the brain an initial impetus. Better nourishment due to meat-eating may also have played a part.[42] Then brain size and language possibly increased together.[43] 'If humans weren't using and refining language I would like to know what they *were* doing with their autocatalytically increasing brains', comments one researcher.[44]

Like the brain of many other animals, the human brain is divided into two halves or hemispheres, each of which has its own tasks. A major advantage is that damage to one side does not inevitably mean lost faculties in the other:

> Much I owe to the Lands that grew –
> More to the Lives that fed –
> But most to Allah Who gave me two
> Separate sides to my head.

says the poet Rudyard Kipling in 'The two-sided man'.[45]

The left hemisphere controls movement in the right side of the body, and also language in most humans. The connection has been known for a long time. In the Bible, a psalm begs: 'If I will forget thee, Jerusalem, let my right hand die – let my tongue stick to the roof of my mouth.'[46] This is a reference to the right-sided paralysis and language impairment which is likely to afflict anyone who has a left hemisphere stroke – regarded in the Bible as a punishment for wrongdoing (see Fig. 7.5).

But exactly how language and handedness are linked is disputed.[47] It's also unclear how this link ties in with our ape cousins. Primates do not show a consistent hand preference, according to some researchers. Others say they change hands, depending on the task, using their right hands for manipulation, and their left hands for reaching.[48] This may have a 'postural origin'. When an animal is clinging in a vertical posture, the right hand is typically used for holding on, the left for stretching and reaching – behaviour seen today in the lesser bush baby, for example, a small primate which clings vertically.[49] This theory does not tie in obviously with language. But it fits in with a claim that speech with its detailed mouth movements would 'come under the direction of the hemisphere already well developed for precise motor control'.[50]

More crucial, perhaps, is the type of specialization found in the human left hemisphere: sequencing is one of its specialities. Perhaps the hemisphere which helped the right hand to place things in a careful left–right order was also the one which came to arrange sounds and words one after the other.[51]

But before humans could voluntarily put things in order, they needed to suppress instinctive vocal responses to external events. Let us consider this suppression more carefully.

The dog that didn't bark

'Is there any point to which you would wish to draw my attention?'
'To the curious incident of the dog in the night-time.'

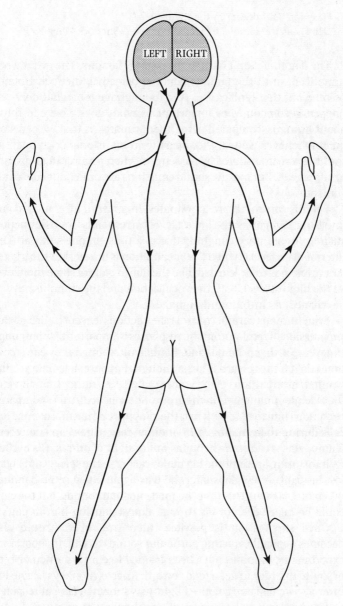

Figure 7.5 Handedness

'The dog did nothing in the night-time.'
'That was the curious incident,' remarked Sherlock Holmes.[52]

The dog that didn't bark in the night is famous. The event went unnoticed, until the famous fictional detective Sherlock Holmes pointed out the significance. And in language too, what does not happen is sometimes as important as what does. One odd thing about humans, compared with other primates, is that we can stay quiet whenever we want to, apart from occasional cries, such as the little screams uttered by passengers when an aircraft drops into an air pocket. But mostly, sound emissions are under our conscious control.

Yet this control is rare in primates. In general, utterances come into three categories: the lowest level corresponds to a reflex action such as involuntary coughing due to a tickle in one's throat. The intermediate level is when the vocalization is innate, but the trigger (stimulus) has to be learned, like the alarm calls of some monkeys. At the highest level, both the vocalization and the stimulus have to be learned, as in human language.[53]

Even humans cannot control reflex actions, except by drugs. But suppression of semi-automatic responses is important for language to develop. Other primates find this difficult, though they can sometimes do it if the reward is large enough. Papoose, a female gorilla, wanted the attentions of the young male Titus, rather than those of the older dominant male in the group. She solicited Titus's company, persuaded him to hide with her, then suppressed normal copulatory calls during their mating.[54] In another case, Figan, an adolescent chimp, was given some bananas out of sight of others. His excited calls instantly brought the big males racing to the scene, and Figan lost his fruit. A few days later, he was again given some bananas when on his own. This time 'he made no loud sounds, but the calls could be heard deep in his throat, almost causing him to gag'.[55]

Once suppression is possible, then the reverse route also becomes available, making particular sounds at will. In laboratory experiments, primates have been trained to emit a particular type of sound in order to get a food reward. Rhesus monkeys learned to utter a *coo*-call if one coloured light was shown, a *bark* in response to another, and to keep quiet at the showing of another.[56]

In language, then, as in many other human activities, suppression of once-automatic responses – the ability NOT to do something – plays an important role.

The language kitchen

Language in the brain should perhaps be envisaged as a restaurant. There's a cooking area where food is prepared, and an eating area where it's consumed. The production of language (the kitchen) is handled primarily by front (anterior) portions of the left hemisphere, an area in both humans and animals which deals with voluntary movement. Comprehension (the eating area) is dealt with mainly by back (posterior) portions, because this is the area which deals with incoming impressions. Traditionally, the anterior production portions are referred to as Broca's area, and the posterior reception portions as Wernicke's area, after the nineteenth-century neurologists who recognized their importance (see Fig. 7.6).

However, Broca's area is not a brain 'unit', and should possibly be regarded as a cover term for a cluster of interconnected areas. At least four subsections can be identified.[57] First, an area which deals with the muscles controlling speech, mainly those of the mouth.

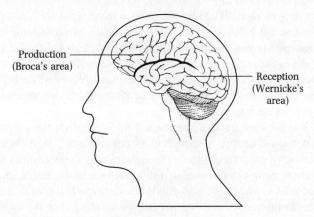

Production (Broca's area)

Reception (Wernicke's area)

Figure 7.6 The human brain: production and reception areas

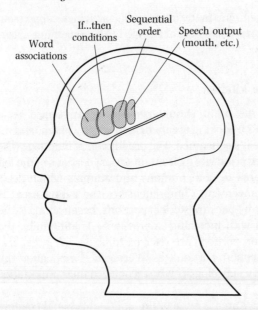

Figure 7.7 Divisions within Broca's area (from Deacon 1992)

Further forward is an area which controls sequential order, that is, the arrangment of things one after the other. Further forward still, another area deals with conditional connections, as in: 'IF it rains, THEN put up an umbrella.' Further forward still, another handles associations between words. The first three of these are probably important in the brains of other primates,[58] though humans have extended their use: 'Language functions have recruited cortical circuits that evolved for very different purposes in our primate ancestry.'[59] (See Fig. 7.7.)

But Broca's area needs to be backed up by contributions from other portions of the brain, including deeper sections.[60] And above all, links between areas matter – the waiters who carry round the plates. Increasingly, neurologists minimize talk of locations, and refer more to messengers: 'Nobody has more than the faintest idea how the brain works', comments one journalist, 'Our brainiest boffins speak almost boastfully about their ignorance... What little they do know suggests that nerve cells secrete chemicals which zip from place to place like motorcycle couriers, dropping tiny electrical parcels as they arrive at their destinations.'[61] Co-ordination of it all may be the key to human language.

The human race may have been able to achieve this degree of co-ordination because of their extended childhood, known as 'neoteny' from the Greek 'young-stretch'. Compared with other primates, human children grow up very slowly. They are born in a helpless state and take longer to reach maturity: they seem to have come into the world too early. The apparent premature birth of humans is due partly to the large size of the human brain, and partly to the narrowing of the birth-canal due to walking on two feet. Consequently, birth would be difficult and dangerous if it was further delayed.

But this tardy maturation has two big advantages. First, the brain does most of its development after birth: a newborn's brain weighs only about one quarter of its final weight. It therefore retains its youthful flexibility for much longer, and allows humans to learn more than they otherwise would.[62] Second, helpless newborns must be kept near their mothers: 'The human infant's brain therefore does most of its forming during a protracted interval of intense social stimulation. It is hard to think of a developmental circumstance that would more favorably affect development of linguistic capacity.'[63]

This raises the question of whether children, as they develop language, can help shed light on the development of language in the human species. This will be the topic of the next chapter.

Summary

This chapter looked at the basic requirements for human language. Sound-producing, sound-receiving, sound-planning and sound-interpreting components are needed.

Sound-receiving mechanisms are shared with our ape cousins, and other primates can distinguish between some human language sounds. Sound-producing equipment – lungs, larynx (voice-box) and mouth – are present in all primates, though they have been greatly modified in humans, perhaps partly because of our upright posture. Only humans can produce the key vowels [i], [a], [u], which act as anchor-points in perception.

The human brain, which contains the sound-planning and sound-interpreting components, has some overall similarities to that of other primates, though the detailed modifications seem to be present only in humans. Humans have an extra-large brain, perhaps partly due to language. They have modified it for language in a number of ways. In particular, humans are able to suppress automatic vocalizations, and produce fine-tuned voluntary ones. Above all, they are able to co-ordinate the multiple strands involved in language in an efficient way. The co-ordination may have become possible because of the extended childhood of humans.

8 Small beginnings:
First steps

> The stammerings of the child in the cradle are the speech of the
> first society before all the resources of man's vocal organism had
> been revealed to his experience ... So there arises thereafter a
> full-fledged society, for it will have a fortress erected against God,
> called *Babel*... A few days later it will have its first book, called
> *Biblion*, and its first empire, *Babylon*.
>
> Charles Nodier, *Elementary notions of linguistics* (1834)

'Every child as he develops is retracing the whole history of
mankind, physically and spiritually, step by step.'[1] This assertion
occurs in a popular twentieth-century manual on child-rearing. Dr
Spock, the author, expresses a widely held belief which dates back
more than a century.[2]

In 1866, Ernst Haeckel, Professor of Zoology at Jena, claimed to
have discovered a 'biogenetic law': 'During its own rapid development ... an individual repeats the most important changes in form
evolved by its ancestors during their long and slow palaeontological
development.'[3] More succinctly, 'Ontogeny is the short and rapid
recapitulation of phylogeny',[4] he stated, using his own invented
terms 'ontogeny' for the development of an individual and
'phylogeny' for the development of a species.

'This is the thread of Ariadne', Haeckel confidently asserted,
'only with its aid can we find any intelligible course through this
complicated labyrinth of forms',[5] likening his supposed insight to
the string which the mythical Ariadne gave to the Greek hero
Theseus to lead him out of an underground maze. The notion that
ontogeny recapitulates phylogeny caught on widely, and Haeckel's
work had enormous influence. But he turns out to be both right
and wrong: ontogeny sometimes recapitulates phylogeny, but it
does not necessarily do so. Modern children do not manufacture
language from scratch, they are exposed to the speech of their
caregivers. And, mentally, they are never blank sheets. Infants

learn continuously,[6] often guided by their elders, who are themselves possibly more sophisticated than early humans. The idea of recapitulation is therefore unlikely to be 'the thread of Ariadne', as Haeckel claimed.

But there are at least two important ways in which language ontogeny may recapitulate phylogeny. The first is physical, the lowering of the larynx. The human larynx is higher in the throat in infants than in adults. Its position is similar to that found in chimps (chapter 7). This enables babies, like chimps, to both feed and breathe at the same time. The larynx descends to its mature location several months after birth.

The second recapitulation is mental, the development of the 'naming insight'. Modern humans just assume things have names. In Mary Shelley's novel *Frankenstein* (1818), her fictional monster is determined to learn the human 'godlike science', their method of communicating via articulate sounds: 'By great application, I discovered the names that were given to some of the most familiar objects of discourse ... "fire", "milk", "bread" and "wood".'[7] The monster took it for granted that the 'godlike science' involved naming.

But youngsters do not automatically know that the sounds coming out of people's mouths might be names for things, they have to discover it. It's something that chimps find hard to grasp, and is an important stage which our ancestors had to go through.

This chapter will discuss the development of the naming insight, both in children and primates. Then it will assess theories about how the first words of humankind might have come into being.

Taming the wilderness

'I have put my faith in language – hence the panic when a simple word eludes me ... I control the world so long as I can name it. Which is why children must chase language before they do anything else, tame the wilderness by describing it, challenge God by learning His hundred names', comments a character in Penelope Lively's novel *Moon tiger*.[8]

Humans need to know the names of things. Yet this naming passion takes time to emerge, as noted earlier. Very young children are unlikely to be naming things when they utter their first 'words':

'The 6-month-old child is faced with having to discover what talking is all about.'[9] The same was true of humans discovering language for the first time.

Babies around ten months old sometimes mouth sounds as they gesture towards an object, activating a brain area used for single words (chapter 6). In spite of the pointing gesture, these youngsters are unlikely to be naming things,[10] and the meaning of these early child vocalizations is fairly wide. A repeated *oo-oo* could be a general attention-getting device, though it may be interpreted by adults as 'Look!' A cry of *ba* may mean 'I want that', but might be assumed by a proud mother to be a word such as 'Mug (containing milk)'. Primitive humans also might have built up a small vocabulary using similar broad 'proto-words', a possible precursor to real language.

Youngsters' first recognizable words – typically uttered around the age of a year – are often bound to a whole situation, rather than an individual item. *Car* might be used only when looking out of a window at a general traffic scene, or *papa* might be uttered when the doorbell rings.[11] The 'naming insight' – narrowing a name down to a single object – takes time to develop.[12]

The 'naming insight' is a major leap. The realization that things have names comes to children at various times, but usually before eighteen months. It seems so normal, most parents do not notice it or comment on it, even though it may lead to a 'naming explosion'[13] – a desire to name everything around.

Late discovery reveals the momentous nature of the naming insight, as in the case of some deaf children. Jean Massieu, an eighteenth-century French boy, was deaf and languageless until the age of almost fourteen, when he came under the care of Abbé Roch-Ambroise Sicard, a pioneer in the education of the deaf. Sicard drew pictures of objects, then wrote their names on the pictures. At first, the boy was mystified. Then quite suddenly, the 'naming insight' came to him. Sicard describes Massieu's subsequent hunger for names:

> We visited an orchard to name all the fruits. We went into a wood to distinguish the oak from the elm ... the willow from the poplar, eventually all the other inhabitants ... He didn't have enough tablets and pencils for all the names with which I filled his dictionary, and his

soul seemed to expand and grow with these innumerable denomina-
tions... Massieu's visits were those of a landowner seeing his rich
domain for the first time.[14]

Helen Keller is perhaps the most famous case. She was deaf and
blind from the age of two. As a child of six, she suddenly understood
that words have meaning, when her teacher held her hand under a
flow of water:

> As the cold stream gushed over one hand she spelled into the other the
> word water, first slowly, then rapidly... and somehow the mystery of
> language was revealed to me. I knew then that 'w-a-t-e-r' meant the
> wonderful cool something that was flowing over my hand. That living
> word awakened my soul, gave it light, hope, joy, set it free!... Everything
> had a name, and each name gave birth to a new thought... every
> object which I touched seemed to quiver with life. That was because I
> saw everything with the strange new sight that had come to me.[15]

Humans, after achieving the naming insight, want to keep
naming things. They enjoy naming for the sake of naming. This is
where humans and primates may differ. Other primates do not
share this enthusiasm for naming, as will be outlined below.

When is a name not a name?

The danger calls used by the vervet monkey may represent a
first stage in the evolution of naming. This agile African animal
with black face, hands, chin and feet, and a long tail, has warning
calls which distinguish different types of predator: at a 'chutter',
vervets stand on their hind legs and look around for a snake; at a
'rraup' they dive into the undergrowth as if hiding from an eagle; at
a 'chirp' they climb a tree, and peer around for a lion or leopard.[16]
But vervets are not alone. Similar specialized alarm calls are
found among South American squirrel monkeys, a long-tailed
species with white rings round their eyes. Some youngsters reared
in isolation responded without teaching to two of them: a 'peep'
warning of a threat in the air caused the animals to freeze, and a
'yap' warning of enemies on the ground such as snakes or cats
made them flee to higher places.[17]
These monkey danger calls are a complex mix of a cry of fear, a

warning to others, and perhaps partly a symbol for the dangerous animal: the calls are not pure naming.[18]

Naming is a major hurdle for chimps who have been taught language-like systems with signs or symbols for words.[19] Kanzi, a bonobo (pygmy chimp) readily learned a set of geometric symbols on a keyboard. But when he pointed to a symbol for *banana*, he expected to get a banana: 'Knowing how to use the symbol "banana" as a way of getting someone to give you a banana is not equivalent to knowing that "banana" represents a banana . . . Full communication would require that the chimp be able to use the symbol "banana" without expecting to receive one.'[20]

Chimps CAN apparently name for the sake of naming. Washoe, a female chimp who was taught signs for words, signed 'toothbrush' on coming across a toothbrush. She was certainly not asking for a toothbrush, since she hated cleaning her teeth. It was an apparently spontaneous naming gesture.[21]

Yet chimps mostly don't WANT to name things just for the sake of it. Naming things for primates is perhaps like swinging in the trees for humans. Humans can sometimes do it, but most of them do not particularly want to. 'You can lead a horse to the river but you can't make him admire the view', commented a character in a novel.[22] Similarly, you can teach a chimp the word for an object, but you cannot make it appreciate the power of naming. And this may be the barrier which has prevented chimps from acquiring language, a barrier stronger than the lack of sophisticated vocal organs.

Early humans acquired the 'naming insight' at some point. How it happened is a mystery.

Suppose some dreaded enemy has been defeated and slain; the whole troop will dance round the dead body and strike up a chant of triumph, say something like 'Tarara-boom-de-ay!'. This combination of sounds, sung to a certain melody, will now easily become what might be called a proper name for that particular event . . . Under slightly altered circumstances it may become the proper name of the man who slew the enemy.[23]

This was the guess of Otto Jespersen in 1922. It is plausible, but still a guess.

And other mysteries surround early human words, such as where the sounds came from in the first place. Inventing new words is a problem. Even today, words which are invented out of nothing are extremely rare: the writer of a book on word formation was able to find only six words of this type, and some of them had been generated by a computer.[24]

The problem of inventing words inspired the 'bow-wow', 'pooh-pooh' and 'yo-he-ho' proposals of earlier writers – that language was in origin either imitation of animals, cries of emotion, or grunts of effort.[25] Let us consider these proposals.

Mrkrgnao!

'May not some unusually wise ape-like animal have imitated the growl of a beast of prey, and thus told his fellow monkeys the nature of the expected danger? This would have been a first step in the formation of language', suggested Charles Darwin.[26] He is echoing the recurring suggestion that early language began by imitating animals, the so-called 'bow-wow' theory.

This view was held by the eighteenth-century German philosopher Johann Gottfried Herder: 'The first vocabulary was . . . collected from the sounds of the world. From every sounding being echoed its name.'[27] Herder imagines the scene:

> The sheep comes again. White, soft, woolly . . . the sound of bleating . . . as the distinguishing mark of the sheep became . . . the name of the sheep . . . And what is the entire human language other than a collection of such words?[28]

Herder extended animal mimicry to other natural sounds: 'The tree will be called the rustler, the west wind the fanner, the brook the murmurer – and there, all finished and ready, is a little dictionary, waiting for the imprint of the speech organs.'[29]

But Herder does not elaborate on how this mysterious 'imprint' materialized. Understandably, primitive hunters might need to decide whether they planned to hunt buffalo or deer, and develop a signal distinguishing them, perhaps based on the animal's bellows or squeaks. Yet speech sounds do not easily correlate with animal squawks, whose representation differs from language to language: English and Spanish pigs go *oink-oink*, but French pigs say *groin groin*, Japanese *buubuu*, Thai *ood ood*, Korean *kkool-kkool* and Ukrainian *hrju-hrju*.[30]

Twentieth-century humans can easily invent onomatopoeic words, because we have a wide range of sounds to express them, and conventional representations such as *moo* as a model. But it would not have been so easy without any infrastructure. Even today, writers find it hard to think up convincing sound sequences for animal noises: 'Mrkrgnao! the cat said loudly...Gurrrhr! she cried, running to lap.'[31] The growls of a dog give equal trouble to a modern cartoonist: 'What can we do on the first of May? Make faces at Pablo and then run away' hums the cartoon cat Bogart: 'Garrrrrr-arrrrrr-arrrrr-rrrr', responds the taunted dog Pablo.[32] (See Fig. 8.1.)

Sometimes, writers give up on representing snorts or squeaks, and compare the noise to some other sound, as with George Orwell's pig: 'So in we goes, an' dere was an old sow lay on her side snorin' like a traction engine.'[33]

Maybe only bird-names consistently arise from onomatopoeia. For example, in one dialect of Ojibwa, an American-Indian language, *baaghaakwaanh* is 'chicken', and *jigjigaaneshiinh* is 'chickadee', an English word which is itself onomatopoeic.[34]

But even if an occasional word such as *cuckoo* is widespread among those who hear cuckoos, one cuckoo doesn't make a language: 'Words of this kind are, like artificial flowers, without a root', commented the nineteenth-century linguist Max Müller. 'The onomatopoeic theory goes very smoothly as long as it deals with cackling hens and quacking ducks; but round that poultry-yard there is a high wall, and we soon find that it is behind that wall that language really begins.'[35]

In short, imitation of animals and other types of sound symbolism may contribute, but probably had a limited use. Cries of emotion – the pooh-pooh idea of language origin (chapter 1) – are also types of sound symbolism. They raise similar problems to animal noises. Other routes to sounds need to be considered.

Figure 8.1 Bogart, *Sunday Times*, 6 May 1991

Pant-hoots and lip-smacks

Chimp-type pant-hoots (chapter 6) may be the forerunners of syllables, and so may the yells of babies. Broadly speaking, syllables are pulses of voiced breath, resulting in vowel-like sounds: *ah! ah! ah!*[36]

In language, syllables usually have some degree of breath obstruction at their onset: typical syllables have a consonant–vowel structure: *ba, ma* and so on. Early consonants in the species were probably developments of primate lip-smacks, and may be similar to those found in the babbling of babies. Infants typically go through a phase when they utter *mamamà, babababa* sequences. Fond parents gleefully assume their child is referring to them, which is why words such as *mama* and *papa* are found the world over as pet names for parents.[37] In fact, the child is instinctively exercising its vocal organs in an enjoyable and non-meaningful way. But all these exercises contribute to the habit of making vocal noises, whether among infants or early humans.

But adults also contribute. The involuntary grunts which emerge from the closing and opening of the vocal folds in effortful heaving and hauling might have promoted this basic syllable shape, which is found in rhythmic work songs the world over. Old sea shanties, for example, which probably accompanied the hauling-up of sails, often ended lines with a grunted exhalation:

> O-ho Jul*yah*!
> Pretty Miss Jul*yah*!
> Take 'em off, Jul*yah*!
> Lay back, Jul*yah*![38]

This ties in with the old 'yo-he-ho' theory of language origin, which proposed that language began with words such as 'Heave!' involving co-operative effort. It's likely to be one among many factors which encouraged the habitual use of vocalization.

But language is not just a sequence of syllables spoken in a monotone: it has additional rhythm and intonation, which are interwoven with the sounds. The next section will consider this aspect.

Singing creatures?

'Words well up freely from the breast', wrote the nineteenth-century German philosopher–linguist Wilhelm von Humboldt, 'and there may well have been no wandering horde in any desert that did not already have its own songs. For man, as a species, is a singing creature.'[39]

The 'primitive song' idea recurs in suggestions about language origin. The eighteenth-century French philosopher Jean Jacques Rousseau claimed that 'the first languages were singable and passionate before they became simple and methodical' (1852/1966) and, in the twentieth century, Otto Jespersen (1922) proposed that: 'The speech of uncivilized and primitive men was more passionately agitated than ours, more like music or song ... the first utterances of speech I fancy to myself like something between the nightly love-lyrics of puss upon the tiles and the melodious love-songs of the nightingale',[40] as pointed out earlier (chapter 1).

This seems unlikely, even though long-range signalling such as yodelling may have developed alongside language, or even prior to it.[41]

But the link between language and song may not be so far-fetched, if singing is taken in a wider sense than may have been intended by these early writers. All languages have some type of 'song'. Either they have tones, that is, different pitch levels for syllables, as in Hausa, an African language, where, for example, *kūkā* 'a cry' and *kūkà* 'baobab tree' are distinguished only by the pitch level of the last syllable. Or they have intonation, that is, different 'tunes' for sentences, as in English. Sometimes, they have both, as in Mandarin Chinese.

In addition, different emotional attitudes can be expressed. Sensitivity to them develops young. At around six months, children react positively to speech melodies expressing approval, and negatively to those expressing disapproval, which seem to be similar across a range of languages.[42] At around eight months, a child heard from the next room may appear to be having a 'real' conversation with himself or herself, but is in fact imitating the 'tunes' of human speech.

Speech tunes and the understanding of emotional nuances are dealt with primarily by the right hemisphere of the human brain, unlike mainstream language skills which are normally located in the left hemisphere (chapter 7).[43]

The perception of pitch and voice gradations appears to be an extension of a similar sensitivity found in chimps. The human race, like human infants, may have produced a range of vocal sounds with a variety of intonations long before language began.

Putting it all together

There's probably no single route by which humans arrived at early words. 'Heave'-type commands used in effort, *mama*-type sounds which evolved from lip-smacks, occasional animal imitations, as well as other intermittent types of sound symbolism probably all contributed. Once a few of these had become accepted in a community, others would follow. Rough equivalents for 'Heave ho!', 'Hi!', 'No!', 'Help!' and several dozen other proto-words might have been in use for a long time. But it's unlikely that there was any systematic sound structure until quite a large number of individual words had been devised.[44]

As this chapter has shown, children can provide occasional pointers to the emergence of language, cases where ontogeny – the development of an individual – may have recapitulated phylogeny – the development of the species.

But right back at the beginning, the infants of the species are unlikely to have initiated language. Adults probably did this, then their tentative speech steps were picked up by the next generation, who expanded their parents' skills.[45] This process can be seen when deaf parents give birth to deaf children. The first generation, the parents, acquire sign language fairly slowly, and never become truly proficient. The second generation, the children, pick up their parents' signing system easily, and eventually carry it on further.[46] Once humans had achieved the 'naming insight', and had started to develop a repertoire of different sounds, there may have been an explosive growth of vocabulary, as with children. Eventually, early humans started to combine these words. This will be the topic of the next chapter.

Summary

Ontogeny – the development of an individual member of a species – only sometimes correlates with phylogeny – the history of the species.

This happens physically with the lowering of the larynx, and it happens mentally in the development of the 'naming insight', the realization that things have names.

Humans were probably already using a range of vocalizations from various sources even before the naming insight. These included work chants which involved consonant-plus-vowel syllables, easy to produce sounds such as *ma* which evolved from lip-smacks, and some imitations of natural sounds.

The naming insight and the development of a large number of words laid the foundations for combining them.

Part 3
Evolution

9 The second word:
The emergence of rules

In the beginning was the word. But by the time the second word was added to it, there was trouble. For with it came syntax, the thing that tripped up so many people.

John Simon, *Paradigms lost*

'Nature unfolds before us a many-hued and... a many-shaped diversity, suffused with a luminous clarity. Our subsequent reflection discovers therein a regularity congenial to our mental pattern', observed the nineteenth-century philosopher–linguist Wilhelm von Humboldt.[1] He may have been struggling to express something which we all take for granted today, that humans do not simply combine sounds and words at random when they talk. Instead, they ring the changes on a relatively few basic patterns.[2]

Humans understand one another because they subconsciously know the patterns found in their own language, which are often referred to as 'rules'. It is a 'rule' of English that the word *the* comes before the noun to which it refers: *the fish* not **fish the* (with an asterisk denoting an impossible sequence), though in Ponapean, a Micronesian language, it would be *mwahmwa-o* 'fish-the' not **o-mwahmwa*.[3] It is another 'rule' of English that you cannot start a word with *mw*, though this is quite all right in Ponapean.

A language needs 'rules'. Communication would break down if there were no agreed ways of combining linguistic units. Random permutations do not make sense, as Gulliver realized when he visited the great academy of Lagado, in the continent of Balnibarbi, in Jonathan Swift's satirical novel *Gulliver's travels* (1726). An optimistic professor had invented a machine which, he hoped, would eventually write books on any topic, by recombining the words of his language:

> The first professor I saw was in a very large room, with forty pupils about him... Observing me to look earnestly upon a frame which took

up the greatest part of both the length and breadth of the room, he said ... the world would soon be sensible of its usefulness; ... The superficies was composed of several bits of wood ... all linked together by slender wires. These bits of wood were covered on every square with paper pasted on them; and on these papers were written all the words of their language in their several moods, tenses, and declensions: but without any order. The professor then desired me to observe ... The pupils, at his command, took each of them hold of an iron handle, whereof there were forty fixed round the edges of the frame; and, giving them a sudden turn, the whole disposition of the words was entirely changed. He then commanded six and thirty of the lads to read the several lines ... and where they found three or four words together that might make part of a sentence, they dictated to the four remaining boys ...

Six hours a day the young students were employed in this labour, and the professor shewed me several volumes in large folio already collected, of broken sentences, which he intended to piece together, and, out of those rich materials, to give the world a complete body of all arts and sciences; which, however, might be still improved and much expedited, if the public would raise a fund for making and employing five hundred such frames in Lagado.[4]

A similar explosion of possibilities occurs at the level of sounds. Even a small number of original sounds can be combined in an enormous number of ways. Consider the problems faced by a character in Umberto Eco's novel *Foucault's pendulum* as he struggled to find a password which he thought might be a permutation of the name of God:

If there were eight letters in the name of God, there would be forty thousand three hundred and twenty permutations, and if ten, there would be three million six hundred twenty-eight thousand eight hundred ... And if the names of God contained twenty-seven letters – in the Hebrew alphabet there are no vowels, but twenty-two consonants plus five variants – then the number of His possible names would have twenty-nine digits. Except that you have to allow for repetitions, because the name of God could be aleph repeated twenty-seven times ... with repetitions you'd have to take twenty-seven to the twenty-seventh power, which is, I believe, something like four hundred forty-four billion billion billion billion. Four times ten with thirty-nine zeros after it.[5]

Any full language has narrowed down the range of overall possibilities to a relatively few allowable combinations. Linguists often refer to the sum total of these permitted patterns as a 'grammar', with the word used interchangeably to mean both the rules subconsciously used by speakers, and those codified by linguists.

At some point, early humans must have started to put words together in a rule-governed way, in an early 'grammar'. Whole words were probably put into some overall order first. The organization of sounds probably came at a later date.[6]

Simple rules have two requirements: first, different types of basic unit must exist; second, ways of combining them must be agreed. This chapter will consider how these requirements might have been fulfilled.

Bundles of things

The mythical professors observed by Gulliver at the great academy of Lagado assumed that words are 'only names for things', and consequently that nouns are in some sense basic:

> We next went to a school of languages, where three professors sat in consultation...
>
> The first project was to shorten discourse by ... leaving out verbs and participles; because, in reality, all things imaginable are but nouns.
>
> The other project was a scheme for entirely abolishing all words whatsoever ... since words are only names for things, it would be more convenient for all men to carry about them such things as were necessary to express the particular business they are to discourse on; ... which hath only this inconvenience attending it, that if a man's business be very great ... he must be obliged ... to carry a greater bundle of things upon his back ... I have often beheld two of those sages almost sinking under the weight of their packs, like pedlars among us: who, when they met in the streets, would lay down their loads, open their sacks, and hold conversation for an hour together; then put up their implements, help each other resume their burthens, and take their leave.[7]

The Lagado professors may be right about the primacy of nouns, as far as the evolution of language is concerned. The 'naming insight' is the main evidence for this, the realization that things have names (chapter 8). This revelation probably caused a naming explosion, and names of things may therefore have outnumbered other types of early words.

The basic status of nouns is supported by other evidence. In the languages of the world, it's normally easy to change a noun into a verb.[8] A noun can often be used directly as a verb, as in numerous English examples:

> Angela *shipped* her car to America
> Henry *bicycled* home
> Betty *bottled* the jam

It's less easy to make a verb into a noun, and usually requires a special ending:

> Paul *discovered* the treasure
> Paul's *discovery* of the treasure...
> Geraldine *met* a bear
> Geraldine's *meeting* with a bear...
> Felix *arrived*
> Felix's *arrival*...

Since this ease of making nouns into verbs is so widespread, but not vice versa, it suggests that nouns may be in some sense primary.

Most languages have many more nouns than verbs. In English, there are approximately three times as many nouns as verbs, according to one count[9] – though this figure perhaps exaggerates the difference: verbs are more polysemous than nouns, that is, each verb has on average approximately three meanings attached to it, but each noun only around two. But there's still an imbalance.

Nouns refer primarily to physical things which we can point at, according to a widely held assumption:

> Every name we call a NOUN
> A *rose*, a *doll*, a *hen*, a *crown*

run the first lines in a *First grammar book for children*.[10] Consequently, people, animals and things have been called 'first-order entities'.[11] Other nouns, which include those such as *truth*, *happiness*, *beauty*, are felt to be less basic, and how they are classified 'may well depend crucially upon the structure of the languages that we use to talk about them'.[12]

Within first-order entities, 'persons are more strongly individualized than animals, and animals more strongly individualized than inanimate things'.[13] The dividing line between persons, animals and inanimates is sometimes unclear. Rivers, winds and mountains are classified in various ways in the languages of the world. A similar fuzzy distinction is found between concrete and abstract.[14] But the message is clear – that 'ordinary things' are basic.

Nouns alone might be useful as a communication device: a primitive grocery list would have its uses. Yet language cannot be properly considered to have emerged until there was at least a primitive grammar. For this, there had to be other words to go with the nouns. A smallish vocabulary relating to verb-like happenings had presumably existed for a long time. Words meaning maybe 'Heave', 'Come', 'Go', 'Eat', 'Open' might have been in use. But they were possibly not as numerous as the names for things, nor were they at first combined with names in a reliable way.

The bare minimum

'That savage saw the tall tree with its mighty crown and sensed the wonder of it: the crown rustled! There the godhead moves and stirs! The savage falls down in adoration! Behold, that is the story of sensuous man, the dark link by which nouns are fashioned from verbs', claimed the German philosopher Herder in the eighteenth century.[15] 'From the verbs it was that the nouns grew and not from the nouns the verbs. The child names the sheep, not as a sheep, but as a bleating creature, and hence makes of the interjection a verb.'[16]

Herder's conviction that verbs came before nouns is unlikely, but nouns and verbs together probably constituted the first 'grammar' – though undoubtedly, humans could mentally distinguish things and people from actions and events for a long time prior to establishing them as nouns or verbs.

But nouns and verbs are not totally distinct, they are on a continuum: 'The *most time-stable* percepts, the ones that change slowly over time . . . are lexicalized as nouns. The *least time-stable* percepts, events, and actions, which involve *rapid change* in the universe, are lexicalized as verbs.'[17] It's a universal tendency.[18]

Nouns tend to be people and objects, which have time stability, verbs to be actions and events which do not:

The dinosaur (N) yawned (V)
Henry (N) swallowed (V) a snail (N)

– though some exceptions can be found: verbs occasionally denote time-stable situations:

The mountain *loomed over* the town

and nouns sometimes involve unstable ones:

There was a sudden *flash* of lightning.

Nouns and verbs are usually regarded as universal categories in language.[19] 'In general, one finds *no* languages without two major classes: *nouns* and *verbs*' claims one researcher.[20] 'The distinction between *nouns* and *verbs* is one of the few apparently universal part-of-speech distinctions ... there are no languages that cannot be said to show a noun–verb distinction', notes another[21] – though Nootka, an American-Indian language, is sometimes claimed to be an exception.[22]

But 'grammar' emerged only when noun-type words were reliably combined with verb-type words. Let us consider how this might have happened.

Nouns plus verbs

The human mind did not burst into bloom with language like a bush suddenly ablaze with blossom in the spring. Putting words together in a rule-governed way might have happened slowly. There are two routes by which nouns and verbs could have been combined: build-ups on the one hand, and re-analysis on the other.

The 'build-up' route assumes that a large number of single words accumulated, but words of different types, some involving things, others actions. Then at a later stage these were combined, just as a child might say *mummy open* as a request: 'Mummy please open this.'

The re-analysis route assumes that words, mainly nouns, were already being combined, but that sometimes more than one interpretation was possible. Take the word *singsing* in Tok Pisin, a pidgin spoken in Papua New Guinea (chapter 1).

A *singsing* is primarily any festival which involves dancing and singing. The words *mi singsing* (me - song and dance) meaning 'I went to the song and dance festival' could easily be reinterpreted as 'I sang and danced.' And there are numerous other similar words, such as:

mi danis	'me - dance'	→	'I danced'
mi bilas	'me - adornment'	→	'I adorned myself'
mi pait	'me - fight'	→	'I fought'
mi wok	'me - work'	→	'I worked'
mi brum	'me - broom'	→	'I swept'

Both the build-up route and the re-analysis route may have been utilized in early language. But there's a missing step. Before either could take place, consistent ordering must have evolved. A repetitious jumble such as *mummy open open mummy, mi danis mi* or *singsing mi singsing* would not provide a basis for any grammar.

There are three types of clue as to how a firm word order might have happened: first, in the signing of chimps; second, in the utterances of Vincent, a hearing child who first learned sign language from his deaf parents before switching to spoken language; third, in the predispositions of humans to think about some things in a particular sequence. Let us examine these.

Nim eat Nim

Nim Chimpsky is a male chimp who was for several years taught a sign language based on ASL (American Sign Language) by Herbert Terrace and his co-workers at Columbia University.[23] When the project ran out of money, Nim was returned to a chimp colony in Oklahoma. Terrace then had time to analyze carefully the huge amount of data from Project Nim.

At first sight, Nim's signing was quite unordered. He signed *Nim eat* almost as often as *eat Nim*. But the order was not completely random, because Nim had some preferences, though they varied in strength. If a food was involved, it was almost always placed first, as in *grape eat, banana Nim eat, apple me eat*. (See Fig. 9.1.)

banana me	97	grape eat Nim	37
sweet Nim	85	banana Nim eat	33
gum eat	79	banana eat Nim	26
grape eat	74	yoghurt Nim eat	20
banana Nim	73	banana me eat	17
		apple me eat	15
		nut Nim nut	15

Figure 9.1 Nim's food requests

Nim always put the word *more* at the beginning in two-word sequences: *more eat, more tickle, more drink*, though '*more* first' was not a firm 'rule', because *me more eat* occurred as often as *more eat Nim* among three-word combinations.

Nim had a mild preference for placing his own name at the end, as in *eat me Nim, grape eat Nim*, but it came in the middle as well, as in *banana Nim eat*, and sometimes at the front, as in *Nim me eat*.[24] (See Fig. 9.2.)

But there's a problem: Nim often repeated words, as in *eat Nim eat, Nim eat Nim*. He may have believed that 'more is better', as in his longest recorded utterance: 'Give orange me give eat orange me eat orange give me eat orange give me you'.

But Nim's intermittent ordering is instructive, because it resembles the process found when a language acquires new word-order rules: mild stylistic preferences change into strong preferences which eventually stablilize. One or two very common utterances become a habit, which forms a pattern which influences the formation of others.

The bonobo, Kanzi, also developed a preferred word order in his use of lexigrams – the symbols on his computer keyboard, often one

play me Nim	81	yoghurt Nim eat	20
eat me Nim	48	more eat Nim	19
eat Nim eat	46	finish hug Nim	18
tickle me Nim	44	Nim eat Nim	17
grape eat Nim	37	eat Nim me	15
banana Nim eat	33	nut Nim nut	15
banana eat Nim	26	drink me Nim	14
me Nim eat	21	hug Nim hug	14
hug me Nim	20	sweet Nim sweet	14

Figure 9.2 Nim's name

geometric shape on top of another, such as a line running across a diamond, which was the sign for 'jello'.[25] (See Fig. 9.3.)

At first he used *hide peanut* as often as *peanut hide*. But he soon picked up on the order used by his English companions, and settled on *hide peanut* as standard. This shows that he is sensitive to order, but does not show how ordering could have developed in the first place.

But Kanzi invented at least one personal ordering rule, a 'lexigram–point' rule. This involved first, a symbol for an action, such as *tickle*, *chase*, then a pointing gesture to indicate who should do the action, perhaps his trainer Sue. He may have invented a second rule, though this is more doubtful: he tended to use the order of occurrence in the game he was playing when two actions

Jello   Yoghurt   Popsicle

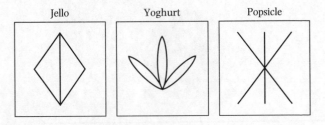

Figure 9.3 Some of Kanzi's signs

occurred together. So *tickle bite* occurred more often than *bite tickle*, and *chase hide* more often than *hide chase*.[26] So Kanzi, like Nim, shows how a preferred order could become a habit which could be regarded as a 'rule'.[27]

You broken car

Vincent was the hearing child of deaf parents who taught him sign language as a first language.[28] He became a fluent signer, but did not speak in spite of regularly watching television, whose accompanying sound effects appear to have had very little effect on him. He was first exposed to 'live' English when he was just over three years old. His speech was barely intelligible at first, though his output slowly became relatively clear.

Most of Vincent's utterances were short: *You - uh-oh* 'You made a mistake', though a few were much longer: *I want puter you go home you* 'I want you to take me to your house'. His vocabulary was sometimes idiosyncratic: *puter* was a general, all-purpose verb, perhaps originally from *put*; *you* sometimes meant 'you', but could also mean 'he', 'she' or 'it'. But the way he put words together was bizarre by ordinary standards.

At first sight, Vincent's strange output looked unanalyzable, especially when sequences such as *You rrr* 'It goes rrr' existed alongside others such as *Rrr car* 'The car was towed'. He also had a tendency to 'copy-around' a word, that is to put one form on both sides of another, as in: *You house you?* 'Do they [those buses] go to your house?'

But when his repeats and copying-around were omitted, a clear word ordering preference appeared. Vincent constructed many sentences according to a basic, but private, plan:

1 Pointing-out word (often a pronoun)
2 Verb-like word
3 Noun-like word or adjective

Sometimes all three elements were present, sometimes only two. The result could be fairly normal:

You Sandra	'You're called Sandra'
I puter keys	'I'll unlock the door'
I see-it fire	'I saw a fireman'

But at other times the result was strange, because he did not consistently put the actor, the person who initiated the action, at the beginning. Sometimes it was at the end:

You daddy	'It's daddy [who's sleeping there]'
You broken car	'The car got broken'
What-do puter Howard?	'Why did Howard do it?'
Where go bus?	'Where do you get the bus from?'
See over-there airplane grandma	'That's the aeroplane grandma flew on'

Vincent, like Nim, shows a pattern seeping through. A default structure underlies his superficially odd utterances. It is not fully consistent. But it reveals a human tendency to categorize words, and to order the categories into a sequence – though one which has not become totally firm.

Both Nim Chimpsky the chimp and Victor the human show that an optional, intermittent word order can become a preferred order, and that a preferred order can become a near-rule. But their output raises a question about where the order came from in the first place.

Human mind-set?

Humans do not consciously decide how to chop the world up, it's already partly done for them by their minds. Philosophers sometimes argue over whether the 'external world' is real. Most of us assume that it is, but that our human mind-set dictates how we see it.

Humans recognize certain broad categories that exist for them, known as 'ontological categories' – with ontology defined as the study of the essence of being, derived from the Greek verb for *to be*. Ontological categories cover notions such as people, things, actions, events.[29] They provide 'a presumably universal initial structure of the language of thought'[30] on which language is superposed.

The innate thought structure covers not only basic categories, but also the way in which they may be combined. Consider the following sentences:

> The cat sat on the mat
> The dog lay under the table
> The train chuffed up the track

Why don't we say instead:

> !The mat lay under the cat
> !The table stood over the dog
> !The track was under the chuffing train

These sentences are not impossible, they're just rather odd – and would be in any language. (An exclamation mark signals an unusual, but not impossible, sentence.) It's normal to locate something small in relation to something large, rather than vice versa. It's not just because the small item is the theme of conversation: it is perfectly possible to envisage the large item as the topic, in which case the sentence order would probably be switched around:

> On the mat sat the cat
> Under the table lay the dog
> Up the track chuffed the train

The location of small onto large may be due to the human way of envisaging things.[31] Indeed, if you ask anyone, they tend to say: 'But it's obvious it has to be that way round, that's the way things are' – confirming the notion of a human mind-set: 'The world is not only queerer than we imagine, it is queerer than we *can* imagine', is an apt remark attributed to the biologist J. B. S. Haldane.

Human thoughts therefore run along pre-ordained grooves, which are likely to affect the order of participants in a grammar. Let us consider what these may be.

Horses before carts

There's a natural tendency to place live things first. This 'animate first' preference is sometimes so strong, that a sentence may get switched around to preserve it. Almost 5,000 English descriptions of an inanimate thing doing something to an animate being were collected by one group of researchers.[32] In almost three-quarters of them, the sentence had been switched into the passive. It was more normal to say:

Patsy was hit on the head by a cabbage

than

A cabbage hit Patsy on the head

The 'animate first' preference is not due to any obvious linguistic factor, such as word length or word rhythm.[33] The human mind-set plays a major role. A 'me first' principle is a possible explanation, a suggestion that humans put first the thing that is most closely connected to them.[34]

Often, the 'animate first' preference ties in with an 'actor (initiator of action) first' principle, partly because in real life animates act on lifeless things more often than vice versa: *Harriet ate the egg*, rather than !*The egg ate Harriet*; *Alfonso chucked a stone*, rather than !*A stone chucked Alfonso*.

In an ingenious experiment, children were shown some carts and horses, each of which were given nonsense names, such as *zot* for a horse and *tep* for a cart. The experiment was carried out in both English and Fijian which, unlike English, places actors at the end of sentences. When asked to recall the horse and cart words, all the children were more likely to recall them in a horse–cart order, even when they had been originally taught them in the cart–horse order.[35] This result suggests that 'animate actor first' may be a strong pre-linguistic preference. However, the fact that 'animate first' and 'actor first' do not always work together shows that natural preferences may sometimes clash. This is one reason why languages do not all end up with the same rules.

Ducks quack, and other natural principles

Ducks quack, frogs jump, and fish swim. A 'participant–event' framework becomes an 'actor–action' sequence which eventually turns into a noun–verb order, according to one scenario.[36]

An actor–action order is overwhelmingly more common than action–actor as a major sentence pattern in the languages of the world. It's a strong preference. English, like many other languages, has the order *The frog jumped*, *The duck quacked*, rather than *Jumped the frog, *Quacked the duck. The reverse is possible: *Up jumped the dog*, *Loudly quacked the duck*, but it is a 'marked' (less normal) order. A few languages even prefer the uncommon order. Welsh regularly starts sentences with verbs, and several languages do so intermittently: in Spanish, *Vino un coche* 'came a car', is more usual than *Un coche vino* 'a car came'.

If two participants are involved, the actor usually comes before the patient, the thing or person to whom something is done. A sequence *Tom hit Jerry*, or *Tom Jerry hit* would be interpreted as Tom hitting Jerry in the languages of the world, unless there was strong evidence to the contrary, such as use of word endings. These Tom and Jerry examples oversimplify the situation, however, because two 'full' nouns tend not to be together as actor and patient in the same clause, at least not in spoken speech: 'Tom arrived, then he hit Jerry', would be more likely, with the 'full nouns' spaced out.[37]

The patient (recipient of action) is normally placed near the action which affects it. In the world's languages, an order *Pigs eat apples* or *Pigs apples eat* is more likely than *Eat pigs apples*. Some languages take this action–patient bonding to extremes, and swallow up patients into the verbs, a process known as 'noun incorporation'. Siberian Koriak, for example, has a verb *qoyanm-* 'to reindeer-slaughter', formed by combining *qoya-* 'reindeer' with *-nm-* 'to kill'.[38] (See Fig. 9.4.)

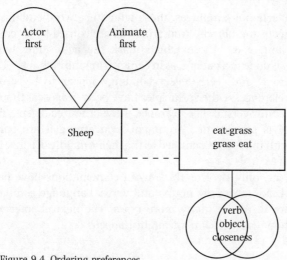

Figure 9.4 Ordering preferences

The 'actor first' and 'action–patient bonding' preferences coincide to produce two likely orders:

ACTOR - ACTION - PATIENT
or ACTOR - PATIENT - ACTION

This partly explains why the majority of human languages have a preferred word order of subject-verb-object, as in English, or subject-object-verb, as in Turkish:

English: Alan cooked the fish
Turkish: Ahmet balığı pişirdi
Ahmet fish cooked

In one sample of 402 languages which were chosen to be representative both of language families and world areas, over 85% came out as one of these two orders:[39]

SOV 180 (45%) SVO 168 (42%)
VSO   37 (9%) VOS   12 (3%)
OVS   5 (1%) OSV   0

These figures are rough ones only, because configurational (strict word order) languages are not inevitable. Word order is sometimes fluid in inflectional languages, those which use word endings to mark subjects and objects. And problems are caused by so-called 'ergative languages', those which mark the actor only when something is done to a patient, as in Guugu Yimidhirr (chapter 3).[40]

'Actor first' and 'verb–object bonding' appear to be strong human preferences. Other principles have been proposed, though these are controversial. For example, a hypothesized 'theme first principle'[41] is problematic: arguments concerning it are partly circular, with the theme identified as the theme mainly because it is placed first.[42]

But so far, only two- or three-word combinations have been considered, and also only nouns and verbs. Language combines many more words, of many more types. The next chapter will consider how this enrichment might happen.

Summary

This chapter examined the emergence of rules. The naming insight possibly stimulated a huge number of names for objects, but true language began when words were combined.

A primitive grammar could have arisen partly out of 'build-ups', putting individual words together, as in *mummy – open*, and partly out of a re-analysis of combined nouns such as *mi danis* 'me dance', which could be interpreted either as two nouns or as a person participating in an action.

At first, many word combinations were possibly repetitive and inconsistent. The chimp Nim Chimpsky, the bonobo Kanzi, and Vincent the hearing child of deaf parents, show how rules may have became fixed: optional orders became strong preferences which became rules.

The original preferences were probably based on pre-linguistic 'mind-sets', which may explain why so many languages show similarities, such as a tendency to place animate actors first, and patients (objects) near the verb affecting them. But sometimes natural principles clash, which partially explains why languages differ.

10 The tower of speech:
Expansion

God woke, but the nightmare
Did not recede. Word by word
The tower of speech grew.
He looked at it from the air
He reclined on. One word more and
It would be level with him.

R. S. Thomas, 'The gap'

Once the ball of language started rolling, it probably kept moving, at first slowly, then faster and faster, like a snowball which accumulates snow, and tumbles ever more quickly down a hill.[1]

But nothing ever comes out of nothing. Humans can adapt only what is already there, both in the human mind, and in the existing language: 'The mind does not manufacture abstract concepts out of thin air ... It adapts machinery that is already available, both in the development of the individual organism and in the evolutionary development of the species.'[2]

And these adaptations are not random. Language, like falling leaves, moves in a predictable direction. 'Do falling leaves make you sad?' asks the cartoon character Charlie Brown. 'Absolutely not', replies his pal Lucy. 'If they want to fall, I say let 'em fall ... It's when you see them jumping back on the tree that you're in trouble.' Similarly, the same patterns recur all over the world, influenced by the human mind-set.

This chapter will consider how our human mind-set affected the expansion of language. It will outline, first, how vocabulary probably grew, and second, how language acquired extra parts of speech, in addition to nouns and verbs.

Inwards and outwards

Humans probably named themselves, their body parts and their immediate environment early in the development of language. As

123

today, the human body, and the space surrounding it, presumably formed the basis of further meaning extensions.[3] Metaphor, 'calling one thing by the name of another', is not a strange poetic event.[4] It is at the heart of language, and the direction of the metaphors is important. The body's influence spreads outwards, to features of the environment, and inwards to the mind.

Words for human body-parts easily move outwards, as shown by pidgins. Take the Tok Pisin word *het* 'head',[5] which has been extended to various natural phenomena:

het bilong diwai	'top of a tree'
het bilong maunten	'top of a mountain'
het bilong wara	'spring, source of water'

Or consider the extensions of *han* (hand, arm):

han bilong diwai	'branch of a tree'
han bilong pik	'front legs of a pig'
han bilong pisin	'bird's wing'
plantihan	'centipede', literally, 'many hands'
han wara	'tributary of a river', literally 'hand water'

But words move inwards also. Outer behaviour is a regular source for talk about the inner mental self, as when physical sight expressions are used for intellectual understanding:

I *see* what Helen means
It all became *clear* to Albert
Can you *enlighten* Betty?
Peter's still *in the dark*

Such examples show that 'Deep and pervasive metaphorical connections link our vocabulary of physical perception and our vocabulary of intellect and knowledge.'[6]

Physical grabbing and holding stretches to mental grasping:

Did you *grasp* what your father meant?
Paul *held on* to his point of view
Fenella *seized* on what Albert said

Travel through space is extended to speech and mental exploration:

Let's *go over* that idea again
How *far have we got* in our plans?

I think Lois is *getting somewhere* with that problem
What conclusion has Henry *reached*?

Differences of detail exist between cultures. Heard utterances
are swallowed among the Dogon of West Africa. In the case of good
speech, the intestines digest the verbal fluid, extract the nutritive
value, and distribute it to other parts of the body[7]. Yet this is not
unlike our own concept of 'inwardly digesting' what is said to us.
The body is still the basis of metaphors about the mind for the
Dogon, even though the exact image differs from our own.

The human body therefore probably always has been and
always will be used to extend language meanings: 'It would have
been ... fantastic for humans not to begin describing the world of
their experience in terms of the human body and its everyday
experiences; this is exactly why languages are anthropocentric.'[8]

Wider patterns

Space affects time: 'Spatial vocabulary universally acquires
temporal meaning rather than the reverse.'[9] Spatial prepositions
get reapplied:

From flower *to* flower → *From* year *to* year
In the garden → *In* the evening
On the table → *On* Saturday

And space has other, far-reaching effects. Some general spatial
schemata may be universal: an up–down verticality scale permeates
our thinking. 'Up' correlates with 'more', and 'down' with 'less':

The crime rate is *rising*
Interest rates are *up* again
House-sales *fell* last month
Export orders are *down*[10]

This schema presumably has a basis in experience: a heap of apples
rises as more are added to it. No essential value is attached, as bad
things such as crime can rise, and good things can decline. Yet,
quite often, verticality involves a value judgment, *up* is good, and
down is bad:

Andrew's going *up* in the world
Marion's *down* on her luck
Helen's *on a real high*
Bob's *down* in the dumps
Nigel always aims *high*
Stella *lowered* her sights

This may have a physical origin: a sick person, or one defeated in battle, is likely to be physically lower than someone who is healthy or a victor.

But verticality is only one example of a general spatial schema, and there are several others. A movement forward and back, or more accurately, in and out, is all-pervasive:

Nathaniel woke suddenly *out* of a deep sleep. He got *into* an argument with his brother, then backed *out* of it by burying his head *in* a book.

A path schema is common, with purpose as a physical goal:

You've still got a *long way to go*
Don't get *sidetracked*
Keep plodding on, you'll get there in the end

And life itself is commonly referred to as a journey, as in the famous first lines of Dante's *Divine comedy* (*c.* 1320):

In the middle of the path of my life,
I found myself in a dark wood,
Through which the direct route had been lost.

The journey of life is sometimes attached to the passage from life to death. In Greek mythology, the ferryman Charon transports the dead across the river Styx. Death is envisaged as a coachman in Emily Dickinson's poem:

Because I could not stop for Death –
He kindly stopped for me –
The Carriage held but just Ourselves –
And Immortality.[11]

In short, humans orient themselves in physical space in predictable and recurring ways, and then apply this space to other areas of experience: 'Image schemata are pervasive, well-defined, and full of sufficient internal structure to constrain our understanding and reasoning.'[12] They 'are not internally "mushy"; on the contrary, they are one of the chief means by which our understanding is structured to give us a more or less comprehensible, patterned world that we can partially make sense of and function within'.[13]

These schemata represent the way humans think about the world. They may have been in existence in embryo even before the origin of language. Language made use of them, and possibly carried them further.

However, more parts of speech were required before full use could be made of the spatial extensions outlined above. This development will be discussed below.

In and out

Linking like a hook and eye, IN and OUT and FOR and BY.
Bird IN nest, and rose ON tree, gift FOR you and sit BY me.

As these lines from a *First grammar book for children*[14] illustrate, links in space are often expressed by a particular type of word, an adposition. This term covers both prepositions, placed in front of a noun, as in English, or postpositions, placed after, as in Hindi:

mez pər
table on
'on the table'

Each language uses primarily either one, or the other, though the major pattern is occasionally supplemented by a few examples of the other. Latin, for example, has mainly prepositions, as in:

ad silvam
towards wood
'to the wood'

but occasional postpositions, as:

honoris causa
of-honour for-the-sake-of
'for the sake of honour'

Adpositions are sometimes separate words, as in English, and sometimes they are bound to the neighbouring noun, as in Turkish:

ev-dan
house-from
'from the house'

Postpositions, it turns out, are more usually bound than prepositions – which will be discussed further in chapter 16.

But there are never many adpositions, maybe twenty or so, as opposed to many thousands of nouns and verbs: roughly 10,000 names for things occur in an average English adult's vocabulary, according to one count.[15] If you ask English speakers why prepositions are so few in number, they usually look baffled and say: 'But how could there be any more? We've got *up, down, in, out,* and so on. After about twenty, we run out of links for prepositions to express.'

The small number is due to the human mind-set.[16] A language with many more can be imagined, in which adpositions standardly include some notion of the objects to which they applied: one word for 'in' might be used when going into something big like a house, another for something small and cosy like a rabbit hole, another for something which is not a container, such as a garden, and so on. A few prepositions are like this, but not many:

!Paul went along the circle

This is weird, because *along* has to refer to something which has length.

!The tight-rope walker walked around the wire

This is odd, because *around* usually requires a space to circulate in or round.

People still tend to say, 'OK, but we don't have many prepositions, because we don't need them.' But this is unconvincing. Language often has multiple possible ways of expressing similar ideas: *wide* and *broad, disease* and *illness, hide* and *conceal,* 'Yesterday it rained' and 'We had rain yesterday.' The limited number of prepositions must be due to the way humans think.[17] Humans re-apply old ones, instead of inventing new ones, as when spatial prepositions are routinely stretched to cover time (p. 125).

Adaptation is the key to prepositions. Consider the history of the English word *along* in Australia and Papua New Guinea. It was at first probably used as a general spatial preposition, as suggested by some Australian records from the last century:

> Boatswain tell me to come up *along* Queensland and work sugar
> 'The boatswain told me to come to Queensland and work the sugar'
> (1885)[18]

Tok Pisin, spoken in Papua New Guinea (see Fig. 10.1),[19] shortened this word to *long* and used it as an all-purpose link word:

mi go *long taun*	'I go to town'
mi kam *long taun*	'I come from town'
mi wokabaut *long taun*	'I walk around in the town'
mi stap *long haus*	'I stayed at home'
mi rait *long pepa*	'I write on the paper'
mi kam *long kanu*	'I came by canoe'
mi paitim dok *long stik*	'I hit the dog with a stick'
mi kam *long nait*	'I came during the night'
mi sori *long yu*	'I'm sorry for you'
mi save *long planti samting*	'I know about a lot of things'

'This word is used... for nearly all the prepositions known in European languages, including: in, on, at, to, from, with, by, about, because of, during, for...', as one dictionary writer noted.[20]

Confusion is usually avoided by paying attention to the surrounding vocabulary: *kam* means 'come towards, arrive', and *go* means 'go away, depart', for example, and other clarifying words can be added:

> mi go *antap long* tri
> I go on-top of tree
> 'I climbed the tree'

> mi sidaun *ananit long* tri
> I sit-down underneath of tree
> 'I sat underneath the tree'

A similar general-purpose preposition might have emerged in the evolution of language, possibly via re-analysis of a verb or noun.

As an example of how a verb can get re-analyzed as a preposition, consider English *belong*. Early Australian records of plantation-workers' speech retain signs of its verbal origin:

> Yes; good fellow gun, box, plenty something *belong a white man*
> 'Yes; a good gun, a box, and lots of the Europeans' things' (1885)[21]

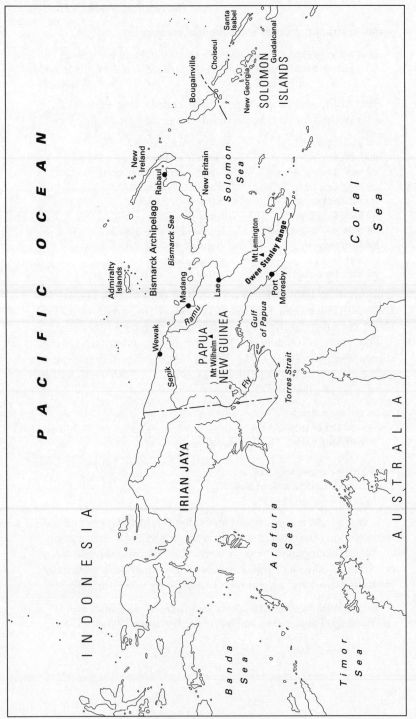

Figure 10.1 Papua New Guinea

In Tok Pisin it surfaced as true preposition *bilong* (of):

papa bilong mi
'father of me,
my father'

han bilong diwai
'arm/hand of tree,
branch of tree'

Bislama, the pidgin spoken in the Republic of Vanuatu, in the southwest Pacific Ocean, provides further examples of verb reinterpretation resulting in prepositions,[22] as with *agensem* (to oppose), where the ending *-em* shows that the word is a verb, even though it probably came from the English preposition 'against' at an earlier stage:

mi no *agensem* yu
I not oppose you
'I am not opposing you'

Huia i toktok *agensem* yu?
Who PRT talk to-oppose you (PRT is a meaningless particle)
'Who spoke against you?'

In the second sentence, *agensem* can be equally well interpreted as a verb 'to oppose' or a preposition 'against'.

The verb *raonem* (to go round), is following a similar pattern:

Bae yumi *raonem* aelan long Sande
FUTURE you-and-i go-round island on Sunday
'We'll go around the island on Sunday'

oli pulum wan fanis raonem yad bilong mi
They put a fence to surround yard of me
'They put a fence round my yard'

Prepositions arise out of verbs quite often, even in English, where *regarding, concerning, following* were once verbs, but are now prepositions:

Cuthbert saw the lawyer *regarding* his claim
Pauline saw the travel agent *concerning* her ticket

Compare:

Bill saw the doctor *about* his knee

But adpositions are not always derived from verbs, sometimes they come from nouns. Hausa, spoken primarily in Nigeria, has prepositions which are derived from body-parts, with *cikin* 'in' coming from the word for 'stomach', and *baayan* 'behind, after' from the word for 'the back'. And a similar pattern is found in several African languages.[23] But the overall picture is clear. Adpositions, when they first developed, were likely to have come from verbs or nouns. At first, there may only have been one or two, which were stretched to cover a wide range. Later, others were added via re-analysis.

Adpositions show two things. First, the human mind has certain inbuilt constraints, which is why there are so few prepositions. Second, language is flexible: it adapts what is already present to express new ideas, which is how so few prepositions get stretched so far.

This is also true of the development of other parts of speech, such as adjectives, as will be considered below.

A swing-category

Nouns are at one end of a continuum, with words which retain their identity through time, such as *dog, mountain, sky*. Verbs are at the other end, with words which involve rapid change, such as *jump, hit, swim* (chapter 9). In the middle come properties, some semi-permanent, as in *a **large** elephant, a **round** pond, a **green** frog*, and some temporary, as in *an **angry** bull, a **happy** baby, a **hot** day*. These property-words are less time-stable than nouns, but more time-stable than most verbs (see Fig. 10.2).

Faced with this in-between group of words, languages follow one of two routes. Some subdivide verbs into those which deal with events, such as *hit, kill*, versus those which deal with states, so called stative verbs, such as *be-green, be-ill*.[24] Mandarin Chinese chooses this path:

tā pǎo   she/he/it run   '(s)he runs'
tā hǎo   she/he/it good   '(s)he's good'[25]

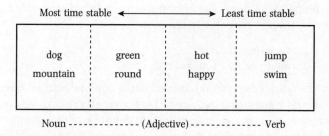

Figure 10.2 Noun–adjective–verb continuum

A similar pattern is found in numerous West African languages, as in Kru, spoken in Liberia:

kpákà   'he is-old'[26]

or Yoruba, spoken mainly in Nigeria:

ó tóbi   'he is-big'

But other languages take a different route. An extra category, adjective, deals with the middle-range words. 'The class of adjectives is a notorious swing-category in languages',[27] it has been said. The border-line between nouns and adjectives, and between adjectives and verbs, often seems arbitrary. Some adjectives seem more like nouns, as in *a* **gold** *watch, a* **tin** *tray*, others more like verbs, as in *a* **lasting** *peace, a* **whistling** *kettle*. As one researcher notes: 'It is, of course, no accident that the lexical class 'adjective' has remained problematic, exhibiting even within the same language some "more noun-like" properties and some "more verb-like" ones.'[28]

Sometimes, it's difficult to decide whether a word is an adjective or a verb describing a state. Tok Pisin shows the dilemma:

mi sik   'I (am) sick'
yu longlong 'you (are) mad'

These could be regarded as stative verbs, 'be-sick', 'be-mad', or as adjectives, with the copula *be* missing, as happens in Russian:

Marija krasivaja 'Mary (is) beautiful'

And similar examples come from the other side of the world, for example Miskito Coast Creole English:

> If yu wud sief, yu wud ron[29]
> 'If you want to be safe, you had better run'

In the early days of language, verbs and adjectives were probably indistinguishable, as in the pidgin/creole examples above. At some point, a verb expressing a state might be reinterpreted as an adjective. But no clear distinction between the two could be formally made until further linguistic devices, such as word-endings, were added.

The lexical mosaic is therefore always being stretched, and always being re-interpreted. The next chapter will consider how this led to more sophisticated linguistic devices, especially markers for verbs and nouns.

Summary

This chapter considered how language expanded. First, language made use of the world, as filtered through human experience. Above all, it made use of the human body and its location in space to move outwards to the surrounding environment, and inwards to inner ideas. This presumably happened at the beginning of language, and is still happening now.

Second, it discussed how language acquired extra parts of speech. Adpositions (prepositions and postpositions) are few in number. Their sparsity is due to the human mind-set, but these few are stretched to cover a wide range. They developed via re-analysis, either of verbs or nouns.

The middle ground between nouns and verbs is handled by languages in two ways: either by subdividing verbs into two types, non-stative and stative, or by developing adjectives, words which deal with properties. Adjectives arose via re-analysis, but they could not be clearly distinguished from verbs until further linguistic devices evolved, some of which will be discussed in the next chapter.

11 Time travelling:
Extra attachments

> The major problem is quite simply one of grammar, and the main work to consult in this matter is Dr Dan Streetmentioner's *Time Traveller's Handbook of 1001 Tense Formations*. It will tell you for instance how to describe something that was about to happen to you in the past before you avoided it by time-jumping forward two days in order to avoid it. The event will be described differently according to whether you are talking about it from the standpoint of your own natural time, from a time in the further future, or a time in the further past ... Most readers get as far as the Future Semi-Conditionally Modified Subinverted Plagal Past Subjunctive Intentional before giving up.
>
> Douglas Adams, *The restaurant at the end of the universe*

'The thing that hath been, it is that which shall be; and that which is done is that which shall be done: and there is no new thing under the sun', runs a famous verse from the Bible.[1] It might well apply to language, where similar events occur in language after language. Such widespread phenomena and how they arise can reveal information about human language in its early stages of evolution.

Ideally, what MUST appear in language should be divided from what MIGHT appear. Yet the essential cannot always be distinguished from the convenient. But some pathways can be predicted. All languages have verbs. And the verbs usually have extra appendages.[2]

Again and again, the same types of *gram* (grammatical marker)[3] get attached to verbs, both in pidgins and creoles, and in full languages. And the attachment always happens in the same way: a full lexical item develops into a gram. This process is known as grammaticization, or grammaticalization, a term coined by the French linguist Antoine Meillet, who defined it as 'the attribution of a grammatical character to a previously autonomous word'.[4]

But how these grams first emerged is controversial. Arguments centre round the amoeba question (chapter 1). Did language start out simple, like an amoeba, and then gradually expand? Or was it a sprawling muddle which was only gradually neatened up into a coherent system?

According to a 'bioprogram view', proposed by the linguist Derek Bickerton, an innate blueprint caused some basic grams to leap into place fast.[5] According to a 'spaghetti junctions' view, early language was like a motorway intersection which provided numerous options. In the long run, several factors converged to make some options more viable than others.[6]

This controversy has centred around the origin of language, and also, more strongly, around pidgins and creoles. As already explained (chapter 1), a pidgin is a subsidiary system used by people with no common language, and a creole is a pidgin learned as a first language. These can show how an embryo system, with minimal resources, expands into a full system, as with the prepositions discussed in the previous chapter.

This chapter will discuss the key topic of verb attachments.[7]

Time and the verb

The fictional Dr Streetmentioner's handbook (in the quotation at the beginning of the chapter) would be quite unnecessary for creoles, which tend to develop three basic appendages: grams for tense, mood and aspect. Tense specifies the time of an action, mood expresses an attitude towards an event, and aspect carries information about the 'contour of an action'.[8]

A typical creole tense–mood–aspect (TMA) system marks three basic distinctions:

TENSE   *anterior* vs non-anterior (before or not before)
MOOD   *non-real* vs real (non-actual or actual event)
ASPECT *non-punctual* vs punctual (non-sudden or sudden)

(See Fig. 11.1.) In each of these three, the meaning placed first is usually marked by a special ending. This pattern is highly probable, though it is not inevitable.[9]

Tense, the time of an event, is perhaps the most straightforward

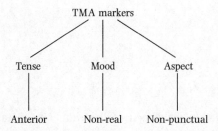

Figure 11.1 Typical creole TMA system

of the verb's attachments. Languages usually specify if the verb's action happened in the past, as in English, which usually adds *-d* on the end: *Drusilla laughed.*

Past tenses everywhere develop via predictable pathways. As a first stage, a word meaning 'finish' is often adapted to express a completed action. This has happened worldwide,[10] from Cocama, spoken in the Andes, to Koho in Southeast Asia, to Tok Pisin:

Kaikai *pinis,* mi go long wok
Food finish I go to work
'After I've eaten, I go to work'

Completion leads to anteriority, the marking of the earlier of two actions, as in the Tok Pisin example above. In English, incidentally, the word *after* is often used for anteriority: '*After* he tripped over the cat, Herbert fell on top of the dog.' According to many,[11] anteriority precedes a true past tense.

But full tense marking takes time to emerge. Typically, such markers start out as optional extras, then become habits, then become obligatory (chapter 9). In pidgins, an action is specified as past only when necessary. Tok Pisin *Mi pundaun* (me fall-down) 'I fell down' need not have a past marker attached, but *mi sik* (me ill) 'I am/was ill' would probably need one. In creoles, grams increasingly get inserted even when they are not essential.

Tok Pisin has evolved a past tense. It followed the 'spaghetti junction' scenario, in that at least two potential past tenses developed, then one of these won out over the other. The competitors were *pinis*, mentioned above, and *bin* from English 'been':

mi kikim pukpuk *pinis*
I kick crocodile finish
'I kicked a crocodile'

mi *bin* sik
I PAST sick
'I was ill'

Historically, *pinis* possibly developed earlier than *bin*. It had several uses. It was used for anteriority, as explained above. It also denoted completion or finality: the word *dai* means 'to faint', but *dai pinis* is 'to die'.

Partly because of these other *pinis* uses, *bin* gradually came to be used as the 'ordinary' past, and won out over *pinis*. This also fitted in with other developing verbal attachments, which were placed in front of the verb. Language, in the long run, tends to be consistent.

At first, *bin* was used only when extra clarity was needed. But gradually *bin* came to be used even when the action obviously happened in the past, as when a secretary described a holiday trip away (PRT is a meaningless particle):

Moskito i bin kaikaim mi nogut tru
Mosquitos PRT PAST eat me no-good truly
'The mosquitos bit me badly'

So in Tok Pisin, two possible past-tense forms were whittled down to one, with the other retained as a useful way of expressing anteriority.

This case history shows how optional features compete. One word becomes relegated to minor uses, the other wins out. The winner becomes used more often, increasingly inserted where it is not strictly necessary. The words *pinis* from 'finish' and *bin* from 'been' were not adopted by chance. Words meaning 'to finish', or 'to be finished, ready, complete' are possibly the commonest source of past tenses in the world's languages, though *be*, *have* and *come* are also prominent.[12]

The general picture is clear. Past tenses start out as full lexical items, which in their origin were often connected with a notion of completion. The idea of finishing something, and ordering it before another event, may be part of the human mind-set. To find it surfacing in language is no surprise.

Non-reality

Many people assume that human languages operate a three-way system, in which time is split into past, present and future. This happens in Latin, but is not particularly common overall. Many languages instead distinguish between fact and probability. A non-reality (*irrealis*) marker expresses something which might happen, rather than something which must happen. In the long run, non-reality markers may turn into future tenses.

Me sow piccaninny taty – *by by* he jump up big fellow!
'I plant little potatoes; in time, they'll grow into big plants'

This use of *by by* by a Western Australian potato planter dates from the mid nineteenth century (1842).[13] It shows an early use of the phrase 'by and by', which developed into an *irrealis* marker in Tok Pisin.

In Tok Pisin, the phrase 'by and by' was borrowed as *baimbai*, then shortened to *bai*. It's found both with future intentions and in hypothetical future events (IR stands for *irrealis*):

Ating *bai* mi watchim ragbi
I-think IR I watch rugby
'I think I'll watch rugby'

Would is the best translation when a hypothetical event is discussed. 'If we were making an underground oven, then we would do the following . . . ':

Bai mipela kisim ol lip
IR we get PLURAL leaf
'We would get leaves'

Na *bai* kamarapim long lip banana gen
And IR cover with leaf banana again
'And we would cover it up with banana leaves again'

The position of *bai* in a sentence is still not fully stabilized. It is found either in front of a pronoun: *bai mi go* 'IR I go' or after it, as in *mi bai go* 'I IR go'. But it is gradually neatening up. Increasingly, it is placed before the pronoun, as in *bai mi go*, perhaps because it tends to get confused with *bin* in fast speech when placed after.

But when *bai* occurs with *em* 'he, she, it', it follows the pronoun more often, as in *em bai go* – perhaps because it would coalesce with *em* if placed in front. So this is not sorted yet, it is taking generations.

But *bai* is not the only future found. A second Tok Pisin construction involving the immediate future is the verb *laik*, which has in some areas been shortened to *la*, with the meaning 'be about to go':

Mi *laik* go 'I want to go'

which has become

Mi *la* go 'I am about to go'

Desire, leading to intention, leading to futurity, is a widespread pattern,[14] found also in the English word *will*, which has followed the same route.

Contours of actions

'You are old, Father William', the young man said,
'And your hair has become very white.
And yet you incessantly stand on your head.
Do you think, at your age, it is right?'

'In my youth', said the sage as he shook his grey locks,
'I feared it might injure the brain.
But now that I'm perfectly sure I have none,
Why, I do it again and again.'[15]

The phrases underlined all provide information about the 'contour' of the action, which in many languages is expressed as an intrinsic part of the verb, its 'aspect'. More widely, 'aspects are different ways of viewing the internal constituency of a situation'.[16] A typical 'contour' is a distinction between an action which happens once, and an ongoing action:

Albert coughed versus *Albert was coughing*

An ongoing action could have several overlapping interpretations, at least:

> Albert coughed *for a long time* (duration)
> Albert coughed *repeatedly* (iteration)
> Albert was *in the habit of* coughing (habituality)

According to the bioprogram view, a single distinction was split into several. According to the spaghetti junction view, several distinctions were streamlined into one, as happened in Tok Pisin.

Tok Pisin started out with a main verb *save* (know), which still exists:

> mi no *save* tumas long kukim
> I not know much about to-cook
> 'I do not know much about cooking'

But when *save* was followed immediately by another verb, its dominant meaning came to be 'know how to', in the sense of 'be skilled at':

> mi *save* kukim kaukau
> I know to-cook sweet-potato
> 'I know how to cook sweet potato' or
> 'I am skilled at cooking sweet potato'

Gradually, 'be skilled at' came to have the weaker meaning of 'be accustomed to', 'habitually do something', though sometimes both meanings would be possible, as in a toothpaste ad (see Fig. 11.2). (PRT is an untranslatable particle):

> Planti switpela kaikai na loli i *save* bagarapim tit hariap
> Lots-of sweet foods and sweets PRT are-skilled-at/are-accustomed-to
> wreck teeth fast
> 'Lots of sweet foods and sweets wreck teeth fast'

But in many cases, only the eventual meaning of 'be accustomed to' is possible:

> Yu *save* smok?
> You know to-smoke
> 'Do you smoke?'

Colgate i save strongim tit bilong yu

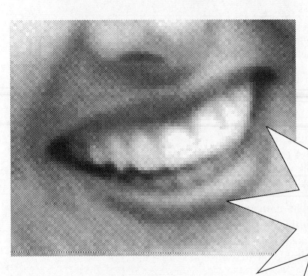

Lukaut: planti switpela kaikai na loli i save bagarapim tit hariap

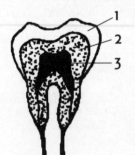

Gutpela tit

1 Skin
2 Bun
3 Hop

Figure 11.2 Toothpaste ad., *Wantok* (Tok Pisin newspaper), 1980

Colgate is accustomed to strengthen teeth of you

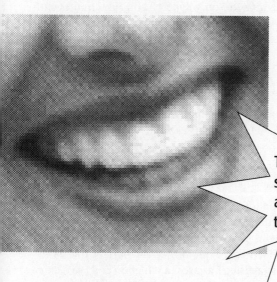

Take care! Lots of sweet food and candy are accustomed to wreck teeth fast

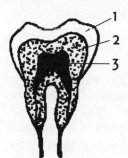

Good teeth

1 Enamel

2 Dentine

3 Nerve

Save in its new meaning of 'be accustomed to' was eventually shortened to *sa*:

> mi *sa* kukim long paia
> I am-accustomed to-cook on fire
> 'I customarily cook it on the fire'

So an original verb *save* split into two: *save* remained as a main verb 'know', but *sa* became a verbal particle which preceded the main verb, meaning 'be accustomed to', 'habitually'. At first, use of *sa* was optional. But, gradually, its use increased, and it was inserted even when habituality was obvious from the context.

But habituality was not the only type of non-punctual event found in Tok Pisin. Long-term and repetitive events could be expressed, but by other methods. The verbs could be repeated:

> mi *singaut singaut*
> I shout shout
> 'I shouted and shouted', 'I kept shouting'

Alternatively, another sequence, often *i go*, sometimes repeated several times, could be added after the verb:

> mi *singaut i go i go*
> I shout PRT go PRT go
> 'I shouted and shouted', 'I kept shouting'

Gradually, this construction is fading, as the *sa* construction starts to cover all non-punctual events. The phrase *i go* may in the long run become a single word *igo* meaning 'and so on', 'continuously', optionally added to a sentence, but no longer part of the basic verbal system. This is suggested by cases in which *sa* and *i go* occur in the same sentence:

> mi *sa* stap long haus *i go i go*
> I customarily stay at home PRT go PRT go
> 'I stayed at home continuously'

To summarize, there has been a 'bleaching' or weakening of the original meaning of the verb, from 'know how to', towards 'be skilled at', ending up as 'be accustomed to'. Once the original meaning had been lost, the word became shortened, and re-analyzed as a particle attached to the verb. It was used increasingly

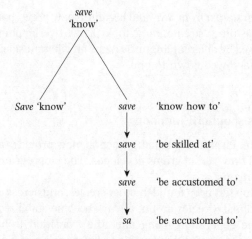

Figure 11.3 Tok Pisin *save* to *sa*

frequently and redundantly, and gradually took over the functions of a postverbal marker expressing repetitive or long-lasting actions (see Fig. 11.3).

Occasionally, *sa* is found in the same sentence with *bin*. When this happens *sa* is nearer the verb, probably because habituality is more closely associated with the events of the verb than the time at which they occurred:

mi *bin sa* stap long haus
I PAST customarily stay at home
'I stayed at home'

Verbs meaning 'know' tend to become grams the world over, though not necessarily with the same final result as in Tok Pisin. In English, a word meaning 'know' was the forerunner of the auxiliary verb *can*. Here, the meaning has bleached (weakened) into 'be able to', rather than the Tok Pisin 'be accustomed to'. In other pidgins, non-punctual markers have resulted from verbs meaning 'stay', 'be there', 'sit', 'sleep' – all common verbs which express a prolonged state.[17]

As Tok Pisin *sa* shows, human language moves in two directions, both splitting and streamlining. Tok Pisin added extra grammatical machinery, as when *sa* split from *save*, and became a new preverbal gram. At the same time, streamlining took place: overlapping distinctions expressed by different linguistic items on different sides of the verb were narrowed down to one.

Bioprogram vs spaghetti junction

In the case of Tok Pisin, the spaghetti junction view provides a realistic account of how verbal grams developed. The bioprogram summarizes the outcome.

Slow neatening up has been found in other creoles, and across a range of constructions: 'Creoles do not always become stabilized systems within one generation. Long after the transition from the . . . pidgin stage, they are still amenable to large scale restructuring . . . The language, as a not yet fully stabilized and relatively young system, is still in search of its mature form', comments a writer on Sranan, spoken in Suriname, on the Atlantic coast of South America. 'Viewed this way, creolization would not be a discrete, one-generation process, but rather one which is gradual, extending over a number of generations'.[18]

Derek Bickerton, the chief 'bioprogram' proponent, would possibly disagree. In his view, Tok Pisin developed too slowly for it to be regarded as a standard pidgin/creole. However, his favoured creoles may not have developed as suddenly as he assumes.[19] So Tok Pisin may not be as abnormal as he has claimed.[20]

Overall, creoles behave no differently from any other language, though their processes of change are accelerated. Splitting and streamlining are found everywhere. So are bleaching, re-analysis and neatening up. And optional grams repeatedly become obligatory. The human mind-set guides language in certain broad directions, and makes some developments more likely than others.

The tense–mood–aspect grams which develop early in creoles are those with the greatest generality: they are widely useful and applicable to a large number of words. But within these broad outlines, there are numerous possibilities. Multiple branches, as it were, sprout out, and are gradually whittled down to a rule-governed system. The end result is a matter of trial and error and compromise, predictable in its outlines, but not in its details. This is true of pidgins and creoles, and is likely to have been true of human language at its outset.

But a language is still not complete with just a few parts of speech, and various attachments for its verbs. Other essential developments will be the topic of the next chapter.

Summary

This chapter considered how verbs acquired attachments. These developed via grammaticization (or grammaticalization), in which a full lexical item developed into a grammatical marker, or gram.

The main evidence comes from pidgins and creoles. Tense–mood–aspect (TMA) systems tend to be similar in all creoles, suggesting that similar events happen whenever a new language comes into being, whether nowadays or when language first emerged.

A basic controversy exists, as to whether a new language starts out simple, and is then elaborated (a bioprogram approach), or whether it is first messy, and then streamlined (a spaghetti junction view).

The developing TMA system in Tok Pisin shows that language develops by sprouting out various options, followed by narrowing down and neatening. The spaghetti junction view represents a more realistic view of what happened than the bioprogram view, which describes the final outcome.

12 Rebuilding on the high seas:
Keeping going

> We are like mariners who have to rebuild their ship on the high seas, without ever being able to strip it down in dock and construct it afresh from the best available components.
>
> Otto Neurath, 'Protocol statements' (1932)

Languages can never start again: they have to patch up and expand what is already there, like the mariners in the quotation above.[1]

But for language, this is not such a disaster. Language has endless possibilities within itself, which it perpetually re-uses: it is an 'inexhaustible store', to quote the nineteenth-century thinker Wilhelm von Humboldt: 'But just as the matter of thinking, and the infinity of its combinations, can never be exhausted, so it is equally impossible to do this with . . . language . . . At every single point and period, therefore, language, like nature itself, appears to man . . . as an inexhaustible storehouse.'[2]

The Port Royal schools, a group of French religious and educational foundations, may have been the earliest to comment coherently on the open-endedness of language. They produced a famous seventeenth-century grammar, which spoke of 'that marvellous invention by which we construct from twenty-five or thirty sounds an infinity of expressions'.[3]

As these linguistic pioneers realized, language possesses the property of *generativity* – the use of a finite number of elementary parts to produce a potentially infinite number of forms and sentences. Generativity may be a basic property of the human mind: 'The generative nature of language is probably parasitic on the generative nature of human cognition.'[4]

But there is more to it than just endlessly re-arranging words within the permissible patterns. More importantly, the rules can be repeatedly re-applied, so that any sentence can in principle go on for ever: 'I know you believe you understand what you think I said.

But I am not sure you realize that what you heard is not what I meant.' This is a notice reputedly found on the wall of a civil servant's office. It is composed of two longish sentences, which have several sub-sentences embedded inside them.

And many more sub-sentences could have been embedded, as in the appalling chain of events described in Scott Smith's novel *A simple plan*:

> I'd shot Jacob because he was going to break down because I'd shot Sonny because I needed to cover up shooting Nancy because she'd been about to shoot me because Jacob had shot Lou because he'd thought Lou was going to shoot me because Lou was threatening me with his shotgun because I'd tricked him into confessing to Dwight Pedersen's murder because Lou'd been blackmailing me because I didn't want to give him his share of the money till the summer because I wanted to make sure no-one was looking for the plane . . . [5]

The eleven 'because' clauses could have been extended to 111 or more. Sentences stop because people get thirsty, or run out of things to say, not because of any linguistic limit.

Language, incidentally, is not the only human ability which involves generativity, it is also found in mathematics. Some researchers suggest that generativity arose first in language, and then spread to other domains.[6] Others, perhaps the majority, assume that the human ability to handle maths arose independently, but made use of some of the same basic capacities as did language.[7]

But the inexhaustibility of language, its generativity, will be the topic of this chapter.

More than a yip-yop

Generativity in its true sense needs to be distinguished from simple repetition. A make-believe insect, a yip-yop, which randomly yipped and yopped all day ('yip, yip, yop, yop, yop, yip, yop, yip, yop') would not qualify as possessing generativity.

There's disagreement over whether any animals have a true generative communication system. Take the song of the chickadee, a North American songbird with grey-black plumage.[8] The songs of these birds contain four basic elements that may be strung together in an open-ended but rule-bound way. The four elements always occur in a particular order, although each element may be repeated any number of times, or may be omitted. Consequently, the authors of the chickadee study claim this system qualifies as 'language'. Others have argued that simple repetition must not be confused with true generativity.[9]

Yet judging from the chickadee, generativity can occur at a very simple level and be indistinguishable from repetition. The mechanisms which underlie it are what matters. Human language makes use of a medley of devices.

An ordering ability is fairly basic, a skill particularly associated with the left hemisphere of the human brain (chapter 7):

The old frog swallowed a very large fly

The order shows that the frog swallowed a fly, not vice versa. Yet keeping to a basic order is not particularly difficult, and even pigeons can be trained to peck at patterns in a particular sequence.

Selective repetition is a step further:

The old old frog swallowed a very very large fly

but not

*The old frog frog caught a very large fly fly

This is more difficult, because it requires an awareness that different types of item are involved. This is a major step towards realizing that language is 'structure–dependent'. Any sentence has an internal structure which has to be subconsciously understood. A division between nouns and verbs may be an early prerequisite (chapter 9), a milestone on the way to structure-dependence.

However, true structure-dependence requires more than this. A speaker must grasp that a group of words can structurally take the place of one: *old frogs, fat old frogs, large fat old frogs, the large fat old frogs who lived in the pond* might take the structural place of the simple word *frogs* (see Fig. 12.1). In short, an awareness of hierarchical structure is necessary. It's possible that the replacement of a single item by an expanded group is part of a general cognitive awareness, which became applied to language.[10] But until this had happened, a major power of language was missing.

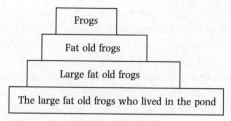

Figure 12.1 Hierarchical structure

Embryo adjectives may have aided this development. Take the Tok Pisin sentences (PRT is an untranslatable particle):

dok bilong yu i longlong, dok bilong mi i gutpela
dog of you PRT mad dog of me PRT good
Your dog is mad, my dog is good

Perhaps the adjective was re-ordered, and used to distinguish between similar nouns:

longlong dok i ranawe, *gutpela dok* i stap long haus
mad dog PRT run-away good dog PRT stay at house
'The mad dog ran away, the good dog stayed at home'

This example shows how one word might become extra-closely associated with another – the basis of hierarchical structure.

But even this does not explain generativity's most important property, the repeated re-application of the same rule. Let us consider this phenomenon.

Re-running the same sentence

Language can re-run the same sentence structure again and again, by repeatedly re-applying the same rules, as in the 'simple plan' example (p. 149). This re-application is known as *recursion*, from the Latin for 'run again'.

This is the frog *which* swallowed the fly *which* settled on the water-lily *which* grew by the river *which* flowed through the fields *which* adjoined the village ...

The potentially endless sentence above illustrates a major type of recursion which is found in all languages. It involves 'relative clauses', which in English begin with words such as *who*, *which*, *that*. They provide further information about a noun. Pidgins – and once again Tok Pisin – show how relative clauses might come into being.

Tok Pisin has a wide variety of possible relative clauses. Different structures compete, and different potential relative clause types predominate in different areas, in a true spaghetti junction situation.[11] But an increasingly common type of relative clause is one which starts with *we*, meaning originally 'where'.

Unlike English, Tok Pisin puts its question words at the end of sentences:

Yu go *we?*
You go where?
'Where are you going?'

Longer sentences are easily made:

Mi go *we* yu go
I go where you go
'I go where you go'

From here, it is a very short step to ambiguous structures which signal the beginning of true relative clauses:

mi drenim aut wara *we* mi boilim pitpit longen
I drain out water where I boil pitpit in-it
'I drain out the water in which (where) I boiled the pitpit (a vegetable)'

ol i go long wanpela ples *we* i gat bikpela tais longen
They PRT go to a place where PRT got big swamp in-it
'They went to a place which had got (where there was) a big swamp in it'[12]

As a next stage, the meaning 'where' has been forgotten, and only the meaning 'which' remains:

pikinini *we* papamama lukautim yet...
Child which parents look-after still...
'A child which its parents still look after...'

Ol i no laikim pater *we* i pulim longpela lotu
They PRT not like priests who PRT drag-out long worship
'They do not like priests who drag out the church service'

Sista *we* wok...
Sister who work
'The nurse on duty'...

This type of relative clause, therefore, has exploited a word *where* which already exists, and adapted it to mean 'which' via ambiguous structures. Its use as a general-purpose relativizer (introducer of relative clauses) was possibly reinforced by *we* from English *when*:

Taim *we* mi bin sik nogut tru...
Time when I was sik no-good truly
'The time when I was very ill...'

It was also probably reinforced by the speech of occasional visitors from the nearby Solomon Islands or from Vanuatu (see Fig. 12.2). Solomon Islands Pijin and Bislama (spoken on Vanuatu) are pidgins which have long used *we* as a relativizer:

waetman *we* i lukaot long stoa long Liro
whiteman where PRT look-out for store at Liro
'The European who looks after the store at Liro'   (Bislama, 1923)[13]

In addition, relative clauses may have been influenced by local Melanesian languages: some sentence patterns look superficially like English relative clauses, even though the basic structure is rather different.[14]

Two major facts about language are revealed by relative clauses beginning with *we* in Tok Pisin: first, re-analysis is not a trivial happening, which affects only single words. It influences whole structures, and allows sentences (potentially) to go on for ever. It is a major tool of generativity. Second, humans are enormously good at pulling together input from numerous sources – the more the merrier, as it were. One source reinforces another cumulatively.

But relative clause construction is not the only type of recursion, as will be discussed below.

Say say

Lapun i tok olsem: 'pukpuk i longlong'
Old-man PRT speak thus crocodile PRT mad
'The old man said: "The crocodile is mad"'

This Tok Pisin sentence suggests another way in which simple

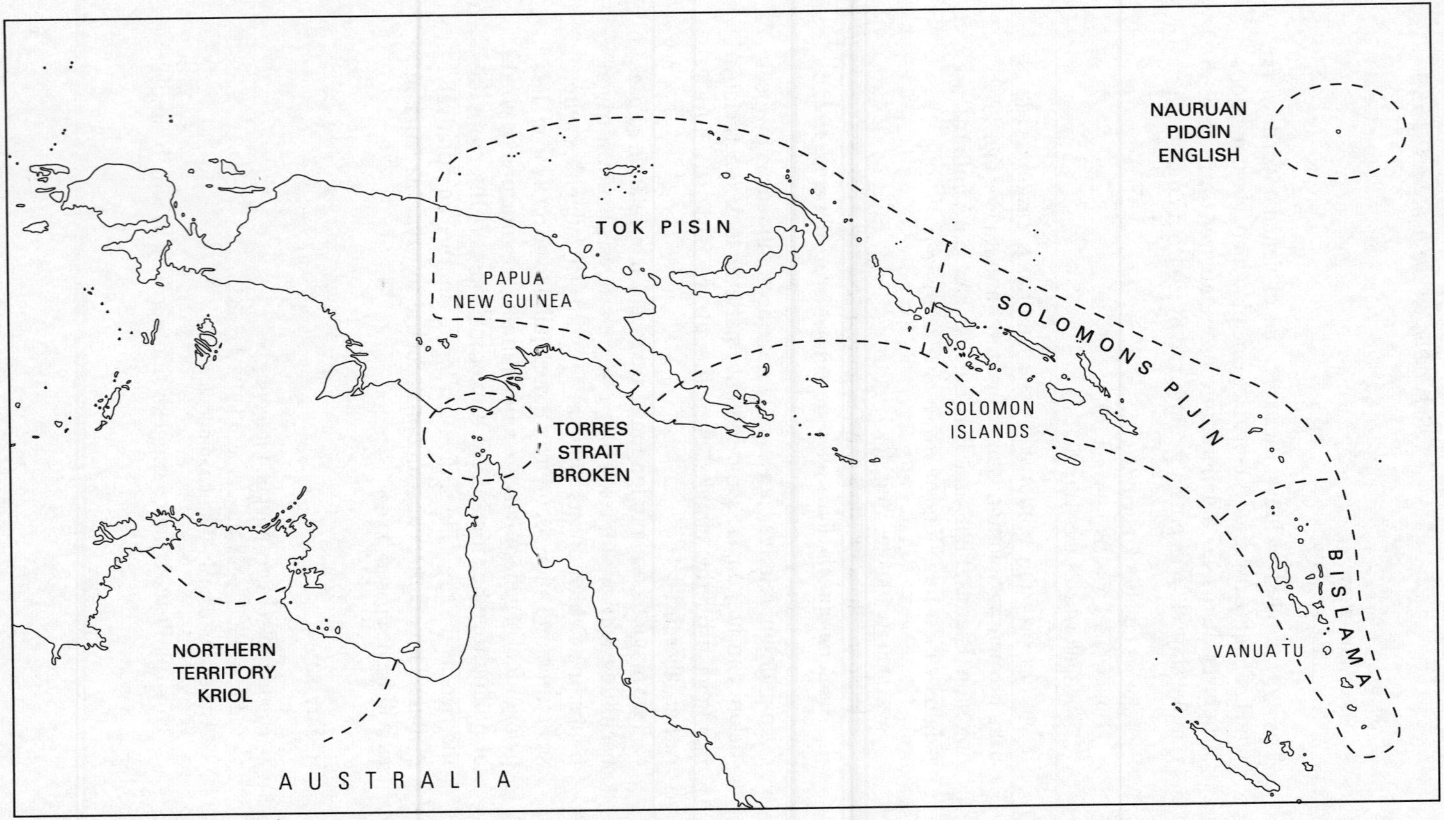

Figure 12.2 Melanesia

sentences can be linked together into one longer structure. *Olsem* is easily re-analyzed as a word introducing indirect speech:

Lapun i tok *olsem* pukpuk i longlong
Old-man PRT speak thus crocodile PRT mad
'The old man said that the crocodile was mad'

At first, the construction was used with the word *tok* (talk). Then it was extended to other verbs:

Na yupela i no *save olsem* em i matmat?
And you PRT not know that it PRT cemetery
'Did you not know that it was a cemetery?'[15]

Sometimes, *olsem* is reduced to *se*:

Em i tok *se* em i laik bilong ol meri yet long maritim waitskin
He PRT say that it PRT desire of PLURAL women still to-marry white-person
'He said that women still wanted to marry a white man'[16]

This Tok Pisin *se* is parallel to another word *se* found in Bislama with the same meaning, but with a different origin.[17] Bislama *se* is probably primarily from an original English word *say*:

Joseph i giaman long mi *se* hem i stap wok
Jospeh PRT lie to me that he PRT is work
'Joseph lied to me that he has a job'

It was supported by the existence of French *c'est* (it is), since it occurs in parallel constructions:

Bislama: Taem *se* vatu
           Time is money

French: Le temps *c'est* de l'argent
           The time it-is of the money
           'Time is money'

In a number of cases, the *say* and *c'est* origins have coalesced, so a Bislama sentence may appear to have been influenced by both:

Wanem mi stap talem *se* mi no finisim work blong mi yet
What I keep say that/it's I no finish work of me yet
'What I am saying is that I haven't finished my work yet'

The *se* constructions show, first, that complex sentences – those with more than one sentence structure inside them – emerge naturally in languages, especially in connection with certain kinds of verb, in this case verbs of saying, extended to verbs of thinking and knowing. Second, they show that new constructions often 'take off' when one source supports another, which may happen by chance.

Wantok

Wantok is the name of a Tok Pisin newspaper, from *wan* 'one' plus *tok* 'talk'. The word *wantok* means a 'fellow countryman', 'someone who speaks the same language'. Similarly, *wanbel* comes from *wan* 'one' and *bel* 'stomach', and it means a 'twin', and *wanlek* from *wan* and *lek* 'leg', meaning a one-legged person.

These examples show that language's 'inexhaustible storehouse' applies also to words. As soon as a language has a supply of basic lexical items, it can use them for explosive expansion. Some examples of Tok Pisin vocabulary were given in chapter 1. But the list is almost endless.[18] Tok Pisin *skru*, for example, is a 'screw' or 'joint'. It gives rise to:

skru bilong lek	(joint of leg)	'knee'
skru bilong fut	(joint of foot)	'ankle'
skru bilong han	(joint of arm)	'elbow'
skru bilong pinga	(joint of finger)	'knuckle'

Or take the word *skin* meaning 'outer covering'. This gives:

skin bilong kiau	(skin of egg)	'eggshell'
skin bilong kokonas	(skin of coconut)	'coconut husk'
skin bilong diwai	(skin of tree)	'bark of tree'
skin bilong trausel	(skin of turtle)	'turtle shell'

Plants and animals also get named, often by describing them, much as we talk about *bluebells* or *goldfish*. In Bislama, *redfis* 'red fish' is a red snapper, *blufis* 'blue fish' is a parrotfish, *bigbel* 'big stomach' is a pufferfish, and *longmaot* 'long mouth' is a barracuda. Some of these coinages may date back a century or more.[19]

These examples of words and sentences show that language,

once it gets going, can easily build and rebuild itself out of its existing resources. It is like a well which constantly replenishes itself: the more is taken out, the more is available for use. But at some point, language spread out across the world. How this happened will be the topic of the next chapter.

Summary

This chapter examined ways in which language keeps going. Language has the property of generativity – the use of finite resources to produce an infinite variety of sentences. It re-uses its own structures, so that there is in principle no end to the length of a sentence.

Languages develop sentences embedded inside other sentences. They do this by re-using words already in use in simple sentences.

They also endlessly form words out of other words.

Part 4
Diffusion

13 The widening circle:
Moving outwards

Turning and turning in the widening gyre
The falcon cannot hear the falconer;
Things fall apart; the centre cannot hold . . .

W. B. Yeats, 'The Second Coming'

Worldwide diffusion followed the origin of language. Language is recognizably language, wherever it has travelled, much to the astonishment of some nineteenth-century travellers: 'The grammar is precise and somewhat complicated . . . ', noted one writer, on encountering the language of the Miskitu Indians in South America, 'it seems strange to find among an uncultivated and uncivilized race rules of grammar as precise and well known as are used by the most cultivated nations of Europe. The Indian who has no literature, no written or defined rules, uses the grammar of his language with uniformity and without confusion. How is this to be explained?'[1]

But the widening circle of language raises two important questions: first, can the early routes of human language diffusion be plotted? Second, can any actual words or syntax be reconstructed for these prehistoric times? These issues will be the topic of this chapter.

Out of Africa

Modern humans are all descended from a fairly small stock of ancestors, who came from Africa (chapter 5). Humans walked out of Africa and into Asia, starting perhaps around 75,000 years ago – though the exact date is disputed.[2] Tribe after tribe filtered outwards and onwards. These new sophisticated humans with their advanced language skills eventually took over the world. The migrants probably came in small groups, one after another.

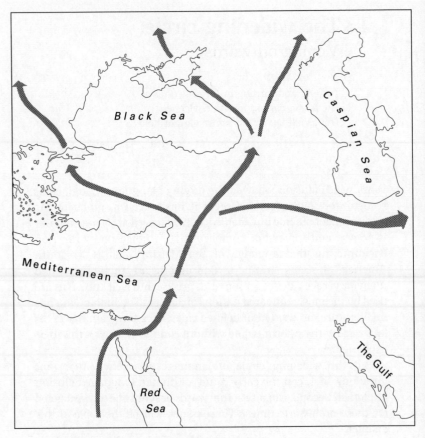

Figure 13.1 Africa to Middle East and onwards

Greater linguistic divergence set in as they moved in different directions (see Fig. 13.1).

The Middle East and particularly Lebanon provided a staging post, judging from the archaeological evidence. Both the skeletons and the tool technology suggest fully modern humans lived there from at least 50,000 BP ('before present').[3] From there, the newcomers moved in various directions.

To the west, a culture of remarkable uniformity and considerable sophistication spread across Europe. Remnants of it have been found in east and southeast Europe dating from around 45,000 BP, Spain around 40,000 BP, and southwest France around 35,000 BP.[4] An archaeologist comments:

> Arguably the most striking feature... is the wide range of different aspects of behaviour which seem to have been affected. The changes range, apparently, into all spheres of culture – the technology of tool production, various forms of symbolic expression, food procurement patterns, demography, social organization and (almost certainly) into the more fundamental realms of communication and the related 'cognitive' structures of the human groups... Indeed, the entire spectrum of... behaviour and culture has a remarkably 'modern' feel (in anthropological terms) which would be hard to visualize without the kind of structures and subtleties of communication which only relatively advanced forms of language could provide.[5]

Technically, this change occurred between the Middle Palaeolithic and the Upper Palaeolithic periods, and is associated with a culture often referred to as 'Aurignacian', named after the contents of a cave found at Aurignac in the Pyrenees.

The new humans did not kill off the existing populations. Peaceful co-existence with some 'acculturation' between them is the most likely scenario.[6] The term 'Neandertal' or 'Neanderthal' is often used to refer to the pre-human population of Europe with whom the new humans interacted.[7] Yet the Neandertals are themselves the subject of controversy. The name was given to a fossil skeleton found in 1857 in the Neander Valley in Germany (*tal* or *thal* 'valley'). The bones are generally assumed to be around 120,000 years old. But nowadays there is considerable discussion as to whether the Neandertals were a previous population, separate cousins, cousins who intermarried, or even modern humans. The main problem is that the original remains were dug up before excavation and dating techniques had been refined.[8]

Other humans moved eastwards from the Middle East, and then southwards to Austronesia, probably in small groups. 50,000 BP is the earliest date proposed for their arrival. The diversity of the mitochondrial DNA (chapter 5) found in Papua New Guinea is paralleled by the diversity of the languages. This may be explained by successive small waves of immigrants, who had spent some time in Asia before moving on to their final destination. No direct link exists between genes and language: the missing link is geographical location. People who are related genetically tend to live together, and consequently speak the same language.

Some humans eventually arrived in America, though when this happened is disputed, as will be explained below.

Into America

Everyone agrees on two things: first, that America was the last of the continents to be populated by humans, and second, on the route the newcomers took (see Fig. 13.2).

Adventurous easterners crossed from northeastern Siberia into northwestern Alaska. They went on foot via Beringia or by boat via the Bering Strait. Given the conditions in the Arctic, multiple entries of smallish groups are more likely than one massive cohort. The migrants may originally have spoken dialects of the same language, or perhaps related languages.

Northeastern Eurasia therefore 'provided seedstock for the languages of the New World. The subsequent differentiation of this seedstock has given rise to the unusually high degree of diversity, both genetic and typological, for languages in the New World.'[9]

But controversy surrounds the date of arrival, with proposed dates ranging from 35,000 BP to 12,000 BP.[10] The archaeological evidence suggests a date at least as early as 30,000 BP.[11]

The diversity of languages found in the Americas points to an early arrival date, according to some recent work by Johanna Nichols, from the University of California at Berkeley.[12] Late-date supporters 'are in the wrong ballpark, given what can be determined about rates of diversification and migration in high-latitude areas like northeastern Siberia',[13] which is the only way the immigrants could have come, she points out.

According to Nichols's calculation, a 'stock' or major language grouping normally lasts at least 5,000 years, and just under 2 daughter languages are likely to survive from it. Approximately 140 Amerind (American-Indian) stocks now exist, so 5,000 years ago there were half that number or 70 stocks, 10,000 years ago only 35, and so on. It would take 35,000 years to reach a figure of

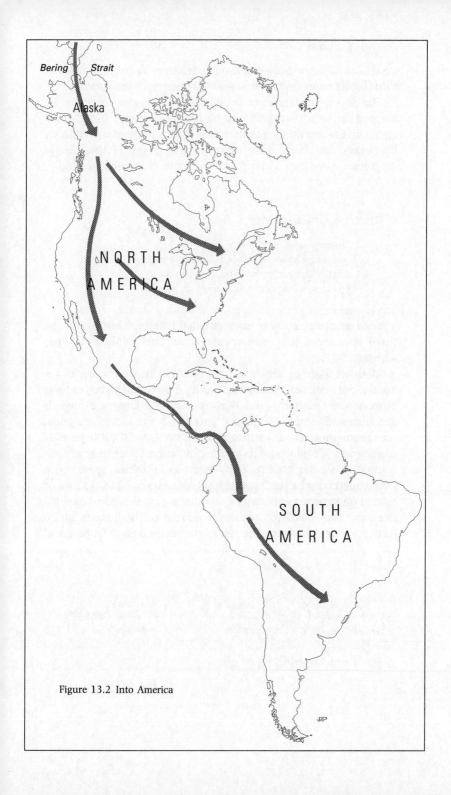

Figure 13.2 Into America

under 2 stocks. The New World must therefore have been settled at least 20,000 and maybe even 40,000 years ago, she concludes.[14]

The spread of language around the globe can therefore be mapped, at least in outline. But this leads to a highly contentious question. Can we do the reverse? That is, can we start with known languages and from them surmise what some of these early languages were like? This will be the topic of the next section.

Reaching backwards

> Philologists who chase
> A panting syllable through time and space,
> Start it at home, and hunt it in the dark,
> To Gaul, to Greece, and into Noah's ark.

For centuries, scholars have pursued language backwards, as these lines from the eighteenth-century poet William Cowper suggest.[15]

Methods of doing this vary. Three of them may be useful for finding out about early language, judging from the claims of their proponents. Comparing relatives – comparing languages which are descended from a common 'parent' – is the oldest and most reliable method, but it cannot go back very far: 10,000 years is usually considered its maximum useful range. Comparing areas – comparing similar constructions across geographical space – is a newer method which may potentially lead back 30,000 years or more. Comparing resemblances – comparing words which resemble one another – is a highly controversial new method: according to its advocates, it leads back to the origin of language. The pros and cons of these methods will be discussed below.[16] (See Fig. 13.3.)

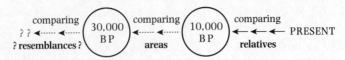

Figure 13.3 Reconstructing the past

Comparing relatives

The 'comparing relatives' method was developed in the nineteenth century, and is known as 'comparative historical linguistics', a name which has replaced its earlier label of 'comparative philology'.

Words from languages known to be 'daughters' of the same 'parent' are inspected, with a view to finding systematic links between them. Compare, for example, some Samoan and Hawaiian words:

Samoan		Hawaiian	
ufi	'yam'	*uhi*	'yam'
afi	'fire'	*ahi*	'fire'
faa	'four'	*haa*	'four'

Samoan *f* repeatedly matches Hawaiian *h*. This is unlikely to be chance. Then a possible earlier common stage can be reconstructed.

Comparative historical reconstruction involves a step-by-step process of deduction. Above all, three guidelines are followed. First, the majority verdict: any route taken by most languages is assumed to be the most likely. Second, phonetic probability: the researcher takes into consideration which sounds are likely to change into which others. Third, language patterns: the reconstructions should be consistent with a plausible linguistic pattern.[17]

In the Polynesian example above,[18] the Proto-Polynesian words can be reconstructed as **ufi* 'yam', **afi* 'fire' and **faa* 'four' mainly because [f] often turns into [h], but the reverse does not normally happen – though for reliable conclusions, evidence must be drawn from many more words, and also other related Polynesian languages.

Distorting features are eliminated as far as possible. Recurring child-language words, such as *papa, mama* (chapter 8), are treated with caution, and so are onomatopoeic words, such as those representing the crowing of roosters, which tends to be represented by [k]-sounds all over the world, from Dutch *kukeleku* to Japanese *kokekokkoo*. Items which could have been borrowed from a near neighbour are discounted, such as English *mutton* from French *mouton* 'sheep'. Isolated resemblances are ignored, as when the English word *bad* reputedly resembles a Persian word with the same meaning.

This method works best with languages which split when their speakers migrated in different directions, as in Polynesia. It can lead back thousands of years, and it has proved especially useful in reconstructing Proto-Indo-European, the language stock to which English belongs, which is presumed to have been spoken around 3,000BC. But, as already mentioned, 10,000 years is usually considered its maximum useful range.

A few optimists have tried to build up a picture of a 'superlanguage', which links several existing language stocks. This hypothetical super-ancestor language is usually called 'Nostratic', from the Latin word for 'our' (language). Tentative attempts began early in the century, but the topic has recently undergone a revival of interest. Nostratic is generally assumed to cover Indo-European, the Dravidian languages of India, the Kartvelian languages of the southern Caucasus, the Uralic family including Finnish and Hungarian, Altaic covering Turkish and Mongolian, and Afro-Asiatic[19] which includes Arabic, Berber and others (see Fig. 13.4).[20]

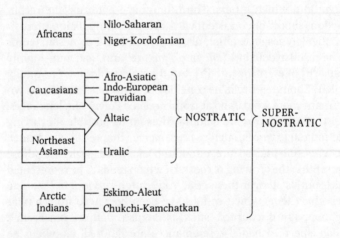

Figure 13.4 Proposed Nostratic groups

Some investigators have proposed an even wider super-grouping, sometimes labelled Super-Nostratic, which adds in extra language stocks such as Eskimo-Aleut from America, Chukchi-Kamchatkan from Siberia, and Niger-Kordofanian and Nilo-Saharan from Africa.[21] Distant links between languages must exist, given that human language sprang from a single source. But at remote time-depths, relationships are hard to establish. One clue that these links may be on the right track is DNA sampling (chapter 5). Some argue that the 'gene trees' correlate well with language stocks[22] – even though genes have no intrinsic connection with languages, as explained earlier (p. 164).

'The distribution of genes corresponds surprisingly well with that of languages', claims a researcher who has spent years matching gene distribution with Nostratic languages.[23] But not everyone agrees with this assessment.[24]

However, hunches about Nostratic may not be the only way to roll back knowledge about language. Other possible methods (mentioned above) will be discussed below.

Comparing areas

A new 'comparing areas' method may lead back more than 30,000 years. Its aim is to find 'principles governing the distribution of structural features among the world's languages'.[25] It seeks out stable and independent linguistic characteristics which might have spread over large areas.

Borrowing via contact is the key to this new approach. Features which are taken over from another language seep in slowly. New words are easily incorporated, but other constructions take time to spread from language to language, and, if found, guarantee a long period of close acquaintance. A bilingual population is usually required for these to take hold, at least on the border between languages.[26]

The new 'comparing areas' method has been developed primarily by Johanna Nichols, who calls it 'population typology'. She treats it 'as a population science, that is, a linguistic counterpart to population biology and population genetics, which analyse variation within and between populations of organisms and use the results to describe evolution'.[27] This wide-ranging geographical approach therefore complements existing attempts to find links between languages.

Population typology is not entirely new, in that 'linguistic areas' have long been recognized, cases where a linguistic feature has spread across unrelated but geographically adjacent languages.[28] Many Indian languages, for example, have 'retroflex' sounds, in which the tongue is curled back against the roof of the mouth. This must have developed via contact, since retroflexion has spread across different language families.

Population typology is innovative in that no serious study has ever before attempted to plot and quantify shared characteristics on a long-term timescale over large sections of the globe. Nichols has sampled a worldwide range of languages, on a number of linguistic features which are independent of one another.

The inclusive/exclusive opposition was one feature examined. Some languages, such as Guugu Yimidhirr in Australia, and Tok Pisin in Papua New Guinea, distinguish between two types of *we*, '*we* inclusive' when *we* includes the other people in the conversation, and '*we* exclusive' when it does not, as in the Tok Pisin sentences below:

Asde *yumi* lukim bikpela snek (*we* inclusive)
'Yesterday we (you and I) saw a big snake'

Asde *mipela* lukim bikpela snek (*we* exclusive)
'Yesterday we (I and some other people) saw a big snake'

The percentage of languages having this opposition increases dramatically towards the east, judging from a representative sample. It occurs in a mere 10% of European and Caucasian languages (one out of ten languages examined), in 56% of South and South East Asian ones (five out of nine), but in a massive 89% of the Australian languages (seventeen out of nineteen).[29]

Plurality neutralization on nouns was another feature scrutinized. That is, cases where the noun did not carry any marker overtly showing it to be plural: plurality was marked primarily on the verb, as in a largish number of North American languages, such as Central Pomo, spoken in California:[30]

yoohtow caac' waada
south-from person go-SINGULAR
'There's a person coming from the south'

yoohtow caac' hlaada
south-from person go-PLURAL
'There are people coming from the south'

Once again, this feature showed an eastwards increase. For this purpose, America is regarded as being 'eastern', since it was populated from the east, via the Bering Strait (p. 164).

An eastward increase was found in a further distinction, between alienable and inalienable possession, that is, things possessed that could be separated from one's person, such as 'my horse', and things that cannot as in 'my foot'.

In summary, for a number of independent language characteristics, there was a superficially puzzling increase: the further east the language, the more likely the feature was to occur, across a range of different language stocks.

A possible explanation runs as follows. In historical times, colonization movements have been primarily from west to east. Therefore if these features were recent ones, one would expect them to be highest in the west, and lowest in the east. If they were old ones, one would expect them to be gradually disappearing as western influence took hold, and so be lowest in the west, and highest in the east, as is the case. In short, the features which show an eastwards increase may be very old, and may reflect early population movements.

The peopling of the world may have happened in three stages, according to Nichols. First, the origin of humans and human language happened in Africa. Then came 'the stage of expansion', in which humans colonized areas within Europe, inner Asia, Australia and America. She dates this to between 60,000 and 30,000 years BP. The third stage followed on, and involved the rise of complex societies and large-scale economies. There was probably a reduction in linguistic diversity, and the spread of a few lineages across the known world.

Some of the features which increase towards the east may represent the 'stage of expansion', she believes. If she is correct, then she has provided glimpses of language at a time-depth far greater than had previously been thought possible. She comments: 'Thus our closest perspective on human language comes from the Pacific and the New World, areas relatively unaffected by the vast spreads in the Old World. The population profile of statistical propensities and diversity of these regions can justifiably be regarded as primordial, and the populations that most clearly show that profile . . . are our best models of human language.'[31]

All languages are equal, in that all languages can express anything they want to express, and all possess similar basic characteristics (chapter 14), so there is no suggestion that these old features are in any sense 'primitive': they merely represent a different way of expressing things from the way most of us are used to.

Nichols has proposed an interesting new method of exploring the past. Inevitably, her claims are controversial, and they have not yet been fully assessed. Hopefully, future research will show whether or not she is right.

Comparing resemblances

The monosyllable *tik* meaning finger is 100,000 years old, according to one optimistic scholar, so are the words *tsuma* 'hair', *kuan* 'dog' and *bur* 'ashes, dust'.[32] The conclusions were reached by a 'lucky dip' approach: trawling through dictionaries, and coming across superficial resemblances between words in far-flung languages. A hypothetical *bur* 'ashes, dust', for example, is claimed to have links with Classical Hebrew *bar* 'field, open space', a word *bur* 'dirty, muddy, dark' from Khalka, a Mongolian language, and a word *pra* 'ashes' in Cayapo, an Amerindian language – to take a sample of the quoted 'evidence'. Most linguists treat these claims with scepticism.

Problems abound with this 'lucky dip' approach, sometimes known as 'the method of mass comparison'.[33] Chance resemblances are easy to find among different languages if only vague likenesses among shortish words are selected. Such words pulled out from a wide time range, across multiple centuries, provide an even greater likelihood of chance similarities.

More importantly, sounds change radically over the centuries.

Words which existed so long ago are unlikely to have survived in anything like their original state. Quite a lot is now known about which sounds tend to be stable over time, and which unstable. At the beginning of a word, *m* is fairly stable, and so is *n*, but most others change hugely over the course of a thousand or so years. To return to *tik*, neither [t] nor [k] are particularly stable sounds, so doubts are raised by the very fact that some modern words similar to *tik* are quoted as relations, as Turkish *tek* 'only', *tek* 'fingernail' from Boven Mbian in Southwest New Guinea, and Greenlandic *tik(-iq)* 'index finger'.[34] For comparison, consider some more traditional etymologies: the English word *tick* 'a kind of mite' has as its possible nearest relatives German *zicke* 'tick', and Irish *dega* 'stag-beetle', while our own word *finger* is usually associated with an old word for 'five', which around 3,000 years ago was probably something like **penkwe* or **kwenkwe*. (An asterisk in reconstructions indicates a word that is presumed to have existed – not to be confused with the asterisks sometimes used to denote an impossible sentence.)

Taboo is a further problem: words for body-parts sometimes involve prohibitions both in primitive societies and in our own. This makes it even harder to be sure of past forms.

To summarize, the 'lucky dip' approach does not make any attempt to eliminate accidental correspondences, nor does it control for phonetic probability or taboo. These basic problems are aggravated by factors inherent in reconstructions of earlier forms of any language: meanings tend to be reduced to fairly simple, straightforward items, with a limited number of phonetic shapes. In these circumstances, chance similarities are likely to play a worryingly high role, and this 'mass comparison' method is unlikely to stand the test of time.

However, the diversity of language, both old and new, leads to another question. Is it possible to identify a 'hard core', a universal base found in every language? This will be the topic of the next chapter.

Summary

This chapter outlined the diffusion of language around the world. Roughly 75,000 years ago, humans moved out of Africa, probably first into Asia Minor, then westwards to Europe, eastwards to the Far East and Australia, and eventually to America via the Bering Strait.

Standard methods of comparing languages can take us back only around 10,000 years, though older links between language stocks have been proposed, and attempts have been made to correlate them with DNA samples. A new method, 'population typology', which plots selected independent constructions, may provide even earlier glimpses.

14 The hidden core:
The hunt for universals

> After a storm the beach has always changed slightly in some way – the sand washed away here to reveal the rocks beneath, then piled up in a swelling dune four hundred yards away. Once, on what had been a wide flat area, a small lagoon formed for a week or so, about sixty feet long behind a solid sandbar. Then came another high tide with a strong wind and the next morning it was gone. The geography of the beach is always changing, yet it always remains the same...
>
> John told me... he was tired of change, and wanted now to study concepts of permanence. He wanted to look at what remained constant in an object... When something is bent, stretched or twisted, he said, certain features of it resist deformation. He wanted to investigate these unchanging features.
>
> William Boyd, *Brazzaville beach*

'100% of the people in this carriage have heads. Therefore this is a good place to advertise hats' ran an ad on the London underground. Similarly, maybe language universals can be detected, a set of basic language characteristics, equivalent to human heads, or the unchanging features of the beach in the quotation above.[1] This is a recurring hope among language researchers.

Any human can learn any language, so something must link all languages together, even though some have been geographically separated from others for at least 50,000 years. But 'language universals' in the sense of 'features which occur in all languages' are extraordinarily elusive. Over fifty years ago, the American linguist Leonard Bloomfield commented: 'Features which we think ought to be universal may be absent from the very next language that becomes accessible'[2] – and similar comments are still being made: 'It is dangerous to speculate about what must be in language, and all too often what appears to be an "obvious" fact

175

about language turns out to be merely a feature of English and familiar (usually European) languages.'[3]

The term 'universal' sounds simple enough, but 'features found in all languages' is not the only possible interpretation. Sometimes, it refers to a universal repertoire, in the sense of 'features which are *available* to all languages', of which any single language will select only a proportion.[4] For example, the 'universal' stock of speech sounds is presumably finite, given the range of sounds which can be produced by the human vocal organs. But each language will contain only a subset of these. The universal store includes noises which are odd to English ears, such as the 'clicks' of Xhosa, a South African Bantu language, which sound to English ears somewhat like 'kissy-kiss' noises, the 'gee-up' encouragement made to horses, and the 'tut-tut' of disapproval.

Just occasionally, the word 'universal' is used in an even wider sense, to mean 'apparently true facts about languages'. The author of a book entitled *A select catalogue of language universals* claims to have gathered together 586 'universals', which include statements such as '14% of the languages of the world have long consonants', and 'Verbs for snoring contain an *r* in many languages.'[5]

But if the term 'universal' is restricted to its narrowest and most obvious sense, that of characteristics shared by all languages, then hardly any can be found. This chapter will consider this problem.

The rarity of absolute universals

Relatively few features are common to all languages. One linguist quoted a presumed six,[6] but critics disputed even some of these, commenting: 'Even though universals in the strictest sense of the word may exist, some of the most likely candidates for strict universality can turn out to be disappointing.'[7]

Of course, it's easy to think up fairly broad 'design features' for languages, if characteristics shared widely with some other animals are included. The linguist Charles Hockett first tried to do this in the 1950s, though his list changed over the years.[8] Hockett's list included, for example, 'interchangeability', meaning that all humans could both send and receive messages.

But, often, features shared with many other animals are too broad to be truly illuminating. Consider the claim that all human languages use outgoing air from the lungs. This is true. It is the main airstream mechanism in all languages, but it is not necessarily the *only* one. Sometimes outgoing air comes from a source higher than the lungs. Hausa, for example, the main language of Northern Nigeria, has 'ejectives', sounds produced by expelling a pocket of air trapped between the tongue and the glottis, the area of the vocal folds. Some languages also use indrawn air. For example, Sindhi, spoken in India and Pakistan, has 'implosives' in which air trapped between the tongue and glottis is pulled inwards. And Xhosa clicks (p. 176) suck back air from within the mouth. No language uses the whole range of possibilities, though Uduk, spoken in southern Sudan, has implosives and ejectives as well as the more usual pulmonic egressive sounds – those produced with outgoing breath from the lungs.

A possible list of 'narrow' absolute universals – features found in all languages – runs as follows.

All languages:

    (1) have consonants and vowels.
    (2) combine sounds into larger units.
    (3) have nouns – words for people and objects.
    (4) have verbs – words for actions.
    (5) can combine words.
    (6) can say who did what to who.
    (7) can negate utterances.
    (8) can ask questions.
    (9) involve structure-dependence (chapter 12).
    (10) involve recursion (chapter 12).

But even these few could be criticized as misleading. For a start, language can be transferred to sign language, which would eliminate the first two.

If spoken language only is considered, then these ten proposed universals are still problematic. For example, some have queried the claim that all languages distinguish nouns and verbs. The noun–verb distinction may be blurred in Nootka, an American-Indian language, spoken in the northwestern USA.[9] At first sight,

Nootka places verbs first in the sentence, followed by a tense ending, and nouns second, often followed by the definite marker.[10]

Mamu·k-ma qu·ʔas-ʔi
work-PRES man-the
'The man is working'

But consider the following, where the order is reversed and the endings also are switched over:

Qu·ʔas-ma mamu·k-ʔi
man-PRES work-the
'The worker is a man'

Sentences such as these have led to claims that Nootka does not have a verb–noun division.

Nootka shows that some languages work in weird ways, by English standards. But Nootka may not be as astonishing as was first thought. In many languages the same word stem can be both a verb and a noun. Consider the English sentences:

Everbody *must work*
Work is a *must* for everybody

In the first sentence, the words *must* and *work* are both verbs, in the second they are nouns. When a verb is used as a noun, the secondary use is often restricted, as shown with *must*. So in English, you can say 'Work is a *must*', but not '*Work is *the must*', or '*Work is *this must*' (with an asterisk marking an ill-formed sentence). The Nootka examples are apparently similar, in that the words are not freely interchangeable.[11]

Another possible interpretation of the Nootka data is that the word order has been been shifted around for emphasis. In this case, *-ma* is not a true present tense, but a 'clitic', a word which attaches itself to another word, here to the first word, even though it may not 'belong' to it in any strong sense.[12]

In short, Nootka nouns ARE distinguishable from verbs, though the distinction is not as clearcut as in English, and Nootka specialists still discuss it: 'While diligent search reveals some characteristics distinguishing these classes, the difference is anything but obvious', comments one researcher.[13] It's a bit like finding some flowers which apparently don't have petals – but on closer inspection, they often do, though petals quite unlike those associated with roses or daisies.[14]

The case of Lisu, spoken in Burma, is perhaps odder. Supposedly, it cannot state clearly who did what to who.[15] In this language, 'even the grammatical relations Agent and Patient cannot be identified',[16] it has been claimed. Take the sentence:

làma nya ánà kyù-a
Tigers TOPIC dogs bite[17]

This could mean either 'Tigers bite dogs' or 'Dogs bite tigers.' The only marker is *nya* which highlights the topic of conversation. So the sentence could be: 'It is tigers that bite dogs' or 'It is tigers that dogs bite'. This is fairly weird, by the standards of most languages.

But Lisu is not quite as peculiar as it seems at first sight. First, many of the ambiguous sentences are clear from the context. Second, and more importantly, a particle *lae* marks the patient in some sentences. So the overall conclusion is that Lisu sometimes marks the difference between agent and patient, but does not do so obligatorily, as do some languages. Furthermore, it's not spectacularly odd to have sentences where the person who did the action is unclear, as in English 'The shooting of the policemen horrified everybody.' Did the policemen shoot, or were they shot? It's impossible to say for sure.

The Nootka and Lisu examples show that neither of these languages is quite as weird as was once thought. But neither of them maintains clearcut boundaries for distinctions which English regards as essential. They show how difficult it is to sort out absolute universals for language even at a basic level, especially as linguists disagree as to how to tackle the problem.

Buried treasure

A tall tree was thus the principal mark ... The top of the plateau was dotted thickly with pine trees of varying height. Every ... man on board the boats had picked a favourite of his own ere we were half way over.[18]

Just as the pirates searching for buried treasure in Robert Louis Stevenson's novel *Treasure Island* cannot agree on where to dig, so linguists argue, often bitterly, about the best way to proceed when they hunt for the linguistic treasure of language universals among the world's 500 or so tongues.

Traditionally, there are two main methods, which can be called shallow scraping and deep delving.[19] Shallow scrapers zap around the world collecting specimens from numerous languages, and then compare them to see what they have in common. Joseph Greenberg is often regarded as the 'father' of the shallow scrapers, whose pioneering work on universals in the 1960s 'set the ball rolling'.[20] Deep delvers, on the other hand, look in depth at the behaviour of one particular language. They then check this against other languages, to see if they have identified common properties. Noam Chomsky and his followers represent the deep delving approach.[21]

Both methods have good and bad points. The advantage of shallow scraping is that it considers a large sample. The method may be useful in the early stages of research, since it gives some idea of the range of data which needs to be accounted for. It takes the inductive approach to knowledge, in which theories are formulated by seeking patterns in a wide array of data.

But shallow scraping contains inherent problems. First, some theory must subconsciously have been formed in order to decide what data to collect, not least about what constitutes a language. Second, patterns are often difficult to detect in disparate arrays of data. In this situation, there is a subconscious temptation to look at only a portion of the evidence, and impose patterns which are not really there.

A third problem with the surface-scraping approach is that the observations are often fairly superficial, because there is not time to look at each language in detail. For example, little can be done with an observation such as 'All languages have the sound *t*', unless it is fitted into a wider framework, such as how many *t*-sounds there are in a language, and which sounds they contrast with: Hindi, for example, has four contrasting types of *t*, compared with English which has only one – and even this one is pronounced in different ways depending on where it comes in a word.

Deep delving represents the deductive approach to knowledge, in which a hypothesis is formulated, and then tested against new evidence. If the hypothesis is disproved, then an amended theory is formulated, and so on.

To take an imaginary non-linguistic example, suppose Yok, a man from Mars, found a dead goldfish up an apple tree. He might first guess that it flew there to eat apples and died from overeating. But he might later discover that goldfish cannot flit through the air, so would reformulate the hypothesis: something took it there. Then he would guess what: maybe a cat, or a large bird, and so on. This is the standard way to proceed. As a linguistic example, a preliminary hypothesis might be: all English sentences must contain a noun phrase (phrase containing a noun) followed by a verb phrase. Then the researcher might find: *Sing!* or *Up jumped the swagman*. The hypothesis would have to be amended or abandoned.

Deep delvers can formulate detailed hypotheses about a particular language, and how its different parts interact. The guesses can then be tested against other languages. But the method also has problems. Its proponents tend to overemphasize the importance of any language they have studied in depth, and so fail to propose hypotheses which might occur to them if they had looked at data from a wider range of languages.

Deep delving also encourages speculation, the postulation of wild ideas which cannot be disproved. Chomsky has suggested that linguists seeking for principles of language are like physicists trying to understand the thermonuclear reactions hidden in the sun's interior.[22] They have to make elaborate guesses about how the sun's heat is converted into light. In some circumstances, as perhaps with the sun, it may be impossible to put forward truly testable hypotheses, but it's important to try.

An untestable hypothesis might be proposed if it was the only suggestion which fitted in with the rest of an otherwise tested theory. If Felix the cat was seen with a goldfish in its mouth, and was also known to be good tree-climber, then a hypothesis that Felix took the goldfish up the tree is highly plausible, if untestable.

But there's always a danger of circularity, especially if more than one researcher is involved. Suppose Yok's friend Yak saw apples floating in a fishpond: her hypothesis is that goldfish eat apples. Yok's original hypothesis was that goldfish climb trees. Yak quotes Yok to back up her proposal, and Yok quotes Yak, and the goldfish–apple myth enters Martian folklore for ever.

It's a true Woozle hunt, as described in a well-known children's storybook:[23] one winter's day, Winnie-the-Pooh, a Bear of Very Little Brain, found paw-marks in the snow which his friend suggested might belong to a Woozle. They decided to follow the trail of this remarkable animal. Soon, the Woozle track was joined by another, then another, then another. Pooh and his friend became increasingly convinced that there was a whole bunch of Woozles in front of them. But they had failed to notice that the growing number of tracks was produced by their own feet as they walked round in circles, and that the initial footprint was one of Pooh's own. An accusation of such 'closed-circuit functioning' is sometimes made against some linguists.[24]

To summarize so far, shallow scraping is important particularly in the early stages of research, in order to explore the data which must be accounted for. Deep delving is a standard method once researchers understand some of the basic questions which need to be asked – though it must take care not to get into a state of closed-circuit functioning.

But whichever method is used, the task is still a mammoth one. The next section will discuss some ways in which a hunt for universals can be made more manageable.

Snark-hunting?

> But the Snark is at hand, let me tell you again!
> 'Tis your glorious duty to seek it!
> To seek it with thimbles, to seek it with care;
> To pursue it with forks and hope

The search for language universals sometimes resembles the hunt for the mythical Snark in Lewis Carroll's poem,[25] in that the searchers do not know the shape of the entity they are pursuing.

A possible step forward is to divide universals into different types. For example, at one time the American linguist Noam Chomsky suggested universals might be either substantive, the substance out of which language is made, or formal, the way in which language is arranged.[26] In outline, this is a good idea, and works in some non-linguistic situations: the beaks of all birds are made out of the same substance, but they differ quite dramatically in form – the beak of a toucan is quite different in shape from that of a parrot or duck. But in language, the division ran into problems. Nobody could agree on whether a statement such as 'All languages have nouns and verbs' was a claim about substance or form, for example.

Two further dimensions have provided a more useful approach. Universals can be looked at via degree of firmness, on the one hand, and degree of independence on the other (see Fig. 14.1, p. 185).

On the firmness dimension, a distinction can be drawn between absolute universals, those true of all languages, which are disappointingly few (pp. 176–7), and statistical universals, those applicable to most languages.

Statistical universals are features which are overwhelmingly likely to be found in a language, but may occasionally be absent. The 'unmarked' situation, the normal, basic one, can then be contrasted with the 'marked' situation, the unusual, exceptional one. For example, nasals – sounds such as m, n – usually involve vibration of the vocal folds. So-called voiceless nasals, without vocal fold vibration, are rare. They occur in a handful of languages only, as in Klamath, a Californian American-Indian language. In one sample of around 300 languages, only 10 were definitely found to have voiceless [m̥], compared with 296 which definitely had voiced [m̥]. This 296 included the 10 which had voiceless [m̥]: no languages had only voiceles [m].[27]

Statistical universals are useful for dealing with languages which appear to 'go mad'. A comforting myth exists that any language somehow balances itself out: a complicated set of vowels is balanced by simple consonants, or vice versa. Or complex word endings compensate for simple syntax, and so on. Sometimes this appears to happen, but not always. Some languages just appear to be 'way out'.

Consider the ratio of consonants to vowels. In the 300-language sample mentioned above, the total number of consonants varied between 6 and 95 with a mean of 22.8. The total number of vowels varied between 3 and 46 with a mean of 8.7.[28] But as a general tendency, the greater the number of consonants, the greater the number of vowels: 'The tendency for vowel inventories to increase in step with increases in consonant inventories is the opposite of the prediction made by a compensation theory.'[29] Another possibility considered was that languages with contrastive stress and several tones might require fewer different sounds. But again this was not borne out: 'The overall tendency appears once again to be more that complexity of different kinds goes hand in hand, rather than for complexity of one sort to be balanced by simplicity elsewhere.'[30] And the same was true of the relationship between number of sounds and syllable structure, that is, large inventories did not result in simple syllables. In short, these investigations suggested 'that complexity of various kinds occurs together in languages, and that languages really do differ in their phonological complexity'.[31]

To take another example, languages streamline their aspectual systems, judging from Tok Pisin (chapter 11). But Central Pomo, an American-Indian language spoken some 100 miles north of San Francisco, has an intricate mesh of fine distinctions. Among its numerous aspectual forms are an imperfective, for unfinished actions, as in 'the ground is drying up'; a habitual imperfective, as in 'children would pack those little fish around in their pockets and eat them like popcorn'; a continuative, as in 'she kept grabbing on to it'; and a frequentative, as in 'Do you go away a lot?' And some of these could be combined further, as in 'I used to talk to him all the time', which involves imperfective, habitual and frequentative. All of these are expressed primarily by combining the consonants [d] and [w] with various vowels, in a system which has around 30 consonants to choose from.[32] For example:

Wá·ymin-wa   ma ?é·y-yo-hduwa·dan ?
often-QUESTION you away-go-FREQUENTATIVE
'Do you go away a lot?'[33]

This frequentative is composed of several different aspectual suffixes, and can be split into yo-h-du-w-a·d-an. In such cases, statistical universals seem essential.

But the independence dimension may be even more important. Universals can be subdivided into unrestricted universals, which encapsulate independent facts, such as 'All languages have vowels', and implicational universals, which have an *if–then* connection: 'If a language has X, then it will also have Y', as 'If a language has voiceless nasals, then it will also have voiced nasals': voiced nasals can exist without voiceless ones, but not vice versa (as explained above).

Implicational universals can reveal important restrictions on languages, as many researchers now realize.[34] A search for restrictions and constraints – things that languages DON'T do – may be the most useful way of tackling the universals problem. This will be the topic of the next chapter.

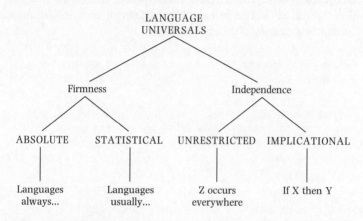

Figure 14.1 Types of universal

Summary

Many linguists hope to find language universals – features common to all languages. Yet this is a problem, apart from the fact that the term 'language universals' is used in more senses than the one above.

Absolute linguistic universals, features common to all languages, are rare, unless one takes an over-broad view of the word 'universal'. Even when apparently found, they differ in details from language to language.

Linguists argue about how to find universals. A shallow scraping approach collects specimens from numerous languages, and attempts to find features which they have in common. A deep delving approach looks at one language, formulates hypotheses about how it might work, and tests the hypotheses against other languages. The first approach is useful for early stages of research, the second for later stages.

Universals can be profitably explored along various dimensions. One is degree of firmness, in which absolute universals are contrasted with statistical universals, features which figure in most languages, but not all. Another is degree of independence, in which independent universals are contrasted with implicational universals: if X, then Y. These can reveal important constraints on language, as will be discussed further.

15 The real magician:
Ruling the rules

> The real magician isn't the bleary-eyed guy who doesn't understand a thing; it's the scientist who has grasped the hidden secrets of the universe.
>
> Umberto Eco, *Foucault's pendulum*

The permitted patterns or 'rules' of all languages constantly change, and new words are continually coming into use. One might expect, sooner or later, a situation of chaos, as envisaged by Alexander Pope, in his 'Essay on Man':

> Let earth unbalanc'd from her orbit fly,
> Planets and suns run lawless thro' the sky;
> Let ruling angels from their spheres be hurl'd,
> Being on being wreck'd and world on world.[1]

'Evolution', a computer program developed by the zoologist Richard Dawkins, shows the basic difficulty.[2] 'Evolution' grew trees. A single vertical line divided into two sub-branches, each of which split into sub-sub-branches, and so on. Minor alterations to the program made the trees more complex: the angle of branching might vary, and so might the length of the branches. Dawkins christened the resulting trees 'biomorphs', and he became entranced by the varied patterns they formed: 'On my wanderings through the backwaters of Biomorph Land, I have encountered fairy shrimps, Aztec temples, Gothic church windows, aboriginal drawings of kangaroos, and, on one memorable but unrecapturable occasion, a passable caricature of the Wykeham Professor of Logic.'[3] But he became increasingly concerned at the zillions of possible biomorphs, noting that 'the number of possible pathways is all but infinite, and the monsters that one encounters are undesigned and unpredictable'.[4] Writing the rules which produced the biomorphs was the easy part of the enterprise, he realized. Controlling the biomorphs was more difficult, stopping them from producing so many trees, and such strange ones.

Language presents a similar problem. Languages appear very different from one another. Yet language never collapses: the rules do not spiral out of control. Each new generation of children can cope with learning their language. And, with a bit of effort, all humans can learn any other human language – though they are baffled when faced with the communication systems of other species:

> The wide world over
> Man with man
> Has talked his own tongue
> Since speech began.
>
> Yet still must sorrow
> Move the mind,
> He understands
> But his own kind

said Walter de la Mare in his poem *Babel*.[5]

It's an odd situation when it's impossible to find more than a few broad language universals. Some principles must rule the rules. Language has 'hidden secrets',[6] reins which keep it in check, and linguists are the would-be magicians, who try to find out what they are. Let us consider the matter further.

Prohibitions vs preferences

Language must have strong constraints, bounds which restrain it. It's easy to think up some things which languages don't do. No language works by simply reversing its words to mean the opposite. That is, *Boris is tired* would not in any language have a word reversal as its negative, **Tired is Boris*, to mean 'Boris is not tired.' But it's less easy to explain why this is so.

Broadly speaking, constraints are of two types, filters and preferences. Filters close off certain possibilities absolutely. 'There are questions we could never get over if we were not dispensed from them by our very nature', said Franz Kafka.[7] Such prohibitions are true constraints. Preferences, on the other hand, provide channels which are easy to flow along. They turn attention away from some non-preferred, though possible, routes. Such pseudo-constraints are often difficult to separate from prohibitions.

Some filters are due to physical limitations: no speech sound can be made by placing a tongue-tip on one's ear, the human tongue is just not long enough. Preferences also may reflect physical make-up. The sound [ʃ] is normally made by placing the upper teeth on the lower lip. But a similar sound can be made by placing the lower teeth on the upper lip. Because the top jaw normally protrudes beyond the lower jaw, the first is an easier and quicker method of producing *f*, and is the one found in all known languages. But occasionally someone with a minor defect, perhaps no top teeth, selects the second way, showing that the standard *f*-route is a preference, rather than a prohibition.

Or take hearing. Humans can perceive only a limited range of sounds. The make-up of their ears prevents them from hearing some high squeaks of bats, or some of the low notes found in whale songs. These are therefore filtered out as possible human speech sounds. To take a preference, no human language has eight different types of *l*, or six different types of *r*, even though physically these would not be impossible to produce. But it would probably be too difficult for humans to pronounce them fast and distinguish them easily. The record, incidentally, is held by Irish, which is reported to have six types of *l* and four types of *r*,[8] though the vast majority of languages have one *l* and one *r*.

In some areas, prohibitions and preferences merge into one another, as in memory restrictions. Humans have a fairly small working memory span – memory for things they do not wish to store permanently: most people can remember a phone number for a few moments, long enough to dial the number after looking it up in the phone book. In line with short-term memory limitations, humans plan and produce speech in smallish chunks. The approximate span is revealed above all by errors: items within a planned span sometimes get confused, as in 'He threw the window through the clock' for 'He threw the clock through the window.' But it's difficult to set an absolute limit.[9]

Ideally, constraints which reflect general human abilities should be separated from those due to special linguistic mechanisms. But in the animal world, constraints due to purpose-built structures cannot always be separated from those caused by more general factors.

Consider the hexagonal shape of the honeycomb cells made by bees. This is the only area of bee-life in which hexagons occur, and one might therefore suppose that bees have an innate knowledge of hexagons, specifically inbuilt to enable them to store their honey in this way, and in no other. But hexagons are the inevitable result of bees pushing with their hemispheric heads from a variety of directions, it turns out.[10] So even unique structures may not be genetically purpose-built.

Possible rediscovery presents a similar problem. All through the ages, humans have probably run away from lions. An innate fear of lions might constrain their actions, and force them down one route rather than another. But it's more likely that they have looked at the teeth and claws and decided that a wrestling match would be too great a risk. To take another example, bows and arrows occur widely around the world. But this does not make them 'innate hunting structures': they represent a recurring thoughtful response to the problem of killing prey that runs faster than humans.[11]

As these examples show, constraints overlap with universals: if humans are prevented from going down alternative paths, they may be inevitably pushed in one particular direction, resulting in an apparent universal.

To summarize, universals and constraints overlap – they are opposite sides of the same coin. Language contains two types of constraints: filters (real constraints) and preferences (pseudo-constraints). And these may work on at least two levels: that of general human abilities, and that of language.

At one time, linguists tried to find absolute, independent constraints. But they proved frustratingly elusive. As time went by, constraining links turned out to be more illuminating, as will be discussed below.

No smoke without fire

'Where smoke, there fire' is a proverb which goes back around 2,000 years, when it's found in the old Indian language Sanskrit.[12]

Similar constraining links (if X, then Y) occur within language (chapter 14), and their importance is enormous in reining in the multiple possibilities of language.

Finding them is a challenge. The evidence has to be treated with care, because superficial correspondences may mislead. To take a trivial example: human eyes and legs come in pairs. But eye structure is not necessarily based on leg structure, or vice versa.

Correlations need to be treated with equal caution. The geographical distribution of bowel cancer in the world correlates broadly with the ownership of telephones. But a significant link between this disease and buying a phone is unlikely. Similarly, growth in children's height normally correlates with language acquisition, but height and language are not directly connected. Two problems therefore exist: first, finding genuine links, second, explaining them.

The study of implicational universals in language dates from the work of the Czech linguist Roman Jakobson over fifty years ago. He suggested, for example: 'The first consonantal opposition[13] is that of nasal and oral stop (*e.g., mama-papa*), which is followed by the opposition of labials and dentals (*e.g., papa-tata* and *mama-nana*). These two oppositions form the minimal consonant system of the languages of the world. These are the only oppositions that cannot be lacking anywhere.'[14] Following his ideas, considerable work has been done on sound-structure implications, over which he was partially right, and partially wrong.[15]

Word-order implications have attracted attention in the last quarter-century, inspired by the work of the American Joseph Greenberg in the 1960s. He proposed a number of links, such as 'With overwhelmingly greater than chance frequency, languages with normal SOV [= subject-object-verb] order are postpositional.'[16]

Most such links are statistical, rather than absolute (chapter 14). This is shown by a recent sample of adpositions, which has been adjusted for geographical distribution and genetic relationship.[17] 70 verb-before-object (VO) languages had prepositions, while only 12 had postpositions. In contrast, 107 object-before-verb (OV) languages had postpositions while 7 had prepositions.[18] Adpositions therefore follow the pattern of verbs: an order of preposition–noun correlates with VO (verb-before-object), and noun–postposition with OV (object-before-verb):

	VO	OV
Prepositions	70	7
Postpositions	12	107

On closer examination, parallel patterns between different word classes occur more extensively, with the 'head' of the phrase (the most important word structurally) tending to be placed in a similar position in different types of phrases:

Peter was   *furious* with his brother
Geraldine was   *out* of the room
Alex was   *thinking* about his mother

This tendency has been labelled the 'principle of cross-category harmony': 'The more the word order co-occurrence sets of languages depart from this "ideal" harmonic ordering, the fewer exemplifying languages there are',[19] comments John Hawkins, who proposed the principle.[20] It has been widely recognized as valid[21] – even though identifying the head of a phrase is sometimes problematic.[22]

Other parallels between different types of phrase have been proposed. For example, some languages may primarily add markers to heads, others to their dependents, it has been suggested.[23] Maltese *bin Alla* 'son of God' marks the head: the word 'son' has been altered from *iben* to *bin* to show the meaning 'son-of'. But English behaves differently: it marks the dependent, as in *son of-God*, or *God's son* – though not everyone agrees that this is a significant distinction.[24]

Noam Chomsky has put forward perhaps the best-known of recent implicational theories.[25] Children, he suggests, have an inbuilt knowledge of some basic language principles. But in addition, they are instinctively aware of some key 'either/or' options. They need to find out which their own language selects. When they discover this, they metaphorically set a switch. Such switch-setting automatically brings in further ramifications, and the whole system clicks into place.

It's as if children were car-drivers who knew in advance that you could drive either on the right, or on the left, of the road. But they have to solve the left or right problem for themselves. Once they decide, extra information follows automatically: which side of

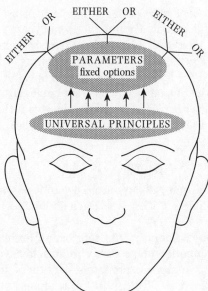

EITHER OR
EITHER OR
EITHER OR
EITHER OR

PARAMETERS
fixed options

UNIVERSAL PRINCIPLES

Figure 15.1 Switch-setting

the car to have the driver's seat, which way to drive round roundabouts (traffic circles), and so on.

Chomsky speaks of this process as 'setting parameters'. A parameter is a fixed property which can vary in particular ways. For example, temperature is a parameter of the atmosphere. The atmosphere must have a temperature, but this alters, going both up and down – which in turn affects day-to-day decisions, such as whether to wear warm clothes, install central heating, and so on (see Fig. 15.1).

Possible linguistic parameters have been much discussed: head-dependent ordering (outlined above) is one, and another overlapping parameter is 'branching direction', that is whether languages attach phrases to the left or right of major lexical items.[26] In addition, predictable differences may exist between 'pro-drop' languages, such as Italian, which allow speakers to drop pronouns at the beginning of sentences – as in: *sono italiano* '[I] am Italian' – and languages such as English, where the pronoun must

normally be included: *I am English*, rather than **am English*.[27]
These discussions will undoubtedly continue for some years.

Parameter setting is important because as Chomsky notes:
'Change in a single parameter may have complex effects, with
proliferating consequences.'[28] More importantly, perhaps: 'A few
changes in parameters yield typologically different languages.'[29]

But switch-setting in an either/or fashion is only one type of link
which might exist within language, as will be discussed below.

Two's company, three's a crowd

If you have fingers, then you will have arms, if you have arms,
then you will have shoulders... This type of chain-link occurs
quite often in language.

An implicational chain is found in the category of number,
which deals with the quantity of people or things involved.
Number can be shown on nouns, pronouns, adjectives and
verbs – either on some or on all of them. In full languages, the
possible number categories are:

singular (one)
plural (more than one)
dual (two)
trial/paucal (three or several)

This whole range is found in Manam, spoken on a small island off
Papua New Guinea.

But the marking of number is not random: if a language has a
trial or paucal, then it will normally also have a dual; if it has a
dual, then it will have a plural; if it has a plural, then it will have a
singular; and all languages have singulars. This implicational
order can be written as:

singular < plural < dual < trial/paucal[30]

This scale is statistical, rather than absolute, and is sometimes
reflected in the way a language marks its plurals. In Kharia, for
example, spoken in north-east India, the extra markedness
(unusualness) of the dual is shown by adding an extra ending onto
the plural:

biloi-ki   'cats'
biloi-ki-yar 'two cats'[31]

But there are other, more complex chains in language. Let us go on to consider one of these.

Who did what to who

> On Wednesday, when the sky is blue,
> And I have nothing else to do,
> I sometimes wonder if it's true
> That who is what and what is who.[32]

These musings of the bear Winnie-the-Pooh[33] might well apply to the thought processes of adults if they ever contemplate grammatical relationships – who did what to who – in different languages.

A 'pecking order' exists among the different roles of noun phrases (phrases containing a noun) within a sentence, resulting in a chain known as the 'grammatical relations hierarchy' (GRH). Complications arise because different languages have different types of chain.

In one variant of this hierarchy, the person or thing initiating the action of the verb is basic and unmarked, while the object of the verb's action is marked, as in Latin:

Caesar puella-m adiuvit
Caesar girl helped
'Caesar helped the girl'

Puella Caesar-em adiuvit
girl Caesar helped
'The girl helped Caesar'

Next on this hierarchy is the indirect object, the person to whom something is given, as in 'Paul sent an orchid *to Felicity*.' This subject < object < indirect object hierarchy shows up in various languages, for example Hungarian:

subject   < object   < indirect object
ember 'man'   ember-t   ember-nek[34]

The hierarchy is completed with 'oblique cases', which refers to relations other than subject, object and indirect object, as in 'Paul arrived *with Felicity.*' This version of the grammatical relations hierarchy (GRH) therefore runs (see Fig. 15.2):

subject < object < indirect object < oblique

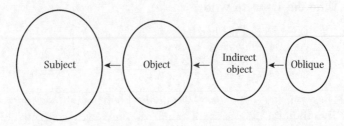

Figure 15.2 Grammatical relations hierarchy, subject–object version

The hierarchy was identified primarily by inspecting various languages, and ranking the markers attached to the noun. But it also shows up in other ways, most notably in relative clauses, which in English often begin with a WH-word (word beginning with *wh-*, such as *who, which*).

The WH-word or phrase in English may be subject (S), object (O), indirect object (IO) or oblique case (OBL) in its clause.

The cat *which* ate the cream ran away (S)
The cook looked for the cream *which* the cat had eaten (O)
The cook wrote to the man *to whom* the cat belonged (IO)
The old man locked the room *in which* the cat slept (OBL)

But languages which do not have this wide set of relative clauses mostly follow the sliding scale of the GRH for what they allow, in a so-called 'noun phrase accessibility hierarchy':

If a language has OBL relative clauses,
    then it will also have IO, O, and S ones.
If a language has IO relative clauses,
    then it will also have O and S ones.
If a language has O relative clauses,
    then it will also have S ones.[35]

Some exceptions to this can be found, but it works in the majority of languages which use the S < O < IO < OBL version of the GRH.[36] But a rather different version of the GRH is also found widely. Consider Dyirbal, an Australian language from north Queensland:

yabu banaganyu
mother returned
'mother returned'

ŋuma *yabu-ŋgu* buran
father mother-ERG saw
'mother saw father'[37]

In this so-called 'ergative' system, a marker is attached only when someone does something which involves someone else. Another Australian example of this phenomenon was given earlier, from the Guugu Yimidhirr language (chapter 3) – though similar ones can be found elsewhere in the world, as in Avar, a Caucasian language:

ins:u-c:a ču bec:uleb bugo
father-ERG horse praising is
'Father is praising the horse'[38]

In these languages, the basic (unmarked) form is the absolutive, which covers both the subject of an intransitive verb (a verb without an object), and the object of a transitive verb (a verb with an object).[39]

In the ergative type of language, the hierarchy runs (see Fig. 15.3):

absolutive < ergative < indirect object < oblique

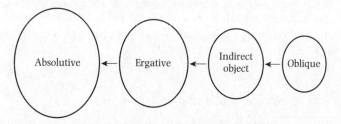

Figure 15.3 Grammatical relations hierarchy, ergative version

The situation is not quite as simple as described here, because many languages mix the hierarchies, having one type of GRH for full nouns and another for pronouns.[40]

Overall, the GRH shows both the importance of finding implicational links within languages, and the difficulty of doing this.

Multiple chains

Chains and hierarchies of various types run throughout language. Grammaticalization chains are another example, which work in the historical dimension (chapters 9-12): Yesterday's discourse is today's syntax; today's syntax will be tomorrow's morphology. This is as valid in all 'full' modern languages, as it is in pidgins and creoles.[41]

Strictly linguistic hierarchies are not the only ones. Others overlap with general cognitive abilities. Eleven basic colour terms exist – white, black, red, green, yellow, blue, brown, purple, pink, orange, grey – and their foci are similar in all languages, according to a claim made by Brent Berlin and Paul Kay, of the University of California at Berkeley, in the late 1960s.[42] They argued for an implicational hierarchy: if a language has two basic colour terms, these will be black and white; if three, red will be added; if five, green and yellow will be included and so on. These claims have been progressively modified, and are still under review.[43] However, controversy still rages as to whether this colour hierarchy truly exists. And, if it does, whether it is based on the human perceptual apparatus, or on the colours found in the physical world – which are in any case filtered through the human eye and brain.

Chains and hierarchies are a major factor in keeping language in check: they help to stop it flying apart in multiple different directions. But their cause is only partially understood, as will be discussed below.

The search for explanations

'There is occasions and causes why and wherefore in all things', says an army officer in Shakespeare's play *Henry V*.[44] And the various constraints on language must not only be described, they need to be explained.

Partially, the answer is clear: language has to be produced and comprehended fairly fast. So some seemingly strange facets of language have a user-and-use or 'processing' explanation: human languages are partly the way they are because of how languages are used. Three explanations of this type will be considered below.

First, look at a slightly odd sentence:

Penelope handed over *the pizza with anchovy, crab and salmon filling* to Fred

Nothing is basically wrong with it, but an alternative order is more readily comprehended:

Penelope handed over to Fred *the pizza with anchovy, crab and salmon filling*

For a long time, it has been known that speakers often move long noun phrases to the end of a sentence, a process known as 'heavy NP shift'. Ease of processing is a possible reason. Sentences may be organized in accordance with a principle of 'early immediate constituents', that is, shortish chunks of speech which are easily recognized as complete constituents or components of the sentence are placed before those which are not so readily identified.[45]

Second, think about words. Extra attachments can be added either by prefixes, added to the front of a word, or by suffixes, added to the end. Swahili, for example, uses prefixes for its nouns *w-imbo* 'song', *ny-imbo* 'songs', whereas English uses suffixes: *song, song-s*. Overall, languages have a suffixing preference: more languages use suffixes than prefixes. According to one count, no object-before-verb (OV) language has only prefixes, but 62% have only suffixes, and 38% have both prefixes and suffixes. Only 10% of verb-before-object (VO) languages have only prefixes, while 17% have only suffixes, and 73% have both:[46]

	OV	VO
Only prefixes	—	10
Only suffixes	62	17
Suffixes & prefixes	38	73

This is a massive vote in favour of suffixes, perhaps because word recognition mostly takes place from the beginning of the word, and prefixes delay early recognition[47] – even though some languages, such as Swahili and Welsh, handle word recognition perfectly well in spite of regularly altering word beginnings.

Thirdly, consider language sounds. Vowel systems tend to be similar across languages, in that they all include a minimum three-vowel system [i], [u], [a] (chapter 7), which is then expanded in predictable ways. It has possibly evolved so as to arrive at a compromise between perception and production: in the sound system as a whole, sufficient perceptual differences have emerged at acceptable articulatory costs.[48]

But there's a puzzle. Function often seems irrelevant, or at least invisible. In some cases, languages have structures which seem even to hinder processing. Take the sentence: 'Who did Penelope say Peter decided to ask to pick up the wine?' in which the word *who* has been moved away from the verb *asked* ('Peter asked who...??'). Even native speakers have to think carefully about who is doing what to who.

As Chomsky comments: 'Language design as such appears in many respects "dysfunctional", yielding properties that are not well adapted to the functions language is called upon to perform.'[49]

This apparently puzzling problem will be discussed in the next chapter.

Summary

Language must have constraints, which prevent it from flying apart in different directions. Some constraints are absolute prohibitions, others are preferences – though distinguishing one from the other is not always easy.

Constraints are hard to find. But a promising approach is the search for constraining links. Language constructions are often linked to one another in implicational chains: if a language has X, it will also have Y. Noam Chomsky's 'parameter setting' is perhaps the best-known implicational theory, but it is not the only one.

Some constraints are related to processing needs, but not all, as will be discussed in the next chapter.

16 Unweaving the rainbow:
Separating the strands

There was an awful rainbow once in heaven:
We know her woof, her texture; she is given
In the dull catalogue of common things.
Philosophy will clip an angel's wings,
Conquer all mysteries by rule and line,
Empty the haunted air, and gnomed mine,
Unweave a rainbow.

John Keats, 'Lamia' (1820)

Language has some similarities to the rainbow.[1] Both can be partially separated from their surroundings: the rainbow from the clouds, and language from a general ability to think (chapter 4). And both language and the rainbow appear to be made out of various strands. To a poet, chopping it all up might seem like pointless pedantry. But for linguists, those professionally concerned with language, this is a necessity, even if the result is unromantic: 'like the end of every rainbow I ever ran to with my sisters, all I ever found was misty rain drops' comments a character in a novel.[2]

Just as a rainbow has different though overlapping colours, so language has developed semi-independent modules within itself. Modular systems tend to be more stable than those which function as wholes (chapter 4). If one part is damaged, the whole system does not collapse.

But unweaving a rainbow may be easier than chopping up language. Two views exist about the splitting, as to whether the result is 'God's truth' or 'hocus-pocus'.[3] 'The God's-truth assumption is that language has a structure that is just there, waiting for the analyst to work it out; uncertainty about the facts bears witness to insufficient observation or defective procedure or both.'[4] The hocus-pocus view is that linguists are imposing their own structure onto language: their divisions are somewhat like the latitude and longitude grids laid over the world by atlases: useful aids when referring to the world, but artificial ones.

Both sides are partially right: a few language components may be separable, but others are so inextricably entwined that any divisions are bound to be inexact. The hard core of a component may be easier to identify than the boundary, as with a rainbow, where pointing to the centre of a colour band is easier than finding where the band stops.

But a more basic problem is the double nature of language. It is a system which has to be used. But it also has to be stored and remembered. Overall, it is a compromise between both these requirements (see Fig. 16.1).

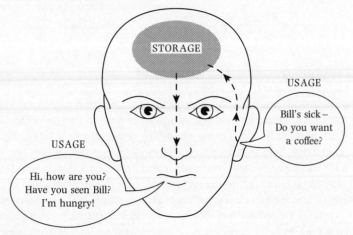

Figure 16.1 Usage vs storage

This chapter will look first at the various strands which make up the stored part of language, and will discuss to what extent they are separable from one another. Then it will consider how they interact in usage.

The strands of language

Language has three basic components, according to most analysts: syntax (word organization), phonology (sound patterns) and semantics (meaning). Morphology (within-word make-up) is usually regarded as a subdivision of syntax. The lexicon (dictionary of words) is attached to all of these (see Fig. 16.2).

PHONOLOGY sound patterns	SYNTAX word organization	SEMANTICS word meaning
LEXICON		dictionary

Figure 16.2 Language sub-divisions

In general the separability of any language component is directly dependent on lack of conscious awareness. The more easily speakers are consciously able to access a strand, the less it can be treated as self-contained. In consequence, phonology is mostly an autonomous system, but semantics is a mixed system, with speakers partially aware and partially unaware of meaning relationships. Take *chase* and *pursue*, words often regarded as synonyms. Few English speakers consciously realize that you *chase* a runaway horse, or a bus, or some other concrete object, often an undesirable one. You *pursue* a hobby or course of action, or similar abstract goal.[5] But speakers can easily be made aware of this, when it is explained.

But syntax is a puzzle. Many people regard it as the core of language, since it is the component which links together the sounds and meaning. It is less accessible to consciousness than semantics, but more so than phonology. So a crucial question is whether it can be regarded as an autonomous system, like phonology, or a mixed system, like semantics. The matter is disputed.

In the following pages, the detachability of phonology will be illustrated. Then the syntax problem will be discussed.

Detached sounds

Key.... oh what do you call them..... oh yeah... you put.... you put... with your.... with your...oh.... with your.... when you.... when someone's stole something.... and.... what do you call them...necklace?... no..... I just don't know the word.[6]

Michael is not an old man, he's a seven-year-old child who can't remember the word *handcuffs*. He knows full well what handcuffs are for, and mentions that they are used 'when someone's stole something'. But he has enormous difficulty remembering the form of words. Sometimes, he manages to get near the word, as in *elilunt*, or *efilunt*, for 'elephant', *telilision, tevilision*, for 'television'. This is a clear case of someone who has a damaged linguistic component: the sound system is partially defective. It has also become detached from the rest of language.

The detachment of sounds from word meaning and syntax is well documented. Elderly people increasingly find that word-forms elude them, even though they may know full well what they want to say. This disability is sometimes extreme in cases of Alzheimer's disease.[7] Take Mary, a 58-year-old patient who was shown a picture of a woman looking out of the window, and allowing a sink to overflow, while a boy reaching for some cookies is about to fall off a stool:

> To me it looks absolutely ridiculous, but still . . . The boy is, while she's looking at the – she must have been looking out of the window I think – and while, during that time, the um boy was taking down the cookie jar and she, the girl, was hand – expecting to get one – and, but the um stool was going to fall, and he was going to fall very quickly and all this (pointing to the water) was going to make it all wet everywhere.[8]

Mary appears unable to access the words *sink, tap (faucet), water*, which would have made her description comprehensible. She could repeat words correctly, showing that she had not lost her grasp of English sounds, but she could not remember the form of words. When tested on pictures, she was able to comprehend most of the pictures she failed to name. Initially, then: 'The naming disorder appears therefore to be one of impaired access from semantic descriptions to the phonological lexicon.'[9]

At a later stage, Mary became progressively more confused, and she was unable to distinguish between similar items, such as a hammer and an axe.[10] But in the early stages of her disease, she showed the independence of word-forms from word meaning.

Phonology (sound structure) is therefore largely detachable, as a variety of studies have shown. It is a relatively independent system, whose patterning is mostly outside human conscious awareness.[11]

The nut-tree question

Many people are aware of bits and pieces of syntax, usually because they have been taught fragments at school: they can often distinguish between nouns and verbs, and have a list of beliefs about what is right and what is wrong. These are often quite odd, several of them dating back to artificial rules imposed by eighteenth-century grammarians, and further promulgated by nineteenth-century etiquette books, which interleaved them with general prohibitions about behaviour:

> Don't drink too much wine. Don't drink from your saucer... Don't wear diamonds in the morning... Don't neglect the small hairs that project from the nostrils and grow about the apertures of the ears... Don't use slang. Don't use profane language. Don't say gents for gentlemen, nor pants for pantaloons. These are inexcusable vulgarisms... Don't use a plural pronoun when a singular is called for. 'Every passenger must show their ticket' illustrates a prevalent error. 'Everybody put on their hats' is another instance. It should be, 'Everybody put on his hat'... Don't say 'It is him,' say 'It is he'. So also, 'It is I,' not 'It is me'... Don't speak of this or that kind of food being healthy or unhealthy; say always wholesome or unwholesome.[12]

But apart from these trivia, many sentences are opaque in structure to the average person, though perfectly comprehensible, as, say: 'The fact that Sebastian's singing in the bath annoys Joanna does not mean that she intends to leave him.' The crucial question, however, is whether syntax always emerges automatically, like the sound structure, or whether it has to be thought through, like the meaning.

The answer is a mixed one. Mostly, syntax is autonomous. But not inevitably. Consider the following children's rhyme:

> I had a little nut-tree,
> *Nothing would it bear*
> But a silver nutmeg
> And a golden pear.

In its second line, this rhyme exemplifies a common rule of English: if you bring a negative towards the front for emphasis, then you need to carry out a further switch, so that the negative is always followed by an auxiliary verb such as *would*, *will*, *do*. That is, you could say:

It would bear nothing

but not:

*Nothing *it would* bear

which must be changed to:

Nothing *would it* bear

(An asterisk denotes an ill-formed sentence.) The switch-over (inversion) is found in sentences such as:

Never *have I* seen such behaviour
Nowhere *could the cat* be found
On no account *may Percy* leave the building

You couldn't say:

*Never *I have* seen such behaviour
*Nowhere *the cat could* be found
*At no time *Percy may* leave the building

This, then, seems like an independent, purely formal rule, which can be applied without conscious thought. But notice the following:

For no money *would Priscilla* dance naked (she wouldn't)
For no money *Priscilla would* dance naked (she would)

Both of these sentences are quite all right, but they have different meanings. As George Lakoff, the linguist who spotted the difference between these constructions, noted: 'This is not a "finer characterization" of a syntactic condition; it is evidence against the claim that syntax is autonomous.'[13] In short, syntactic rules cannot be applied mindlessly, meaning has to be taken into consideration at all times. The rules of language cannot be treated as a completely independent system – even though in many ways the link-up with the world has become quite indirect.

Let us now consider a further claim sometimes made about syntax, that the morphological component within it can be detached.

One wug, two wugs

'This is a wug', said the researcher, showing a birdlike creature. 'So these are...?' she asked, showing two of them. The woman being tested 'looked totally confused and laughed nervously and responded, "How should I know?" ' After some prompting she said 'These are wug.'[14]

Putting endings onto nonsense words is a task which normal children find easy.[15] Yet the adult above found it enormously difficult, even though she was not an infant, nor was she ill. She is one of an extended family, of whom about half cannot easily cope with providing plurals for words. To *zat* she responded, 'These are zacko.' When asked about *sas* 'she smiled broadly, ... and responded *sasez*... She then added *ez* to all the rest of the items: *zoop* goes to *zoopez*, *tob* to *tobez*, and *zash* goes to *zashes*.'[16] Another family member 'corrected' 'The boy eats three cookie' to 'The boy eat four cookie'.[17]

Verb endings provide equal problems for these family members. One given the sentence 'Every day he walked eight miles. Yesterday he __?' responded: 'had a rest'. After being prompted to use the word *walk*, the subject replied *walks*. Yet all of the subjects were able to produce past tenses some of the time, but often inconsistently, as in:

She *remembered* when she *hurts* herself the other day
Then we *went* canoeing really fast and then I *fall* in three times[18]

Perhaps these family members just cannot think fast enough when they talk, is an immediate response. Yet their written language also contained errors of this type. An eleven-year-old girl wrote in her diary, on different occasions:

Carol *is cry* in church
I *walking* down the road[19]

But it's not just word endings. The afflicted individuals, who could be either male or female, have other problems. They prefer to repeat nouns, rather than use pronouns:

> The lady's pointing at the bird and the man is watching her. The man is climbing the tree looking at the birds in their nest. The lady is crying because the man what fall off the tree and the bird frowd away. The neighbors phone the ambulance because the man fall off the tree. The ambulance come along and put the man into the ambulance to the hospital, and he's got a broken leg in the hospital.[20]

This description of a set of pictures contrasted strongly with that of a family member with normal speech who said: 'He climbs up the tree and the branch breaks... So he falls on the ground and he breaks his leg. So she runs indoors to call an ambulance... The ambulance comes. They get in the van and he's in the hospital.'[21]

Speaking is difficult for those affected: 'They find using language very stressful and tiring. They report that they often plan what they are going to say and, when possible, avoid situations in which they must speak.'[22] Yet they could perfectly well follow commands such as: 'Here are three crayons. Drop the yellow one on the floor, give me the blue one, and pick up the red one.'[23]

Controversially, a defective gene was originally proposed as the cause of the problem: 'It is not unreasonable to entertain an interim hypothesis that a single dominant gene controls for those mechanisms that result in a child's ability to construct the paradigms that constitute morphology'[24] – though this explanation is now thought to be oversimple, especially as the difficulty covers more than morphology – segments of words.

Language uses more than one type of skill: first, an ability to store items, to recall them, and place them one after the other. The impaired family members can do this. Second, an ability to adjust the form of these items as they are spoken. This, it seems, is difficult for the family members with defective speech: they just cannot 'get the hang of it'.

In brief, these impaired speakers can memorize whole lexical items, but they cannot perform normal 'on-line' manipulations. They learned past-tense forms one at a time, and only in response to specific corrections. For example, one diary entry referred to the previous weekend's activities:

On Saturday I watch TV and I watch plastic man and I watch football[25]

The teacher inserted -*ed* after each occurrence of *watch*. The subject got *watched* right the next time he used it, but he did not mark the past tense on other verbs:

> On Saturday ... I wash myself and I get dress and I eat my breakfast and I watched TV all day ...

Families with this defect therefore show that language is a complex interaction between static components and processing needs.[26] As an analogy, it's as if the family members with the disorder have a full bone-structure for the leg – but they just cannot flex the knee-joint fully.

Beyond the rainbow

The analogy of language as a rainbow may be too simple. It is more like a whole body. The human body can be discussed in terms of fixed organs: heart, lungs, liver and so on. But it can also be described in terms of the functional systems which utilize these organs: circulation, breathing, digestion:[27] 'These two systems are in a many-many relation with each other. One particular type of cell tissue can be involved in carrying out two or more functions, and each function draws on several types of anatomical structure.'[28] Furthermore, these systems have evolved in tandem. Function strongly influences structure, yet at some point the structure becomes a semi-independent entity.

Much the same structure–function interaction appears to have happened in language, even though there are no 'language organs' as such: language circuits would be a better term (chapter 4, chapter 7). Yet arguments arise because those investigating language disagree about which facet is the most important.

Traditionally, linguists work on stable basics. They regard language as a complex system, formed out of numerous interacting sub-systems.[29] These are themselves simple, yet affect one another in important but predictable ways. In general, linguists pay attention to the relatively unchanging basics, the components which are available for use, and how they interact in principle.

They are less concerned with how these are actually used. To follow up the body imagery, linguists might describe the heart or liver in some depth, and the blood vessels which join them, but would be less likely to track a litre of blood pumping round the body.

Psychologists, on the other hand, are more concerned with the moving aspects of language, the way in which people learn it and process it in day-to-day usage. Humans have a powerful ability to 'mop up' information, whether they are children acquiring language, or adults exposed to new words. As language is used, multiple concurrent connections are activated. These links and how they are formed have been a major concern recently, so much so that 'connectionism', the overall name given to this type of study, has received massive attention.[30] But there has been less interest in the way such links might be integrated into an overall system, and how the system might develop its own independence. To return to the blood analogy, psychologists would be intrigued by how a litre of blood spread itself round the body, but the structure of the heart might not interest them so much.

Linguists and psychologists therefore traditionally look into different aspects of the same system, even though this is something of an oversimplification: an increasing number of 'functional linguists' try to understand language by looking at usage, as many discussions in this book have shown.[31]

But even 'shaking them all up in a bag' oversimplifies what might be happening. It leaves out of account speakers' own interaction with the system, which works in two opposing ways: on the one hand, speakers become aware of parts of language which they had not thought about before. On the other hand, they become better at handling chunks of language automatically, without thinking about it: 'Development thus seems to involve two opposite processes: on the one hand, the progressive access to knowledge previously embedded in procedures and, on the other hand, the progressive modularization of parts of the system.'[32]

Language is therefore a highly complex system, which both 'works under its own steam', and also responds to immediate needs. The more complex a system, the more likely it is to have evolved into a relatively stable state as far as its overall design goes. Parts of the system may alter, but there is sufficient leeway within it for language to rebalance any changes without collapsing. As the linguist Roman Jakobson said over fifty years ago: 'A sense of equilibrium, and a simultaneous tendency towards breaking it, are indispensable properties of language as an entity.'[33]

Summary

Traditionally, language has three basic components: phonology (sound structure), syntax (word organization) and semantics (meaning). The level of autonomy of these relates to conscious awareness. Meaning interacts with conscious thought, but sound patterns mostly do not. Syntax comes somewhere between the two.

But language does not always split itself neatly into these components, as is shown by a family who can use some linguistic structures, but cannot handle on-line processing.

Structure and processing interact in language – though some current controversies exist because linguists tend to examine stable components, whereas psychologists concentrate on processing.

17 The endless stair:
Past and future

Lead us, Evolution, lead us
  Up the future's endless stair;
Chop us, change us, prod us, weed us.
  For stagnation is despair:
Groping, guessing, yet progressing,
  Lead us nobody knows where.

C. S. Lewis, 'Evolutionary hymn'

Evolution is sometimes claimed to be the most powerful idea that has ever arisen on earth. And Charles Darwin initiated an intellectual revolution with his theory of natural selection, which aimed at explaining how evolution works.[1] Darwin himself apparently believed that everything was getting better and better: 'Natural selection is daily and hourly scrutinizing, throughout the world, every variation, even the slightest; rejecting that which is bad, preserving and adding up all that is good.'[2]

Yet this is impossible: there are inevitable trade-offs. Animals with arms can't have wings. Humans have a streamlined throat, good for sound production, but this streamlining makes them liable to choke. People who are naturally protected against malaria are vulnerable to a blood disease, sickle-cell anaemia, and so on.

But trade-offs cannot always be found: marsupials produce more embryonic babies than they can nourish. Mother wolf-spiders carry a hundred or so babies around on their backs for about six months, during which time the young do not eat or grow. Humans have long hair on top of their heads, and relatively little anywhere else.[3]

Some oddities can be explained because unwanted remnants fade away very slowly. The human appendix no longer has a function, but has not yet disappeared. But other oddities remain a puzzle. In a complex organism, there are conflicting messages. It's impossible to see 'function' as governing all. The overall requirements of a semi-stable system may override a quick response to a short-term need, as happens with language.

And organisms can proceed only along grooves which fit in with their existing predispositions. These tracks are one-way paths, with an inbuilt directionality. As the Urdu poet Iqbal said:

> Behold tomorrow in the lap of its today...
> Thy present takes its birth from thy past,
> And thy future emerges out of thy present.

This is true of human language, both now, and in its early days.

But where, if anywhere, is language going? This question can be considered first, by summarizing the findings of earlier chapters, and then by asking if any new developments might affect human language in the future.

A brief summary

Part 1, 'Puzzles', considered some of language's puzzling features. Chapter 1 pointed out that human language is bizarre, in that it has more in common with birdsong than with the communication systems of other primates. Chapter 2 examined the role of language, and noted that it was particularly good at social roles: influencing others and maintaining friendly relations. Chapter 3 queried why languages differed so much: it explained that language is a category of innately guided behaviour, in which the framework is provided by nature, but the details are filled in by learning. This allows a range of variation. Chapter 4 discussed cases in which language had been apparently separated from general cognitive abilities, and concluded that language was largely an independent system.

Part 2, 'Origin', explored how language probably originated. Chapter 5 outlined the 'East Side story', which suggests that humans separated from apes when they were stranded on the east side of Africa, after the Great Rift Valley split the terrain. Humans were forced to live on their wits in a harsh landscape, and began to develop language. Chapter 6 examined the prerequisites for language, which are shared with our ape cousins: first, friendly involvement with others and a predisposition for grooming;

second, an aptitude for tactical deception, or lying, which depends on 'a theory of mind', an ability to understand the intentions of others. Chapter 7 considered the basic requirements for speech, many of which are present in other primates. Sound-receiving mechanisms are shared with apes, though sound-producing ones differ, perhaps because of our upright posture, which in the long run enabled humans to produce a range of finely tuned sounds. Human brains allowed our ancestors to suppress automatic vocalizations, and to co-ordinate multiple strands of language in an efficient way. Chapter 8 noted that ontogeny, the development of the individual, only sometimes correlates with phylogeny, the development of the species. Two ways in which these coincided were the lowering of the larynx, and the development of the 'naming insight', an understanding of the power of naming.

Part 3, 'Evolution', examined how language might have evolved. Chapter 9 looked at ways in which words could have been combined. At first, many sequences were possibly repetitive and inconsistent. But, gradually, strong preferences may have become rules. These preferences were based on pre-linguistic 'mind-sets'. Chapter 10 looked at how language expanded, and showed how it makes use of the human body and its location in space for extending word meanings. The evolution of different parts of speech occurred probably via re-analysis: adjectives and prepositions both grew out of re-interpretation of nouns and verbs. Chapter 11 considered attachments to verbs. Multiple options possibly arose, then these were slowly narrowed down to a fairly typical tense, mood and aspect system. Chapter 12 examined generativity, the use of finite resources to produce an infinite variety of sentences. Such structures arose from re-analysis of existing structures.

Part 4, 'Diffusion', considered the spread of language around the world, and discussed why languages have not become unlearnably different from one another. Chapter 13 outlined the route taken as humans moved out of Africa, and considered the possibility of reconstructing glimpses of language as it might have been more than 30,000 years ago. Chapter 14 examined the difficulties and frustrations of hunting for language universals. Chapter 15 pointed out that looking for constraints, things that languages don't do, might be more enlightening. Implicational links, it noted, are important for keeping language in check. Such links are partially due to processing needs, but partly also to the overall structure of the system. Chapter 16 outlined the components within the language system, and emphasized that these interacted with usage of the system in a complex way.

Maxims of language evolution

Language evolution can be largely summarized in four key maxims, which apply also to language change today:[4]

(1) Nothing comes out of nothing
(2) Multiple births are the norm
(3) Changes are unidirectional
(4) More of the same

First, 'Nothing comes out of nothing.' Just about all innovations are re-analyses of existing constructions, or borrowings. In the earliest stages, the first words probably came out of 'natural' sounds: lip-smacks, pant hoots, or grunts as the vocal chords open after effortful action. Some of these sounds became conventional, with an agreed meaning. But the 'nothing out of nothing' maxim may account for the slow take-off at the beginning of language – perhaps allied with the need for the 'naming insight'. As more words became established and combined, more could be re-analyzed.

Second, 'Multiple births are the norm.' Language branches out in numerous new directions, then slowly neatens itself up. In the early stages, language was probably very messy, with repeated words, and little sign of 'rules'. Various human preferences tended to make certain orders probable, but many more possible. Then as now proliferation was followed by slow smoothing-out, alongside further proliferation.

Third, 'Changes are unidirectional.' Just as rivers do not flow backwards, so language changes move in predictable directions. 'Language moves down time in a current of its own making. It has a drift... The linguistic drift has direction',[5] said the linguist Edward Sapir in 1921. He may have been struggling to express the insight that certain changes are possible and likely, and others apparently impossible and unlikely.[6]

Fourth, 'More of the same'. Each language tends to repeat and extend its own patterns. This is broadly known as analogy, sometimes defined as 'reasoning from parallel cases'. It causes both levelling (the smoothing-out of differences), and extension (expanding an existing pattern by bringing in new similar examples).

Flexibility and leaps

The maxims of language evolution demonstrate two crucial aspects of human minds, their flexibility and their tendency to jump to conclusions.

Human concepts have fuzzy edges, rather than hard boundaries. Humans repeatedly look for resemblances, and they allow latitude in what they regard as 'similar'. They require rough matches only. Such underspecification is an important property of language.[7]

Using this fuzziness, humans place sounds and words into flexible categories. They also extract new patterns out of old material: in short, they can restructure.

The restructuring often takes place in leaps: a few pieces of evidence are combined, and a jump is made: 'Logical deduction is not our strong suit', two researchers note, 'What we are good at is jumping to conclusions – taking two or three bits of evidence and extracting a pattern or rule that makes us feel we've got that problem in the bag and can go on to the next one.'[8]

These abilities were built into language. Language spent a long time getting established. It finally took off and expanded quite fast, then gradually emerged into a fairly stable system, at least in its overall design. No 'language organ' exists, but specialized brain circuits have evolved, which were at first adaptations of neural structures found also in primates. These are inherited by any child born today, though exposure to language is required for the circuits to be fully activated.

The system has grown up piecemeal, so that any human language is a complex mosaic: 'Our language can be seen as an ancient city', said the philosopher Wittgenstein, 'a maze of little streets and squares, of old and new houses, and of houses with additions from various periods; and this surrounded by a multitude of new boroughs with straight regular streets and uniform houses.'[9]

This piecemeal development raises a question about language and thought: how did they interact as language emerged? A philosopher, Neil Tennant, has expressed it well:

> There could be staccato talk without thought.
> There had to be thought before structured talk.
> Once established, structured talk could be mastered with less thought.
> Once mastered, structured talk makes for more thought.[10]

But eventually, language took off on its own route. In its modern state, the various components of language are semi-independent, each with its own particular organization, and its own 'rules'. 'Rules conveniently short-cut our dealings with the details of the world, thereby saving our energy for other matters.'[11] But a long-term tension exists between language structure (the system) and language processing (its day-to-day usage).

But one critical question needs to be asked about language today: are languages and speakers 'equal'?

The equality question

The equality question is really two questions: first, are all languages equal? Second, are all humans equal in their ability to speak them?

All languages are equal, as far as we can tell, in that any language can express everything it needs to express.

Of course, languages differ in the number of vocabulary distinctions they draw, as shown by the numerous words for sitting, standing and lying found in Mam (chapter 3) – though the commonly heard claim that Eskimos have numerous words for 'snow' has been much exaggerated. Eskimos and British skiers possibly equal one another in the types of snow they can name, as explained in an article aptly entitled: 'The great Eskimo vocabulary hoax'.[12] And languages also show considerable structural diversity (chapters 3, 15).

Such observations lead to another commonly asked question – whether language differences can affect thought in any deep way.

'Human beings...are very much at the mercy of the particular language which has become the medium of expression for their society...The worlds in which different societies live are distinct worlds, not merely the same world with different labels attached',[13] Edward Sapir claimed in a famous speech in 1928.

As Sapir pointed out, humans tend to think along the grooves of their own language, and the mental mind-set imposed by one language can lead to misunderstandings in others. Yet linguistically aware speakers can detect problems, and mismatches can be pointed out. In an evolutionary perspective, misunderstandings between languages are relatively unimportant, in that they can be put right. No language differences have been identified which could not potentially be understood by any speaker of any language. Problems remain because speakers have never been made aware of the divergences, not because they are incapable of grasping them.[14]

Moving on to the second type of equality, all humans are equal in that any normal human can learn any language as a first language. Children may find some aspects of their own language easier to grasp than others, in that they seem to have certain expectations about language which are not always immediately met,[15] much as bees have expectations about flowers which need to be honed by experience (chapter 3). The occasional claim that some languages are more 'difficult' than others is thought to be a mirage: languages just seem complicated to learners who try to acquire a second language which is structurally different from their own.

But not all people can handle language equally well, even leaving aside anyone brain-damaged. One half of the human race, the female half, may be 'better' at language than males. Women perform better than men on a wide range of verbal skills, though men outperform women at spatial tasks.[16] This difference is apparently due to hormonal differences which affect the embryo, though the details are disputed. One long-standing view is that men's brains are more 'lateralized', with abilities more firmly located in one hemisphere than the other, though recent studies have not all supported the lateralization claim.[17] A controversial evolutionary interpretation is that early human hunter-gatherers may have taken on different roles. Perhaps men were responsible for hunting large game, which may have required long-distance travel and an ability to find their way about. Women gathered food near the home, looked after children, and talked to them and to each other.[18] But this is speculation.

The future

A long line of humans have become dissatisfied with language, and assumed that it is on the decline.[19] The seventeenth-century pedagogue John Amos Comenius, for example, proposed to institute a new universal language, which would be 'a universal antidote to confusion of thought . . . For the men of earlier ages, the authors of that language which has been handed down to us, were not so accurate in their investigation of things as to remark all their peculiar qualities and differentiae, and so to express them in exact and appropriate terms.'[20] Yet language adjusts itself to its requirements, far better than any invented system, above all because of its flexibility.

The grumblers complain for various reasons. Some have not realized that the artificial prescriptions they were taught in their youth are irrelevant (chapter 16). Others wonder whether human developments can wreck language. Occasionally telephones are blamed, or newspapers, or television, or more recently the Internet.

Above all, the media are a convenient target for people's discontent. But the media hardly ever initiate a change, though they may spread the use of a new word, such as *wimp* 'feeble male'.[21] They may also appear to sanction a change: 'It must be all right to say *damn*, I heard it on the radio.' Overall, the media can only push language further along paths it is already travelling. The Internet is unlikely to influence language any more than the telephone: conversations in this medium develop their own conventions. This does not alter a normal person's speech any more than learning to write a business letter affects them.

Yet while 'language worriers' agitate about minutiae within their own language, global language patterns are changing radically.

Language death

'The coming century will see either the death or the doom of 90% of mankind's languages', according to one prediction.[22] This gloomy forecast was reached as follows: 6,000 was assumed to be 'not an unreasonable round estimate' for living languages in the last decade of the twentieth century.[23] Of these, half will perish, based on a calculation of 'moribund' languages, those no longer learned as a first language by the new generation of speakers. A further 2,400 will come near extinction, on the assumption that any language with fewer than 100,000 speakers is in the unsafe zone. This leaves 600, or 10% of the current total, in the safe category.

'I am always sorry when any language is lost, because languages are the pedigree of nations', said the eighteenth-century lexicographer Samuel Johnson.[24] Johnson's concern is unusual. More people nowadays worry about endangered species in the biological world, where figures of loss are much lower: the total number of threatened mammals has been estimated at 10%, and birds at 5%.[25]

A relatively few languages therefore may remain. These will spread across the world. Once diffused, they are likely to split into separate languages, much as Latin split into French, Spanish, Italian and so on. Already, some varieties of English, for example, differ quite widely from one another.[26]

But the structural variety found will inevitably be reduced. Arguably, the massive disappearance of so many languages represents 'irretrievable loss of diverse and interesting intellectual wealth, the priceless products of human mental industry'.[27]

Lifting the veil

> And how can one imagine oneself among them
> I do not know;
> It was all so unimaginably different,
> And all so long ago.[28]

These lines by the poet Louis MacNeice were written about the people of ancient Athens. But they are equally applicable to any attempts to write about earlier stages of human language. The origin and evolution of human language cannot be recreated in any detail. But the general outline of events is slowly becoming clearer. The remark made by Jakob Grimm in 1851 is still relevant today:

The veil which conceals the origin of speech is lifted but not fully raised.[29]

Hopefully, future generations will raise it further still.

Symbols used in the text

* An asterisk marks *either* a reconstructed form *or* an ill-formed one. The text makes it clear which of these is intended.

Phonetic symbols have been kept to a minimum. When these occur in the text, they are put in square brackets, e.g. [t].

[ʔ] a so-called 'glottal stop', as in some pronunciations of the English word *butter* (*bu'er*), is found in some linguistic examples.

When examples are quoted of a language which is not English, the form of the text is that given by the researcher whose work is being reported. On the whole, examples with complex sounds have been avoided.

Notes and suggestions for further reading

Where two dates appear together, e.g. Herder 1891/1966, the first is the date of the original publication of the work, the second the date of the edition to which reference is made.

Foreword

1 Grimm 1851/1984: 24.
2 Garner 1891-2/1996: 321.
3 Allen 1948.
4 Genesis 2.19.
5 Helmont 1594, in Rée 1999.
6 Whitney 1893: 279.
7 Hurford 1990a: 736.
8 Pinker and Bloom 1990: 727.
9 J. G. Farrell (1973/1975). *The siege of Krishnapur*. London: Penguin, p. 115.

1 A natural curiosity: How did language begin?

1 S. Milligan (1959/1968). *Silly verse for kids*. Harmondsworth: Penguin, p. 41.
2 *Scientific American*, December 1989, p.18.
3 Methods of reconstructing early languages are outlined in chapter 13.
4 J. Webb (1669). (In Yaguello 1984/1991.)
5 Yaguello 1984/1991.
6 Fano 1962/1992: 155.
7 Yaguello 1984/1991: 145-6.
8 In Lyons 1988: 141.
9 Whitney 1893: 279.
10 Hewes 1977.

11 Holloway 1976: 330.
12 Ruhlen 1987: 261.
13 Genesis. 2.19-20.
14 Rousseau 1852/1966. Rousseau was writing around 1750, though his essay on language origin was not published until 1852. It has recently been reprinted (1966).
15 Owren, Seyfarth and Hopp 1992: 103.
16 Owren, Seyfarth and Hopp 1992: 103.
17 E. Hahn, *New Yorker*, 24 April 1978.
18 Nottebohm 1975.
19 Nottebohm 1975; Gould and Marler 1987; Marler 1991b. On similarities and differences between other types of animal communication and language, see Aitchison 1998.
20 Lester and Boukydis 1991.
21 Marler 1991b: 38.
22 For summary, see Aitchison 1998.
23 Nottebohm 1975.
24 Marler 1991a.
25 Merton, Morris and Atkinson 1984.
26 Nottebohm 1975. The kakapo's behaviour is more like communicatory yodelling than true speech (Hall-Craggs 1969).
27 Jespersen 1922: 434.
28 Nottebohm 1975: 86.
29 Diamond 1959: 272.
30 C. Marlowe (1564-93). 'The passionate sheepheard to his love', in J. Hayward (ed.) (1956). *The Penguin book of English verse*. London: Penguin.
31 A. Christie (1957/1993). *Evil under the sun*. London: Harper Collins, pp. 167-8.
32 Thucydides. *History of the Peloponnesian War* I.22, my translation. On pidgins and creoles in general, see Aitchison 1991, 1994a; Arends, Muysken and Smith 1995; Mühlhäusler 1986; Romaine 1988.
33 In Mackay 1991: 198.
34 Anon. in E. O. Parrott (ed.) (1984). *The Penguin book of limericks*. London: Penguin.
35 The three types of theory were first summarized by the German linguist F. Max Müller; they possibly became widely known via Jespersen 1922.
36 Rousseau 1852/1966.
37 Jespersen 1922: 420.
38 E.g. Bickerton 1981, 1984, 1990.

39 Aitchison 1989b; Bybee, Pagliuca and Perkins 1994.
40 The amoeba question will be discussed primarily in chapter 11.
41 Wang 1982: 16. The myth was originally a Greek one, in which Pallas Athene sprang from the head of Zeus. Noam Chomsky is the main supporter of the mutation view, e.g. 1972: 70, and Stephen Jay Gould of the 'brain causes language' view, e.g. Gould and Lewontin 1979.
42 The rabbit-out-of-a-hat question will be discussed primarily in chapters 5 and 6, and its relation to the development of creoles in chapter 11.
43 Whitney 1872, in Nerlich 1990: 36.

2 A peculiar habit: What is language for?

1 Morris 1967.
2 J. Locke 1690/1975.
3 Cushing 1994.
4 In Nerlich 1990: 43.
5 This list is based on Holmes 1992: 286, where the functions are labelled referential, directive, expressive, phatic, poetic and metalinguistic. Many such lists are based on work by Michael Halliday (e.g. Halliday 1978).
6 In W. H. Auden and L. Kronenberger (1962/1970). *The Faber book of aphorisms*. London: Faber Paperbacks.
7 J. Toghill (1979). *Knots and splices*. Steyning, W. Sussex: Fernhurst Books.
8 A. Draffen, R. Strauss and D. Swaney (1992). *Brazil: a survival kit*. 2nd edn. Hawthorn, Vic., Australia: Lonely Planet, p. 160.
9 M. Amis (1989/1990). *London Fields*. London: Penguin, p. 349.
10 S. Orbach. When disappointment strikes, *Guardian Weekend*, 27 May 1994, p. 12.
11 Lord Byron. 'Childe Harold's Pilgrimage' c. IV, st. 178.
12 From 'Matilda, who told Lies, and was Burned to Death', in H. Belloc (1940/1964). *Selected cautionary verses*. London: Pelican.
13 W. S. Gilbert (1885/1992). *The Mikado*. New York: Dover.
14 P. Kerr (ed.) (1994). *The Penguin book of lies*. London: Penguin.
15 In K. Amis (ed.) (1987). *The new Oxford book of light verse*. Oxford University Press.
16 K. Whitehorn, *Observer*, 24 October 1993.
17 De Villiers and de Villiers 1978: 165.
18 Malinowski 1935: 9.

19 S. Johnson (1761). *The Idler.* London: J. Newbery, no. 11.
20 Raj 1990.
21 Tannen 1989: 57.
22 A. Bennett (1982). *Objects of affection.* London: BBC Publications, pp. 110-11.
23 J. Austen, *Pride and prejudice,* ch. 14.
24 M. Dobbs (1989). *House of cards.* London: Collins/Fontana, p. 245.
25 In J. Green (ed.) (1989). *Pan dictionary of contemporary quotations.* Revised edn. London: Pan.
26 Orwell 1946/1962: 156.
27 In J. M. Cohen and M. J. Cohen (1980). *Dictionary of modern quotations.* 2nd edn. London: Penguin.
28 W. S. Gilbert (1891). *Patience,* Act 1.
29 W. Collins (1993). *Computer one.* Harpenden, Herts.: No Exit Press, pp. 3-4.
30 Catania 1990.

3 The bother at Babel: Why do languages differ so much?

1 Comrie 1989.
2 Joos 1957: 96.
3 Mithun and Chafe 1979.
4 Canger 1986.
5 Canger 1986: 20.
6 Haviland 1979.
7 In Guugu Yimidhirr, as in many other languages, the ergative system affects full nouns, rather than pronouns. Further examples of ergative languages will be discussed in chapter 15.
8 Genesis 11. 9.
9 Gould 1983/1984: 46.
10 Gould 1984.
11 Sebeok 1965.
12 Rapoport 1990.
13 Rapoport 1990: 200.
14 Rapoport 1990: 201.
15 G. Orwell (1949/1954). *Nineteen eighty-four.* London: Penguin, p. 45.
16 Of course, some limited standardization may be useful within a language, otherwise its speakers might fail to understand one another: but this cannot normally be easily imposed, though it may happen naturally in the course of time. On this question see Aitchison 1991, Milroy and Milroy 1991.

17 Cosmides 1993.
18 Aitchison 1998.
19 Shettleworth 1975; see also Gallistel, Brown, Carey, Gelman and Keil 1991. On the soft-wired versus hard-wired distinction, see Medin, Ahn, Bettger, Florian, Goldstone, Lassaline, Markman, Rubinstein and Wisniewski 1990.
20 Morris 1967 argues that snake fear is innate.
21 This eyesight is also partially soft-wired, in that it takes practice to develop it.
22 Gould and Marler 1987: 62.
23 Isaac Watts (1674-1748). *Divine songs for children.* xx. 'Against idleness and mischief'.
24 Gould and Marler 1987.
25 Gould and Marler 1987.
26 Gould and Marler 1987: 73.
27 Lenneberg 1967; for a summary, see Aitchison 1998.

4   Distinct duties: Is language an independent skill?

1 Spencer in Mackay 1991.
2 Technically, the occipital lobe.
3 Sacks 1995.
4 Lecours and Joanette 1980: 5.
5 Lecours and Joanette 1980: 6.
6 Lecours and Joanette 1980: 10.
7 Lecours and Joanette 1980: 12.
8 Lecours and Joanette 1980: 13.
9 Curtiss 1977, 1988; Rymer 1993; summary in Aitchison 1998.
10 Yamada 1990: 58.
11 Curtiss 1988.
12 Cromer 1991.
13 Cromer 1991: 133.
14 Smith and Tsimpli 1991, 1995.
15 Bellugi, Bihrie and Corina 1991.
16 Bellugi, Bihrie and Corina 1991: 386.
17 Plato. *Phaedrus* 265e.
18 See Cosmides and Tooby 1994, Garfield 1987, Maratsos 1992 for general discussions of modularity; also Fodor 1983, 1985, 1990.
19 Shallice 1984.
20 Shallice 1988.
21 Chomsky 1986: xxvi.

22 Chomsky 1986: 13.
23 Chomsky 1979: 83.
24 Karmiloff-Smith 1991: 183.
25 Posner and Raichle 1994.
26 In Posner and Raichle 1994: 129.
27 Karmiloff-Smith 1991: 182.

5   The family tree: The evolutionary background

1 E. R. Burroughs (1912/1972). *Tarzan of the apes*. London: Flamingo
   Books, p. 50. The epigraph at the top of the chapter comes from 'St.
   George and the Dragon', in M. Marshall (ed.) (1979). *The Stanley
   Holloway Monologues*. London: Elm Tree Books.
2 Gould 1993/1994; Pinker 1994.
3 Johanson and Edey 1981/1990; Leakey 1994.
4 T. D. White, Suwa and Asfar 1994. Ramid means root among the
   Afars who live in the region.
5 For a brief summary of the arguments surrounding this and other
   early hominids, see Wavell 1995.
6 Johanson and Edey 1981/1990: 24.
7 Johanson and Edey 1981/1990: 24.
8 Lieberman 1984.
9 R. White 1985; Mellars 1993. For a useful outline account, see
   Lewin 1993. This technological advance will be discussed further in
   chapter 13.
10 Mayr 1991/1993: 7.
11 Mayr 1991/1993: 1.
12 Darwin 1859/1964: 61.
13 Darwin 1859/1964: 471.
14 Darwin 1859/1964: 84.
15 See Mayr 1991/1993 for an account of the arguments; see also
   Dawkins 1995, Dennett 1995, Ridley 1993, for outline overviews of
   evolution.
16 Grant 1986; for popular accounts, see Grant 1991, Weiner 1994.
17 Coppens 1994.
18 Coppens 1994: 69.
19 Aiello and Wheeler 1995.
20 F. Weldon (1989). *The cloning of Joanna May*. London: Fontana, p.
   156.
21 Wilson and Cann 1992.
22 Wilson and Cann 1992: 23.
23 Not all researchers agree with the clock rate, or the notion of a small

stock, e.g. Thorne and Wolpoff 1992.
24 Cann, Stoneking and Wilson 1987; Wilson and Cann 1992. See Lewin 1993 for a useful summary of the evidence.
25 Wilson and Cann 1992: 23.
26 Cavalli-Sforza 1991.
27 Chomksy 1972: 70.
28 Eldredge and Gould 1972. See also Eldredge and Gould 1988, Gould and Eldredge 1977.
29 This example was pointed out by Weizenbaum 1976/1984: 32.
30 Possible evidence for this will be discussed in chapters 6 and 7.
31 W. Golding (1955/1961). *The inheritors*. London: Faber and Faber, p. 16.
32 W. Golding (1955/1961). *The inheritors*. London: Faber and Faber, pp. 144-5.
33 Cronin 1991: 382.
34 Language diffusion will be discussed in chapter 13.
35 This viewpoint is well summarized in Gazzaniga 1992, also Piatelli-Palmarini 1989. Within evolution in general, proliferation followed by paring down is discussed in Gould 1989/1991.
36 From 'The road not taken', in R. Frost (1971). *The poetry of Robert Frost*. (Ed. E. C. Lathem). London: Jonathan Cape, p. 105.

6 A devious mind: The basic requirements

1 Hume 1739/1978.
2 D. Adams (1992/1993). *Mostly harmless*. London: Pan, p. 91.
3 Glezer and Kinzey 1993.
4 Morris 1967.
5 F. S. Fitzgerald (1965). *The crack-up with other pieces and stories*. Harmondsworth: Penguin.
6 Profile of Tina Brown, *Sunday Times*, 9 April 1995. No author attribution.
7 Dunbar 1993.
8 Hyland 1993.
9 J. L. Locke 1995: 289; cf. J. L. Locke 1993.
10 Small 1994: 33.
11 Reported in Small 1994.
12 Homer. *Odyssey* I.1.
13 Replying to Samuel Wilberforce, Bishop of Oxford, in a debate on Darwin's theory of evolution. Several versions of this comment exist. This version is from the *Oxford dictionary of quotations*.
14 Lorenz 1950/1977: 167.

15 R. W. Byrne and Whiten 1988, 1992: 612.

16 R. W. Byrne and Whiten 1992: 614.

17 R. Rendell (1993/1994). *The crocodile bird*. London: Arrow Books, p. 250.

18 The term 'theory of mind' is the commonest label for insight into the minds of others, though several other names are found, for example, 'metarepresentation', 'mindreading', 'the intentional stance'. A fuller list of labels is given in Baron-Cohen, Ring, Moriarty, Schmitz, Costa and Ell 1994.

19 Baron-Cohen, Leslie and Frith 1985; Baron-Cohen 1990; Frith 1993; Baron-Cohen, Ring, Moriarty, Schmitz, Costa and Ell 1994; Baron-Cohen 1995.

20 R. W. Byrne and Whiten 1992.

21 R. W. Byrne and Whiten 1988; R. W. Byrne 1994a.

22 Machiavelli's treatise *Il Principe* ('The Prince') was completed in 1513.

23 R. W. Byrne and Whiten 1992.

24 R. W. Byrne and Whiten 1992: 525.

25 For a discussion of other thought processes which may be related to language, see Donald 1991, 1993.

26 Kimura 1976; Lyons 1988; Corballis 1992; Armstrong, Stokoe and Wilcox 1995.

27 Condillac (1715-80) wrote De l'origine et du progrès du langage (1746), part 2 of Essai sur l'origine des connaissances humaines (Condillac 1798/1947). His views are summarized and discussed in Wells 1987.

28 Condillac 1798/1947: 263; Wells 1987: 9.

29 Condillac 1798/1947: 263; Wells 1987: 9.

30 Lyons 1988: 149.

31 Lyons 1988: 156.

32 Lyons 1988: 159.

33 In Lane 1984: 181.

34 In Wells 1987: 26.

35 Corballis 1992: 215-16.

36 Van Cleve 1987.

37 The achievements of Washoe and other signing chimps are outlined in Aitchison 1998, Wallman 1992.

38 Dever 1974.

39 Petitto and Marentette 1991.

40 Kimura 1976.

41 Posner and Raichle 1994.

42 Passingham 1982: 78.

43 Dan Everett, on Linguist.
44 Gould and Lewontin 1979; the view is supported also by Piatelli-Palmarini 1989.
45 Gould and Lewontin 1979.
46 Hockett and Ascher 1964: 141.
47 Pinker and Bloom 1990.
48 As suggested, e.g., by Deacon 1992.

7 Broken air: Inherited ingredients

1 Geoffrey Chaucer *The house of fame*, ll.765-70. *The works of Geoffrey Chaucer*. Oxford University Press, 1966. Translation: 'Sound is nought but air that's broken, and every utterance that's spoken, loud or private, foul or fair, in its substance is but air; just as flame is lighted smoke, so too sound is air that broke.'
2 W. S. Gilbert (1885/1992). *The Mikado*. New York: Dover Publications.
3 Deacon 1988, 1992.
4 W. Boyd (1990/1991). *Brazzaville beach*. Harmondsworth: Penguin, pp. 61-2.
5 Lieberman 1984: 134.
6 Ploog 1992. See also Petersen 1982.
7 Mehler, Jusczyk, Lambertz, Halsted, Bertoncini and Amiel-Tison 1988.
8 Symmes and Biben 1992.
9 Seyfarth and Cheney 1986.
10 Darwin 1871: 54.
11 Work on categorical perception dates back to the 1950s. Liberman, Harris, Hoffman and Griffith 1957 was highly influential, and there is now a huge literature – for a summary, see J. Miller and Jusczyk 1990; work on infants is particularly associated with Eimas and his colleagues, e.g. Eimas, Siqueland, Jusczyk and Vigorito 1971 – for a summary see Eimas 1985. For an overview of categorical perception, see Harnad 1987.
12 For a summary, see Kuhl 1987, Molfese and Morse 1991.
13 Eimas, Siqueland, Jusczyk and Vigorito 1971.
14 Primates, of course, are not the only animals with sensitive ears: barn owls, for example, also show acute perceptual discrimination, with an ability to form perceptual equivalence classes from variable input stimuli; Sussman 1989.
15 Differences between human and monkey perception are discussed in Kuhl 1987, Molfese and Morse 1991, Ploog 1992. See also Savage-Rumbaugh, Murphy, Sevcik, Brakke, Williams and Rumbaugh 1993.

16 Owren, Seyfarth and Hopp 1992.
17 On this imbalance, see also Savage-Rumbaugh, Murphy, Sevcik, Brakke, Williams and Rumbaugh 1993.
18 Wind 1983.
19 Marler 1976.
20 Etcoff 1989.
21 For details and their relation to evolution, see Aiello and Dean 1990.
22 Liem 1988; this is well summarized by Gould 1993/1994: 114.
23 Ploog 1992.
24 Lenneberg 1967.
25 Du Brul 1977.
26 E.g. Lieberman 1984.
27 Summary in Wind 1983.
28 Darwin 1859/1964: 191. On the larynx, see Aiello and Dean 1990; Lieberman 1984, 1991, 1992. Also Corballis 1991, 1992.
29 Houghton 1993.
30 Lieberman 1984: 129.
31 Lieberman 1992.
32 Lieberman 1984, 1991.
33 Lieberman 1984, 1991.
34 E. R. Burroughs (1912/1972). *Tarzan of the apes*. London: Flamingo Books, p. 40.
35 Lieberman 1991.
36 The English word *hundred*, for example, came from an earlier word *k̥mtom* (with an asterisk marking a reconstructed form); [m̥] is an *m* which forms a whole syllable, as in *blossom*.
37 The muscle, according to Laver 1994, is the posterior cricoarytenoid muscle.
38 Snowden, Brown and Petersen 1982.
39 Thelen 1991: 339.
40 Barber and Peters 1992: 344.
41 See Falk 1991, Lewin 1993 for figures.
42 Aiello and Wheeler 1995.
43 Deacon 1992.
44 Falk 1989: 142; Gibson 1994 argues controversially that quantitative expansion is the key to language.
45 R. Kipling, (1927). *Rudyard Kipling's verse*. London: Hodder and Stoughton.
46 Psalms 135. 5-6.
47 Aitchison 1998, Springer and Deutsch 1993 outline the link between handedness and language, including a discussion of left-handedness.

48 MacNeilage, Studdert-Kennedy and Lindblom 1987.
49 MacNeilage 1991.
50 Kimura 1979: 203.
51 On handedness in general, see Springer and Deutsch 1993.
52 A. Conan Doyle (1894/1981). Silver blaze, in *The memoirs of Sherlock Holmes*. In *The complete Sherlock Holmes*. London: Penguin, p. 347.
53 Jürgens 1992a.
54 Byrne 1994b.
55 Goodall 1986: 125.
56 Sutton 1979; Jürgens 1992b;
57 Deacon 1992.
58 Deacon 1992.
59 Deacon 1988: 376.
60 Posner and Raichle 1994; in particular, the basal ganglia are thought to be deeply involved in speech.
61 D. Newnham. Pills and hope, *Guardian Weekend*, 18 February 1995.
62 On neoteny, see Gould 1977.
63 Locke 1995: 287.

8 Small beginnings: First steps

1 Spock 1968: 229.
2 The quotation at the top of the chapter is from Nodier, in Yaguello 1984/1991: 144.
3 Haeckel 1866: vol. II, 300, translation from Gould 1977: 77.
4 Haeckel 1866: vol. II, 330, translation from Gould 1977: 76.
5 Haeckel 1874: 9, translation from Gould 1977: 77.
6 Carey 1985, Keil 1989.
7 M. Shelley (1818/1981). *Frankenstein*. London: Bantam Classic, pp. 96-7.
8 P. Liveley (1987/1988). ·*Moon tiger*. London: Penguin, p. 51.
9 Griffiths 1986: 281.
10 Halliday 1978; Griffiths 1986; Carter 1979.
11 Barrett 1995.
12 Aitchison 1994c provides a summary.
13 McShane 1980.
14 Excerpts from Sicard's book in Lane 1984: 83-126.
15 H. Keller (1903). *The story of my life*. New York: Doubleday.
16 Seyfarth, Cheney and Marler 1980a, 1980b.
17 Ploog 1992.
18 Scherer 1992; Marler, Evans and Hauser 1992.

234 Notes and suggestions for further reading

19 The abilities of these chimps are summarized in Aitchison 1998, Wallman 1992.

20 Savage-Rumbaugh and Lewin 1994: 67.

21 Gardner and Gardner 1969.

22 N. Rush (1991). *Mating*. New York: Knopf/Vintage, p. 195.

23 Jespersen 1922: 440.

24 Bauer 1983.

25 Chapter 1. As mentioned in the notes to chapter 1, these ideas were commonplace, though were possibly first summarized by Max Müller, and made widely known via Jespersen 1922.

26 Darwin 1871: 85.

27 Herder 1891/1966: 132.

28 Herder 1891/1966: 117.

29 Herder 1891/1966: 130.

30 Information about the sounds of the world's animals on the World Wide Web, http://www.georgetown.edu/cball/animals/animals2.html.

31 J. Joyce (1922/1993). *Ulysses*. Oxford University Press, p. 54.

32 *Sunday Times* cartoon 6 May 1991.

33 G. Orwell (1964). *A clergyman's daughter*. Harmondsworth: Penguin, p. 147. See Chapman 1984 on the representation of sounds in literature.

34 Rhodes 1994.

35 Müller, in Jespersen 1922: 414. Against this view, Hinton, Nichols and Ohala 1994a argue that sound symbolism plays a larger role in language than has been hitherto recognized.

36 The definition of the syllable is highly problematic, e.g. Laver 1994.

37 Jakobson 1962/1971.

38 In A. L. Lloyd (1967). *Folk song in England*. London: Lawrence & Wishart, p. 297.

39 Humboldt 1836/1988: 60.

40 Jespersen 1922: 420/434.

41 On the characteristics of long-range signalling, see Hall-Craggs 1969.

42 Fernald 1992.

43 On the complex relationship of language to music, see Handel 1989, Lerdahl and Jackendoff 1983, Rosner 1995.

44 Studdert-Kennedy 1991.

45 On the role of an early 'sensitive period' for language, see Aitchison 1998; on the evolution of a sensitive period, see Hurford 1991, Newport 1990, 1991.

46 Newport 1990.

9 The second word: The emergence of rules

1 Humboldt 1836/1988: 61.
2 Sound patterns are known as phonology, word patterns as syntax. The quotation about syntax at the head of the chapter is from Simon 1981: 111.
3 Ponapean example from Hopper and Thompson 1984.
4 J. Swift (1726/1952). *Gulliver's travels*. London: Dent, pp. 173-4.
5 U. Eco (1988/1990). *Foucault's pendulum*. London: Picador, p. 35
6 Studdert-Kennedy 1991.
7 J. Swift (1726/1952). *Gulliver's travels*. London: Dent, pp. 174-6.
8 Hopper and Thompson 1984.
9 G. A. Miller and Fellbaum 1991.
10 Anon., *First grammar book for children*. London: Walker, n.d.
11 Lyons 1977: 442-3; Lyons 1989. Lyons first distinguished between first-, second- and third-order entities in 1977. He rediscussed the matter in 1989, drawing a slightly different division between second- and third-order entities.
12 Lyons 1977: 443.
13 Lyons 1989: 169.
14 Lyons 1989.
15 Herder 1891/1966: 133.
16 Herder 1891/1966: 132.
17 Givón 1979: 321.
18 Hopper and Thompson 1984.
19 Robins 1952; Hopper and Thompson 1984.
20 Givón 1979: 320.
21 Schachter 1985: 7.
22 As will be discussed in chapter 14 on universals.
23 Terrace 1979.
24 Terrace 1979: 212-13.
25 For Kanzi's lexigram board, see Greenfield and Savage-Rumbaugh 1990: 548-9.
26 Greenfield and Savage-Rumbaugh 1990; Savage-Rumbaugh and Lewin 1994.
27 Care has to be taken when comparing short utterances of different types, see Aitchison 1995a.
28 Todd and Aitchison 1980.
29 Jackendoff 1983, 1993/1994.
30 Braine 1992: 90.
31 Landau and Jackendoff 1993; Jackendoff 1993/1994.

32 Bock, Loebell and Morey 1992.
33 McDonald, Bock and Kelly 1993.
34 Cooper and Ross 1975.
35 B. Byrne and Davidson 1985.
36 Hopper and Thompson 1984.
37 Du Bois 1987.
38 Mithun 1984
39 Tomlin 1986; (S = Subject, mostly corresponding to Agent; O = Object, mostly corresponding to Patient, V = Verb); on the difficulties involved in identifying a sentence subject, see Keenan 1976, Dixon 1989.
40 For further examples of ergative languages, see chapter 15. On word order in general, see Payne 1992a, 1992b, Mithun 1992.
41 Tomlin 1986.
42 For critical reviews of Tomlin 1986, see Noonan 1988, Blake 1988.

10   The tower of speech: Expansion

1 The quotation at the head of the chapter is from R. S. Thomas (1978). *Frequencies*. London: Macmillan, p. 7.
2 Jackendoff 1983: 188-9.
3 Johnson 1987.
4 On metaphor, see Lakoff and Johnson 1980, Ortony 1993, Gibbs 1994.
5 Tok Pisin is a pidgin/creole spoken in Papua New Guinea, as noted in chapter 1.
6 Sweetser 1990: 21.
7 Reported in R. Harris 1990.
8 Remark attributed to Keith Allan, unpublished paper, quoted by Heine, Claudi and Hünnemeyer 1991: 123.
9 Sweetser 1990: 9.
10 Johnson 1987.
11 E. Dickinson (1890/1970). No. 712 in *The complete poems of Emily Dickinson*. (Ed. T. H. Johnson.) London: Faber and Faber, p. 350; quoted and discussed in Lakoff and Turner 1989.
12 Johnson 1987: 126.
13 Johnson 1987: 127.
14 Anon., *First grammar book for children*. London: Walker, n.d.
15 Landau and Jackendoff 1993.
16 Landau and Jackendoff 1993.
17 Landau and Jackendoff 1993; Jackendoff 1993/1994.
18 Crowley 1991: 397.
19 See chapter 1.

20 Mihalic 1971: 123.
21 Crowley 1991: 397.
22 Crowley 1990b.
23 Heine, Claudi and Hünnemeyer 1991.
24 Dixon 1982.
25 Hopper and Thompson 1984: 729.
26 Holm 1988: 85.
27 Givón 1979: 13.
28 Givón 1979: 14.
29 Holm 1988: 85.

11 Time travelling: Extra attachments

1 Ecclesiastes 1.8.
2 As satirized in the quotation at the head of the chapter, from D. Adams (1980). *The restaurant at the end of the universe*. London: Pan, pp. 79-80.
3 Bybee, Perkins and Pagliuca 1994.
4 Meillet 1912/1948: 131. On grammaticization, see Traugott and Heine 1991, Hopper and Traugott 1993.
5 Bickerton 1981, 1984, 1990. For a review of Bickerton 1981, see Aitchison 1983.
6 Aitchison 1989b.
7 On Tok Pisin in general, which will figure largely in the discussions, see Dutton 1973, Dutton and Dicks 1985, Mühlhäusler 1985, 1986, Wurm and Mühlhäusler 1985.
8 On tense, mood, aspect in general see Hopper 1982, Binnick 1991, Comrie 1976, 1985.
9 Muysken 1981; Givón 982; for a fuller account of the developments discussed in this chapter, see Aitchison 1989b; see also Bybee, Perkins and Pagliuca 1994, Singler 1990.
10 Bybee, Perkins and Pagliuca 1994.
11 E.g. Bickerton 1981.
12 Bybee, Perkins and Pagliuca 1994.
13 P. Baker (1995). Australian and Melanesian Pidgin English and the *fellows* in between (Ms.).
14 Bybee, Perkins and Pagliuca 1994.
15 L. Carroll (1865/1982). *Alice in Wonderland*, in *The complete works of Lewis Carroll*. London: Penguin, p. 16.
16 Comrie 1976: 3.
17 Givón 1982.
18 Arends 1986: 117.

19 Goodman 1985.
20 On the speed controversy, see also Bickerton 1991.

12 Rebuilding on the high seas: Keeping going

1 Otto Neurath, Protokollsätze, *Erkenntnis* 3 (1932), p. 206.
2 Humboldt 1836/1988: 61.
3 In Sacks 1989/1991: 76.
4 Bloom 1994: 181.
5 S. Smith (1994). *A simple plan.* New York: Doubleday/Corgi Books, p. 269.
6 E.g. Corballis 1992.
7 Wynn and Bloom 1992.
8 Hailman and Ficken 1986.
9 E.g. Corballis 1992.
10 Cromer 1991.
11 Mühlhäusler 1985; Aitchison 1992.
12 The examples are taken from Mühlhäusler 1985 and Aitchison 1992.
13 Crowley 1990.
14 Keesing 1988.
15 Woolford 1979b: 118.
16 Mühlhäusler 1985: 414.
17 Crowley 1989.
18 Examples are taken from Mihalic 1971, Mühlhäusler 1979, Crowley 1992a.
19 Crowley 1992a.

13 The widening circle: Moving outwards

1 Bell 1899: 309.
2 Various figures have been proposed between 100,000 and 50,000-75,000 is average.
3 Mellars 1993.
4 Mellars 1993.
5 Mellars 1993: 2, 7.
6 Mellars 1993.
7 E.g. Mellars 1993.
8 Johanson and Edey 1981/1990: 24. On the discovery of a 'Neandertal' hyoid bone, see chapter 7.
9 Nichols 1990: 476.
10 35,000 is the date in Nichols (1990), earlier than most. Greenberg (1987) proposes a much later date, and is now thought by many to be mistaken.

11 Fortescue 1995.
12 Nichols 1990.
13 Nichols 1990: 476.
14 Nichols 1990.
15 W. Cowper, 'Retirement', in J. D. Baird and C. Pryskame (eds.) (1980). *The poems of William Cowper*. Oxford: Clarenden, ll. 619-72.
16 A number of other, well-established methods of reconstructing the past also exist, but they take us back at most only a few thousand years. For these methods, see Aitchison 1991, Crowley 1992b, Fox 1995.
17 For further details see Aitchison 1991, Crowley 1992b, Fox 1995.
18 Crowley 1992b.
19 Sometimes known as Hamito-Semitic.
20 For a summary, see Ross 1991:75; see also Ruhlen 1992, Kaiser and Shevoroshkin 1988.
21 Kaiser and Shevoroshkin 1988: 309-10.
22 Cavalli-Sforza 1991; Cavalli-Sforza, Piazza, Menozzi and Mountain 1988; Cavalli-Sforza, Minch and Mountain 1992; Cavalli-Sforza, Menozzi and Piazza 1993.
23 Cavalli-Sforza 1991: 76.
24 E.g. Nei and Roychoudhury 1993.
25 Nichols 1992: 2.
26 For a summary of borrowing, see Aitchison 1991; for a more extensive survey, see Thomason and Kaufman 1988.
27 Nichols 1992: 2.
28 For an outline account, and further references, see Aitchison 1991.
29 Nichols 1992: 124.
30 Mithun 1988.
31 Nichols 1992: 281.
32 Ruhlen 1994.
33 See Salmons 1992, who lists a number of problems.
34 Ruhlen 1994: 322.

14 The hidden core: The hunt for universals

1 W. Boyd (1990/1991). *Brazzaville beach*. Harmondsworth: Penguin, p. 365.
2 Bloomfield 1933: 20.
3 Palmer 1994: 22.
4 Chomsky 1965.
5 Décsy 1988: 60. See also Aitchison 1988 for review of Décsy 1988.
6 Bolinger 1968: 18.

7 Mallinson and Blake 1981: 9.
8 For a discussion of design features, see Aitchison 1989a. See Hockett and Altmann 1968 for one of the later versions.
9 Swadesh 1939.
10 Examples from Schachter 1985: 11.
11 Schachter 1985.
12 Anderson 1985a.
13 Anderson 1985a: 155.
14 Schachter 1985 notes that Tagalog, in the Philippines, has some similarities to the Nootka case.
15 Li and Thompson 1976. For an overview of grammatical relations, see Palmer 1994.
16 Li and Thompson 1976: 472.
17 Example from Li and Thompson 1976: 473.
18 R. L. Stevenson (1883/1985). *Treasure island.* Oxford University Press, pp. 171-2.
19 The terms 'shallow scraping' and 'deep delving' are my own, Aitchison 1986 and Aitchison 1989a, though the controversy is one of long standing. The two approaches are well explained, though not labelled, in Comrie 1989.
20 E.g. Greenberg 1963/1966. Greenberg's tradition has been carried on by others, e.g Comrie 1989.
21 E.g. Chomsky 1980, Coopmans 1984.
22 Chomksy 1980.
23 A. A. Milne (1926/1965). *Winnie-the-Pooh.* London: Methuen, ch. 3.
24 Gross 1979: 966.
25 L. Carroll (1876/1967). *The annotated snark.* London: Penguin, p. 68.
26 Chomksy 1965.
27 Maddieson 1984.
28 Maddieson 1984.
29 Maddieson 1984: 17.
30 Maddieson 1984: 21.
31 Maddieson 1984: 23.
32 Mithun 1995.
33 Example from Mithun 1995.
34 E.g. Chomsky 1986.

15 The real magician: Ruling the rules

1 A. Pope (1733/1966). *Pope: Poetical works.* Oxford University Press, Epistle 1, ll.251.
2 Dawkins 1986/1988.

3 Dawkins 1986/1988: 60.
4 Dawkins 1986/1988: 60.
5 W. de la Mare (1973). *Selected poems*. London: Faber and Faber. Walter de la Mare lived 1873-1956.
6 U. Eco (1988/1990). *Foucault's pendulum*. London: Picador, p. 370.
7 F. Kafka (1994). *The collected aphorisms*. Harmondsworth: Penguin, no. 56. Kafka lived 1883-1924.
8 Maddieson 1984.
9 On working memory and language, see Gathercole and Baddeley 1993; on memory in general, see Baddeley 1990.
10 Bates 1984.
11 D. Everett (3 June 1995) on the electronic bulletin board *Linguist*.
12 Carr 1986.
13 In child language.
14 Jakobson 1941/1968: 48.
15 Maddieson 1984 provides an up-to-date list of sound-structure implications.
16 Greenberg 1963/1966: 79; on adpositions (prepositions and postpositions), see chapter 10.
17 Dryer 1992.
18 Dryer 1992.
19 Hawkins 1983: 134.
20 Hawkins 1983.
21 For example, it is a tenet of 'X-bar syntax' within transformational generative grammar; for an outline account see Radford 1988.
22 On the 'head' problem, see Corbett, Fraser and McGlashen 1993.
23 Nichols 1986; Vincent 1993.
24 Dryer 1992 disputes the usefulness of the head- and dependent-marking distinction within linguistic typology.
25 E.g. Chomsky 1986, for a readable version.
26 Dryer 1992.
27 Rizzi 1986; Hyams 1986.
28 Chomsky 1981: 6.
29 Chomsky 1986: 152.
30 Some people put implicational arrows the other way round, but this direction is followed in Croft 1990.
31 Croft 1990: 99.
32 A. A. Milne (1926/1965). *Winnie-the-Pooh*. London: Methuen, p. 90.
33 A bear in the widely read children's book.
34 Croft 1990: 10.
35 Comrie 1989.

36 Comrie 1989.
37 Dixon 1994: 10.
38 A. C. Harris and Campbell 1995: 189.
39 The term 'ergative' is used here in its most widely used sense, as in Dixon 1994. But following on from Burzio 1986, transformational grammarians have used it in a rather different sense: for an outline account, see Radford 1988.
40 Dixon 1994. See Keenan 1976, Dixon 1989 on subject/object identification problems.
41 E.g. Heine 1992.
42 Berlin and Kay 1969.
43 E.g. Kay and McDaniel 1978, Kay, Berlin and Merrifield 1991, Davidoff 1991.
44 William Shakespeare, *Henry V*, V:i.
45 Hawkins 1994.
46 Hall 1992: 42; Hawkins and Gilligan 1985, 1988; Hawkins and Cutler 1988; Bybee, Pagliuca and Perkins 1990.
47 Marslen-Wilson 1989.
48 Lindblom, MacNeilage and Studdert-Kennedy 1984.
49 Chomsky 1991: 448. The form vs function dilemma has a massive literature. See Comrie 1984, Hawkins 1988a, Hurford 1990 for overviews.

16 Unweaving the rainbow: Separating the strands

1 Keats's rainbow is in 'Lamia' II, ll. 231-7 in J. Keats (1908). *The poetical works of John Keats*. Oxford University Press.
2 J. P. Donleavy (1978). *The destinies of Darcy Dancer*. London: Allen Lane.
3 This distinction supposedly originated with Householder, but it became widely known via Joos 1957.
4 Joos 1957: 80.
5 Aitchison and Lewis 1996.
6 Constable, Stackhouse and Wells 1994: 1.
7 Strictly speaking, DAT: Dementia of Alzheimer type.
8 Funnell and Hodges 1991: 174.
9 Funnell and Hodges 1991: 176.
10 Funnell 1992.
11 See Lindblom, MacNeilage and Studdert-Kennedy (1984) for a discussion of the evolution of sound patterning, Anderson (1985b) for an outline of twentieth-century approaches to phonology,

Goldsmith (1995) for recent phonological theory.
12 Censor (*c.* 1880/1982). *Don't: A manual of mistakes and improprieties more or less prevalent in conduct and speech.* 2nd edn. Whitstable: Pryor Publications.
13 Lakoff 1991: 58.
14 Gopnik and Crago 1991: 19.
15 Berko 1958.
16 Gopnik and Crago 1991: 19.
17 Gopnik and Crago 1991: 35.
18 Gopnik 1994: 123.
19 Gopnik and Crago 1991: 41.
20 Gopnik and Crago 1991: 43.
21 Gopnik and Crago 1991: 44.
22 Gopnik and Crago 1991: 46.
23 Gopnik and Crago 1991: 19.
24 Gopnik and Crago 1991: 47.
25 Gopnik 1994: 128.
26 Gopnik and Crago 1991 and Gopnik 1994 provide useful accounts of the disorder; Matthews 1994 contains a wide-ranging set of working papers on the topic; Vargha-Khadem, Watkins, Alcock, Fletcher and Passingham 1995 suggest that the deficit may go beyond language.
27 Newmeyer 1991 proposes this analogy.
28 Newmeyer 1991: 22.
29 E.g. Chomsky 1986.
30 For an outline, see Bechtel and Abrahamsen 1991, Morelli and Brown 1992; on its application to child language acquisition, see Plunkett 1995.
31 E.g. Hopper and Thompson 1984; the linguistic structure/function debate is discussed in relation to language evolution in Newmeyer 1992.
32 Karmiloff-Smith 1991: 186.
33 Jakobson 1949/1978: 120, my translation.

17 The endless stair: Past and future

1 See chapter. The quotation at the top of the chapter is from C. S. Lewis, 'Evolutionary hymn', in K. Amis (ed.) (1987). *The new Oxford book of light verse.* Oxford University Press, p. 234.
2 Darwin 1859/1964: 84.
3 Wesson 1991 lists these examples.
4 Cf. A. C. Harris and Campbell 1995 who try to reduce syntactic

change to three broad principles, which partially overlap with these; on language change in general, see Aitchison 1991.

5 Sapir 1921: 150, 155. See also Whorf 1956.
6 The meaning of Sapir's cryptic comment has been much discussed.
7 See Aitchison 1994c for a discussion of fuzziness and prototypes in relation to word meaning.
8 Barber and Peters 1992: 344.
9 Wittgenstein 1958: 8.
10 Tennant 1984: 102.
11 Barber and Peters 1992: 344.
12 Pullum 1991.
13 Sapir 1929/1949: 162.
14 Aitchison 1995b.
15 Slobin 1985.
16 Kimura 1992, Halpern 1992.
17 For a useful survey of lateralization, see Springer and Deutsch 1993.
18 Kimura 1992.
19 On this, see Aitchison 1991.
20 Comenius, *Via lucis*, in Slaughter 1982: 114.
21 Aitchison 1994a.
22 Krauss 1992: 7. Krauss 1992 is part of Hale, Craig, England, LaVerne, Krauss, Watahomigie and Yamamoto 1992, which is a more extensive exploration of dying languages.
23 Krauss 1992: 5. Around 5,000 was an estimate quoted in chapter 3.
24 Reported in James Boswell (1785/1924). *The journal of a tour to the Hebrides*. Oxford University Press, p. 310.
25 According to Krauss 1992.
26 Burchfield 1994.
27 Hale 1994: 6.
28 L. MacNeice (1939). *Autumn journal*. London: Faber and Faber, p. 39.
29 Grimm (1851) in Wells 1987: 53.

References

Aiello, L. C. & Dean, C. (1990). *An introduction to human evolutionary anatomy*. London: Academic Press.

Aiello, L. C. & Wheeler, P. (1995). The expensive-tissue hypothesis: the brain and the digestive system in human and primate evolution. (With comment). *Current Anthropology*, 36, 199–221.

Aitchison, J. (1983). On roots of language. *Language and Communication*, 3, 83–97.

(1986). Review of John Hawkins, *Word order universals*. *Lingua*, 70, 191–7.

(1988). Review of G. Décsy, *A select catalogue of language universals*. *General Linguistics*, 28, 227–8.

(1989a). Hidden treasure: the search for language universals. In J. Montangero & A. Tryphon (eds.), *Language and cognition* (vol. x). Geneva: Fondation Archives Jean Piaget.

(1989b). Spaghetti junctions and recurrent routes: some preferred pathways in language evolution. *Lingua*, 77, 151–71.

(1991). *Language change: Progress or decay?* (2nd edn). Cambridge University Press.

(1992). Relative clauses in Tok Pisin: is there a natural pathway? In M. Gerritsen & D. Stein (eds.), *Internal and external factors in linguistic change*. Berlin: Mouton de Gruyter.

(1994a). *Language joyriding*. Inaugural lecture at Oxford University. Oxford University Press.

(1994b). Pidgins, creoles and change. In R. E. Asher (ed.), *The encyclopaedia of language and linguistics*. (vol. VI, pp. 3181–6). Oxford and Aberdeen: Pergamon Press and Aberdeen University Press.

(1994c). *Words in the mind: An introduction to the mental lexicon* (2nd edn). Oxford: Blackwell.

(1995a). Chimps, children and creoles: the need for caution. In S. Puppel (ed.), *The biology of language*. Amsterdam and Philadelphia: John Benjamins.

(1995b). Free or ensnared? The hidden nets of language. In E. Barker (ed.), *LSE on freedom*. London: LSE Books.

(1995c). Tadpoles, cuckoos and multiple births: language contact and models of change. In J. Fisiak (ed.), *Linguistic change under contact conditions*. (Proceedings of international conference on language contact and linguistic change, Rydzyna, Poland, 1991.) Berlin: Mouton de Gruyter.

(1998). *The articulate mammal: An introduction to psycholinguistics* (4th edn). London: Routledge.

Aitchison, J. & Lewis, D. (1996). The mental word-web: forging the links. Swedish Academy.

Allen, W. S. (1948). Ancient ideas on the origin and development of language. *Transactions of the Philological Society*, 35–60.

Anderson, S. R. (1985a). Inflectional morphology. In Shopen (1985c).

(1985b). *Phonology in the twentieth century*. University of Chicago Press.

Ardrey, R. (1970/1972). *The social contract*. London: Fontana.

Arends, J. (1986). Genesis and development of the equative copula in Sranan. In P. Muysken & N. Smith (eds.), *Substrata versus universals in creole genesis*. Amsterdam and Philadelphia: John Benjamins.

Arends, J., Muysken, P. & Smith, N. (1995). *Pidgins and creoles: An introduction*. Amsterdam: John Benjamins.

Armstrong, D. F., Stokoe, W. C. & Wilcox, S. E. (1995). *Gesture and the nature of language*. Cambridge University Press.

Arnold, D., Atkinson, M., Durand, J., Grover, C. & Sadler, L. (1989). *Essays on grammatical theory and universal grammar*. Oxford: Clarendon Press.

Baddeley, A. (1990). *Human memory: Theory and practice*. Hove and London: Lawrence Erlbaum.

Baker, P. (1995). Australian and Melanesian Pidgin English and the *fellows* in between (Ms.).

Bar-Adon, A. & Leopold, W. F. (eds.) (1962/1971). *Child language: A book of readings*. Englewood Cliffs, NJ: Prentice-Hall.

Barber, E. J. W. & Peters, A. M. W. (1992). Ontogeny and phylogeny: what child language and archaeology have to say to each other. In Hawkins & Gell-Mann (1992).

Baron-Cohen, S. (1990). Autism: a specific cognitive disorder of 'mind-blindness'. *International Review of Psychiatry*, 2, 81–90.

(1995). *Mindblindness: An essay on autism and theory of mind.* Cambridge, MA: MIT Press.

Baron-Cohen, S., Leslie, A. M. & Frith, U. (1985). Does the autistic child have a 'theory of mind'? *Cognition*, 21, 37–46.

Baron-Cohen, S., Ring, H., Moriarty, J., Schmitz, B., Costa, D. & Ell, P. (1994). Recognition of mental state terms: clinical findings in children with autism and a functional neuroimaging study of normal adults. *British Journal of Psychiatry*, 165, 640–9.

Barrett, M. (1995). Early lexical development. In P. Fletcher & B. MacWhinney (eds.), *The handbook of child language*. Oxford: Blackwell.

Bates, E. (1984). Bioprograms and the innateness hypothesis. *Behavioral and Brain Sciences*, 7, 188–90.

Bauer, L. (1983). *English word-formation*. Cambridge University Press.

Bechtel, W. & Abrahamsen, A. (1991). *Connectionism and the mind: An introduction to parallel processing networks*. Oxford: Blackwell.

Bell, C. N. (1899). *Tangweera: Life and adventures among gentle savages*. London: Arnold.

Bellugi, U., Bihrie, A. & Corina, D. (1y991). Linguistic and spatial development: dissociations between cognitive domains. In Krasnegor, Rumbaugh, Schiefelsusch & Studdert-Kennedy (1991).

Berko, J. (1958). The child's learning of English morphology. *Word*, 14, 150–77. (Also in Bar-Adon and Leopold (1971))

Berlin, B. & Kay, P. (1969). *Basic color terms: Their universality and evolution*. Berkeley: University of California Press.

Bickerton, D. (1981). *The roots of language*. Ann Arbor: Karoma.

(1984). The language bioprogram hypothesis. *Behavioral and Brain Sciences*, 7, 173–221. (Includes peer commentary.)

(1990). *Language and species*. University of Chicago Press.

(1991). On the supposed 'gradualness' of creole development. *Journal of Pidgin and Creole Languages*, 6, 25–8.

Binnick, R. L. (1991). *Time and the verb: A guide to tense and aspect*. Oxford University Press.

Blake, B. J. (1988). Review of Tomlin (1986). *Journal of Linguistics*, 24, 213–17.

Bloom, P. (1994). Generativity within language and other cognitive domains. *Cognition*, 51, 177–89.

Bloomfield, L. (1933). *Language*. New York: Holt, Rinehart, Winston.

Bock, J. K., Loebell, H. & Morey, R. (1992). From conceptual roles to structural relations: bridging the syntactic cleft. *Psychological Review*, 99, 150–71.

Bolinger, D. L. (1968). *Aspects of language.* New York: Harcourt, Brace and World.

Braine, M. D. S. (1992). What sort of innate structure is needed to 'bootstrap' into syntax? *Cognition,* 45, 77–100.

Burchfield, R. (1994). *The Cambridge history of the English language* (vol. V: *English in Britain and overseas*). Cambridge University Press.

Burzio, L. (1986). *Italian syntax.* Dordrecht: Reidel.

Butterworth, B., Comrie, B. & Dahl, O. (eds.) (1984). *Linguistics 21. Explanations for language universals.* The Hague: Mouton.

Bybee, J. L., Pagliuca, W. & Perkins, R. D. (1990). On the asymmetries in the affixation of grammatical material. In W. Croft, K. Denning & S. Kemmer (eds.), *Studies in typology and diachrony.* Amsterdam and Philadelphia: John Benjamins.

Bybee, J. L., Perkins, R. D. & Pagliuca, W. (1994). *The evolution of grammar: Tense, aspect and modality in the languages of the world.* University of Chicago Press.

Byrne, B. & Davidson, E. (1985). On putting the horse before the cart: exploring conceptual bases of word order via acquisition of a miniature artificial language. *Journal of Memory and Language,* 24, 277–389.

Byrne, R. W. (1994a). The ape legacy: the evolution of Machiavellian intelligence and interactive planning. In E. Goody (ed.), *Social intelligence and interaction.* Cambridge University Press.

(1994b). The evolution of intelligence. In P. J. B. Slater & T. R. Halliday (eds.), *Behaviour and evolution.* Cambridge University Press.

Byrne, R. W. & Whiten, A. (1988). Towards the next generation in data quality: a new survey of primate tactical deception. *Behavioral and Brain Sciences,* 11, 267–71.

(1992). Cognitive evolution in primates: evidence from tactical deception. *Man,* 27, 609–27.

Canger, U. (1986). What the eye sees. In M. S. Flier & S. Karlinsky (eds.), *Language, literature and linguistics: In honor of Francis J. Whitfield on his seventieth birthday March 25, 1986.* Berkeley, CA: Berkeley Slavic Specialities.

Cann, R. L., Stoneking, M. & Wilson, A. C. (1987). Mitochondrial DNA and human evolution. *Nature,* 325, 31–6.

Carey, S. (1985). *Conceptual change in childhood.* Cambridge, MA: MIT Press.

Carey, S. & Gelman, R. (eds.) (1991). *The epigenesis of mind: Essays on biology and cognition.* Hillsdale, NJ: Lawrence Erlbaum.

Carr, M. W. (ed.) (1986). *A selection of Telegu proverbs.* New Delhi: Asian

Educational Series.

Carter, A. L. (1979). Prespeech meaning relations: an outline of one infant's sensorimotor morpheme development. In P. Fletcher & M. Garman (eds.), *Language acquisition: Studies in first language development*. Cambridge University Press.

Catania, A. C. (1990). What good is five percent of a language competence? *Behavioral and Brain Sciences*, 13, 729–31. (Open peer commentary on Pinker & Bloom (1990))

Cavalli-Sforza, L. L. (1991). Genes, people and languages. *Scientific American*, 265(5), 72–8.

Cavalli-Sforza, L. L., Menozzi, P. & Piazza, A. (1993). Demic expansions and human evolution. *Science*, 259, 639–46.

Cavalli-Sforza, L. L., Minch, E. & Mountain, J. (1992). Coevolution of genes and languages revisited. *Proceedings of the National Academy of Science USA*, 89, 5620–4.

Cavalli-Sforza, L. L., Piazza, A., Menozzi, P. & Mountain, J. (1988). Reconstruction of human evolution: bringing together genetic, archaeological and linguistic data. *Proceedings of the National Academy of Science USA*, 85, 6002–6.

Chapman, R. (1984). *The treatment of sounds in language and literature*. Oxford: Basil Blackwell.

Chomsky, N. (1965). *Aspects of the theory of syntax*. Cambridge, MA: MIT Press.

(1972). *Language and mind* (enlarged edn). New York: Harcourt Brace Jovanovich.

(1979). *Language and responsibility*. Sussex: The Harvester Press.

(1980). *Rules and representations*. Oxford: Basil Blackwell.

(1981). *Lectures on government and binding*. Dordrecht: Foris.

(1986). *Knowledge of language: Its nature, origin and use*. New York: Praeger.

(1991). Some notes on economy of derivation and representation. In R. Freidin (ed.), *Principles and parameters in comparative grammar*. Cambridge, MA: MIT Press.

Comrie, B. (1976). *Aspect*. Cambridge University Press.

(1984). Form and function in explaining language universals. In Butterworth, Comrie & Dahl (1984).

(1985). *Tense*. Cambridge University Press.

(1989). *Language universals and linguistic typology: Syntax and morphology* (2nd edn). Oxford: Blackwell.

Condillac, E. B. de (1798/1947). Essai sur l'origine des connaissances humaines, ouvrage où l'on réduit à un seul principe tout ce qui concerne l'entendement. In *Oeuvres philosophiques de Condillac*. Paris: Georges Leroy.

Constable, A., Stackhouse, J. & Wells, B. (1994). The case of the missing handcuffs: phonological processing and word finding difficulties in a boy with specific language impairment. *Work in Progress: The National Hospital's College of Speech Sciences*, 4, 1–27.

Cooper, W. E. & Ross, J. R. (1975). World order. In R. E. Grossman, L. J. San & T. J. Vance (eds.), *Papers from the parasession on functionalism*. Chicago Linguistic Society.

Coopmans, P. (1984). Surface word order typology and universal grammar. *Language*, 60, 55–69.

Coppens, Y. (1994). East Side story: the origin of humankind. *Scientific American*, 270(5), 62–79.

Corballis, M. C. (1991). *The lopsided ape: Evolution of the generative mind*. Oxford University Press.

(1992). On the evolution of language and generativity. *Cognition*, 44, 197–226.

Corbett, G. G., Fraser, N. M. & McGlashen, S. (eds.) (1993). *Heads in grammatical theory*. Cambridge University Press.

Cosmides, L. (1993). The evolution of reasoning. (Paper presented at conference on Evolution and the human sciences. LSE, London, June 1993.)

Cosmides, L. & Tooby, J. (1994). Beyond intuition and instinct blindness: toward an evolutionarily rigorous cognitive science. *Cognition*, 50, 41–77.

Croft, W. (1990). *Typology and universals*. Cambridge University Press.

Cromer, R. F. (1991). *Language and thought in normal and handicapped children*. Oxford: Blackwell.

Cronin, H. (1991). *The ant and the peacock*. Cambridge University Press.

Crowley, T. (1989). *Say, c'est* and subordinate constructions in Melanesian Pidgin. *Journal of Pidgin and Creole Languages*, 4, 185–210.

(1990a). *Beach-la-mar to Bislama: The emergence of a national language in Vanuatu*. Oxford: Clarendon Press.

(1990b). Serial verbs and prepositions in Bislama. In J. W. M. Verhaar (ed.), *Melanesian Pidgin and Tok Pisin*. Amsterdam: John Benjamins.

(1991). Genesis of a preposition system in Bislama. In R. Harlow (ed.), *Western Austronesian and contact languages* (Papers from the 5th International Conference on Austronesian Linguistics). Auckland: Linguistic Society of New Zealand.

(1992a). Derivational morphology and structural complexity in nineteenth century Melanesian Pidgin. *Te Reo*, 35, 3–18.

(1992b). *An introduction to historical linguistics* (2nd edn). Oxford University Press.

Curtiss, S. R. (1977). *Genie: A psycholinguistic study of a modern-day 'wild child'*. New York: Academic Press.

(1988). Abnormal language acquisition and the modularity of language. In F. Newmeyer (ed.), *Linguistics: The Cambridge survey* (vol. II). Cambridge University Press.

Cushing, S. (1994). *Fatal words: Communication clashes and aircraft crashes*. University of Chicago Press.

Darwin, C. (1859/1964). *On the origin of species*. Cambridge, MA: Harvard University Press.

(1871). *The descent of man and selection in relation to sex* (vols. I–II). London: John Murray.

Davidoff, J. (1991). *Cognition through colour*. Cambridge, MA: MIT Press.

Dawkins, R. (1986/1988). *The blind watchmaker*. Harmondsworth: Penguin.

(1995). *River out of Eden*. London: Weidenfeld and Nicolson.

Deacon, T. W. (1988). Human brain evolution: 1. Evolution of language circuits. In H. J. Jerison & I. Jerison (eds.), *Intelligence and evolutionary biology* Berlin: Springer.

(1992). Brain–language coevolution. In Hawkins & Gell-Mann (1992)

Décsy, G. (1988). *A select catalogue of language universals*. Bloomington, IN: Eurolingua.

Dennett, D. (1995). *Darwin's dangerous idea*. London: Allen Lane.

Dever, R. B. (1974). Discussion summary: non-speech communication. In R. L. Schiefelbusch & L. L. Lloyd (eds.), *Language perspectives: Acquisition, retardation and intervention*. Baltimore: University Park Press.

De Villiers, J. G. & de Villiers, P. A. (1978). *Language acquisition*. Cambridge, MA: Harvard University Press.

Diamond, A. S. (1959). *The history and origin of language*. London: Methuen.

Dixon, R. M. W. (1982). *'Where have all the adjectives gone?' and other essays in semantics and syntax*. Berlin: Mouton.

(1989). Subject and object in universal grammar. In Arnold, Atkinson, Durand, Grover & Sadler (1989).

(1994). *Ergativity*. Cambridge University Press.

Donald, M. (1991). *Origins of the modern mind: Three stages in the evolution of culture and cognition*. Cambridge, MA: MIT Press.

(1993). Origins of the modern mind. *Behavioral and Brain Sciences*, 16, 737–91. (Includes peer commentary.)

Dryer, M. S. (1992). The Greenbergian word order correlations. *Language*, 68, 81–138.

Du Bois, J. W. (1987). The discourse basis of ergativity. *Language*, 63, 805–55.

Du Brul, E. L. (1977). Origin of the speech apparatus and its reconstruction in fossils. *Brain and Language*, 4, 365–81.

Dunbar, R. I. M. (1993). Co-evolution of neocortex size, group size and language in humans. *Behavioral and Brain Sciences*, 16, 681–735. (Includes peer commentary.)

Dutton, T. (1973). *Conversational New Guinea Pidgin. Pacific Linguistics: D-12*. Canberra: Australian National University.

Dutton, T. & Dicks, T. (1985). *A new course in Tok-Pisin. Pacific Linguistics Series: D-67*. Canberra: Australian National University.

Eimas, P. D. (1985). The perception of speech in early infancy. *Scientific American*, 252(1), 34–40.

Eimas, P. D., Siqueland, E., Jusczyk, P. & Vigorito, J. (1971). Speech perception in infants. *Science*, 171, 303–6.

Eldredge, N. & Gould, S. J. (1972). Punctuated equilibria: an alternative to phyletic gradualism. In T. J. M. Schopf (ed.), *Models in palaeobiology*. San Francisco, CA: Cooper & Co. Punctuated equilibrium prevails. *Nature*, 332, 211–12.

Etcoff, N. L. (1989). Asymmetries in recognition of emotion. In F. Boller & J. Grafman (eds.), *Handbook of neuropsychology* (vol. III). New York: Elsevier Science Publishers.

Falk, D. (1989). Commentary. *Current Anthropology*, 30, 141–42. (1991). 3.5 million years of hominid brain evolution. *Seminars in the Neurosciences*, 3, 409–16.

Fano, G. (1962/1992). *The origins and nature of language*. Bloomington: Indiana University Press. (Trans. Susan Petrilli. Originally *Origini e natural del linguaggio* (1962 & 1973))

Fernald, A. (1992). Meaningful melodies in mothers' speech to infants. In H. Papousek, U. Jürgens & M. Papousek (eds.), *Nonverbal vocal communication: Comparative and developmental approaches*. Cambridge University Press.

Fodor, J. A. (1983). *The modularity of mind*. Cambridge, MA: MIT Press. (1985). The modularity of mind. *Behavioral and Brain Sciences*, 8, 1–42. (Summary of Fodor, J. A. (1983). *The modularity of mind*. Includes peer commentary.) (1990). *A theory of content and other essays*. Cambridge, MA: MIT Press.

Fortescue, M. (1995). Eskimo-Aleut and Chukotko-Kamchatkan pronouns and verbal inflection: skeletal Proto-Siberian. Ms., Department of

Eskimology, University of Copenhagen.

Fox, A. (1995). *Linguistic reconstruction: An introduction to theory and method.* Oxford University Press.

Frith, U. (1993). Autism. *Scientific American*, 268(6), 78–84.

Funnell, E. (1992). Progressive loss of semantic memory in a case of Alzheimer's disease. *Proceedings of the Royal Society of London*, B243, 287–91.

Funnell, E. & Hodges, J. R. (1991). Progressive loss of access to spoken word forms in a case of Alzheimer's disease. *Proceedings of the Royal Society of London*, B 243, 173–9.

Gallistel, C. R., Brown, A. L., Carey, S., Gelman, R. & Keil, F. C. (1991). Lessons from animal learning for the study of cognitive development. In Carey & Gelman (1991).

Gardner, R. A. & Gardner, B. T. (1969). Teaching sign language to a chimpanzee. *Science*, 165, 664–72.

Garfield, J. L. (ed.). (1987). *Modularity in knowledge representation and natural-language understanding.* Cambridge, MA: MIT Press.

Garner, R. L. (1981–2). The simian tongue. In Harris (1996).

Gathercole, S. E. & Baddeley, A. D. (1993). *Working memory and language.* Hove, Sussex: Lawrence Erlbaum.

Gazzaniga, M. S. (1992). *Nature's mind: The biological roots of thinking, emotions, sexuality, language and intelligence.* New York: Harper Collins.

Gibbs, R. W. (1994). *The poetics of mind: Figurative thought, language and understanding.* Cambridge University Press.

Gibson, K. R. (1994). Continuity theories of human language origins versus the Lieberman model. *Language and Communication*, 14, 97–114.

Givón, T. (1979). *On understanding grammar.* New York: Academic Press.

(1982). Tense–aspect–modality: the creole proto-type and beyond. In P. J. Hopper (ed.), *Tense–aspect: Between semantics and pragmatics* Amsterdam and Philadelphia: John Benjamins.

Glezer, I. I. & Kinzey, W. G. (1993). Do gossip and lack of grooming make us human? *Behavioral and Brain Sciences*, 16, 704–5.

Goldsmith, J. A. (1995). *The handbook of phonological theory.* Oxford: Blackwell.

Goodall, J. (1986). *The chimpanzees of Gombe: Patterns of behavior.* Cambridge, MA: Harvard University Press.

Goodman, M. (1985). Review of Bickerton (1981). *International Journal of American Linguistics*, 51, 109–13.

Gopnik, M. (1994). Impairments of tense in a familial language disorder. *Journal of Neurolinguistics*, 8, 109–33.

Gopnik, M. & Crago, M. B. (1991). Familial aggregation of a developmental language disorder. *Cognition*, 39, 1–50.

Gould, J. L. & Marler, P. (1987). Learning by instinct. *Scientific American*, 256(1), 62–73.

Gould, S. J. (1977). *Ontogeny and philogeny*. Cambridge, MA: Harvard University Press.

(1983/1984). *Hen's teeth and horse's toes*. Harmondsworth: Penguin.

(1989/1991). *Wonderful life: The Burgess Shale and the nature of history*. London: Penguin.

(1993/1994). *Eight little piggies*. London: Penguin.

Gould, S. J. & Eldredge, N. (1977). Punctuated equilibria: the tempo and mode of evolution reconsidered. *Palaeobiology*, 6, 383–96.

Gould, S. J. & Lewontin, R. C. (1979). The spandrels of San Marco and the Panglossian paradigm. A critique of the adaptionist programme. *Proceedings of the Royal Society of London*, 205, 281–8.

Grant, P. R. (1986). *Ecology and evolution of Darwin's finches*. Princeton University Press.

(1991). Natural selection and Darwin's finches. *Scientific American*, 263(4), 60–5.

Greenberg, J. (1963/1966). Some universals of language with particular reference to the order of meaningful elements. In J. Greenberg (ed.), *Universals of language* (2nd edn). Cambridge, MA: MIT Press.

(1987). *Language in the Americas*. Stanford University Press.

Greenfield, P. M. & Savage-Rumbaugh, E. S. (1990). Grammatical combination in *Pan paniscus*: processes of learning and invention in the evolution and development of languages. In S. Taylor Parker & K. R. Gibson (eds.), *'Language' and intelligence in monkeys and apes*. Cambridge University Press.

Griffiths, P. (1986). Early vocabulary. In P. Fletcher & M. Garman (eds.), *Language acquisition: Studies in first language development* (2nd edn). Cambridge University Press.

Grimm, J. (1851). Über den Ursprung der Sprache. In L. Speidel (ed.), *Aus den kleineren Schriften von Jacob Grimm*. Berlin, 1911.

Grimm, J. K. L. (1851/1984). *On the origin of language*. Leiden: Brill. (Trans. R. A. Wiley).

Gross, M. (1979). On the failure of generative grammar. *Language*, 55, 859–85.

Haeckel, E. (1866). *Generelle Morphologie der Organismen* (vols. I & II). Berlin: George Rymer.

(1874). *Anthropogenie*. Leipzig: W. Engelmann.

Hailman, J. P. & Ficken, M. S. (1986). Combinatorial animal communication with computable syntax: chick-a-dee calling qualifies as 'language' by structural linguistics. *Animal Behaviour*, 34, 1899–1901.

Hale, K. (1994). Resisting language loss: the human value of local languages. Ms., Massachusetts Institute of Technology.

Hale, K., Craig, C., England, N., LaVerne, J., Krauss, M., Watahomigie, L. & Yamamoto, A. (1992). Endangered languages. *Language*, 68, 1–42.

Hall, C. J. (1992). *Morphology and mind: A unified approach to explanation in linguistics*. London: Routledge.

Hall-Craggs, J. (1969). The aesthetic content of bird song. In R. A. Hinde (ed.), *Bird vocalizations: Their relations to current problems in biology and psychology*. Cambridge University Press.

Halliday, M. A. K. (1978). *Language as social semiotic: The social interpretation of language and meaning*. London: Edward Arnold.

Halpern, D. F. (1992). *Sex differences in cognitive abilities*. New York: Erlbaum.

Handel, S. (1989). *Listening: An introduction to the perception of auditory events*. Cambridge, MA: MIT Press.

Harnad, S. R. (1987). *Categorical perception: The groundwork of cognition*. Cambridge University Press.

Harnad, S. R., Horst, D., Steklis, D. & Lancaster, J. (eds.). (1976). *Origins and evolution of language and speech*. Annals of the New York Academy of Science: 280. New York Academy of Science.

Harris, A. C. & Campbell, L. (1995). *Historical syntax in cross-linguistic perspective*. Cambridge University Press.

Harris, R. (1990). On 'folk' and 'scientific' linguistic beliefs. In S. L. Tsohatsidis (ed.), *Meanings and prototypes: Studies in linguistic categorization*. London: Routledge.

Harris, R. (ed.) (1996). *The origin of language*. Bristol: Thoemmes Press.

Haviland, J. B. (1979). How to talk to your brother-in-law in Guugu Yimidhirr. In T. Shopen (ed.), *Languages and their speakers*. Cambridge, MA: Winthrop.

Hawkins, J. A. (1983). *Word order universals*. New York: Academic Press.
   (1988a). Explaining language universals. In Hawkins (1988b).
   (ed.) (1988b). *Explaining language universals*. Oxford: Blackwell.
   (1994). *A performance theory of order and constituency*. Cambridge University Press.

Hawkins, J. A. & Cutler, A. (1988). Psycholinguistic factors in morphological asymmetry. In Hawkins (1988b).

Hawkins, J. A. & Gell-Mann, M. (eds.) (1992).*The evolution of human languages*. Santa Fé Studies in the Science of Complexity: 11. Reading, MA.

Hawkins, J. A. & Gilligan, G. (1985). The suffixing preference: a processing explanation. *Linguistics*, 23, 723–58.

(1988). Prefixing and suffixing universals in relation to basic word order. *Lingua*, 74, 219–59.

Heine, B. (1992). Grammaticalization chains. *Studies in Language*, 16, 335–68.

Heine, B., Claudi, U. & Hünnemeyer, F. (1991). *Grammaticalization: A conceptual framework*. University of Chicago Press.

Herder, J. G. (1891/1966). On the origin of language. In J. H. Moran & A. Gode (eds.), *On the origin of language* (essays by Rousseau and Herder, translated, with afterwords, by John H. Moran and Alexander Gode). Chicago and London: University of Chicago Press.

Hewes, G. W. (1977). Language origin theories. In D. M. Rumbaugh (ed.), *Language learning by a chimpanzee: The Lana project*. New York: Academic Press.

Hinton, L., Nichols, J. & Ohala, J. J. (1994a). Introduction: sound-symbolic processes. In Hinton, Nichols & Ohala (1994b).

(eds.) (1994b). *Sound symbolism*. Cambridge University Press.

Hockett, C. F. & Altmann, S. (1968). A note on design features. In T. Sebeok (ed.), *Animal communication: Techniques of study and results of research*. Bloomington: Indiana University Press.

Hockett, C. F. & Ascher, R. (1964). The human revolution. *Current Anthropology*, 3, 135–47.

Holloway, R. L. (1976). Paleoneurological evidence for language origins. In Harnad, Horst, Steklis & Lancaster (1976).

Holm, J. A. (1988). *Pidgins and creoles* (vol. I). Cambridge University Press.

Holmes, J. A. (1992). *An introduction to sociolinguistics*. London: Longman.

Hopper, P. J. (ed.) (1982). *Tense–aspect*. Amsterdam and Philadelphia: John Benjamins.

Hopper, P. J. & Thompson, S. A. (1984). The discourse basis for lexical categories in universal grammar. *Language*, 60, 703–52.

Hopper, P. J. & Traugott, E. C. (1993). *Grammaticalization*. Cambridge University Press.

Houghton, P. (1993). Neanderthal supralaryngeal vocal tract. *American Journal of Physical Anthropology*, 90, 139–46.

Humboldt, W. von (1836/1988). *On language: The diversity of human language structure and its influence on the mental development of mankind.* Cambridge University Press.

Hume, D. (1739/1978). *A treatise of human nature* (2nd edn, ed. P. H. Nidditch). Oxford: Clarendon Press.

Hurford, J. (1990a). Beyond the roadblock in linguistic evolution studies. *Behavioral and Brain Sciences* 13, 736–7.

(1990b). Nativist and functional explanations in language acquisition. In I. M. Roca (ed.), *Logical issues in language acquisition.* Dordrecht: Foris.

(1991). The evolution of the critical period for language acquisition. *Cognition,* 40, 159–202.

Hyams, N. (1986). *Language acquisition and the theory of parameters.* Dordrecht: Reidel.

Hyland, M. E. (1993). Size of human groups during the Paleolithic and the evolutionary significance of increased group size. *Behavioral and Brain Sciences,* 16, 709–10.

Jackendoff, R. (1983). *Semantics and cognition.* Cambridge, MA: MIT Press.

(1993/1994). *Patterns in the mind: Language and human nature.* New York: Basic Books.

Jakobson, R. (1941–1968). *Child language, aphasia and phonological universals.* The Hague: Mouton.

(1949/1978). Principles of historical phonology. In P. Baldi & R. N. Werth (eds.), *Readings in historical phonology.* Philadelphia: Pennsylvania State University Press.

(1962/1971). Why 'mama' and 'papa'? In Bar-Adon and Leopold (1962/1971).

Jespersen, O. (1922). *Language, its nature, development and origin.* London: Allen and Unwin.

Johanson, D. C. & Edey, M. A. (1981–1990). *Lucy: The beginnings of mankind.* London: Penguin.

Johnson, M. (1987). *The body in the mind: The bodily basis of meaning, imagination and reason.* University of Chicago Press.

Joos, M. (1957). *Readings in linguistics I: The development of descriptive linguistics in America 1925-56.* University of Chicago Press.

Jürgens, U. (1992a). Introduction and review. In Papousek, Jürgens & Papousek (1992).

(1992b). On the neurobiology of vocal communication. In Papousek, Jürgens & Papousek (1992).

Kaiser, M. & Shevoroshkin, V. (1988). Nostratic. *Annual Review of Archaeology,* 17, 309–29.

Karmiloff-Smith, A. (1991). Beyond modularity: innate constraints and developmental change. In S. Carey & R. Gelman (eds.), *The epigenesis of mind: Essays on biology and cognition.* Hillsdale, NJ: Lawrence Erlbaum.

Kay, P., Berlin, B. & Merrifield, W. R. (1991). Biocultural implications of systems of color naming. *Journal of Linguistic Anthropology*, 1, 12–25.

Kay, P. & McDaniel, C. K. (1978). The linguistic significance of the meanings of basic color terms. *Language*, 54, 610–46.

Keenan, E. L. (1976). Towards a universal definition of 'subject'. In C. Li (ed.), *Subject and topic*. New York: Academic Press.

Keesing, R. (1988). *Melanesian Pidgin and the Oceanic substrate.* Stanford University Press.

Keil, F. C. (1989). *Concepts, kinds and cognitive development.* Cambridge, MA: MIT Press.

Kimura, D. (1976). The neurological basis of language qua gestures. In H. Whitaker & H. A. Whitaker (eds.), *Current trends in neurolinguistics*. New York: Academic Press.

(1979). Neuromotor mechanisms in the evolution of human communication. In H. D. Steklis & M. J. Raleigh (eds.), *Neurobiology of social communication in primates*. New York: Academic Press.

(1992). Sex differences in the brain. *Scientific American*, 267(3), 80–7.

Krasnegor, N. A., Rumbaugh, D. M., Schiefelbusch, R. L. & Studdert-Kennedy, M. (eds.) (1991). *Biological and behavioral determinants of language development.* Hillsdale, NJ: Lawrence Erlbaum.

Krauss, M. (1992). The world's languages in crisis. *Language*, 68, 4–10.

Kuhl, P. T. (1987). The special-mechanisms debate in speech research: categorization tests on animals and infants. In S. Harnad (ed.), *Categorical perception: The groundwork of cognition*. Cambridge University Press.

Lakoff, G. (1991). Cognitive versus generative linguistics: how commitments influence results. *Language and Communication*, 11, 53–62.

Lakoff, G. & Johnson, M. (1980). *Metaphors we live by.* Chicago University Press.

Lakoff, G. & Turner, M. (1989). *More than cool reason: A field guide to poetic metaphor*. Chicago University Press.

Landau, B. & Jackendoff, R. (1993). 'What' and 'where' in spatial language and spatial cognition. *Behavioral and Brain Sciences*, 16, 217–65. (Includes peer commentary.)

Lane, H. (ed.) (1984). *The deaf experience: Classics in language and education.* Cambridge, MA: Harvard University Press. (Trans. Franklin Philip)

Laver, J. (1994). *Principles of phonetics.* Cambridge University Press.

Leakey, R. (1994). *The origins of humankind.* London: Weidenfeld and Nicolson.

Lecours, A. R. & Joanette, Y. (1980). Linguistic and other aspects of paroxysmal aphasia. *Brain and Language*, 10, 1–23.

Lenneberg, E. H. (ed.) (1967). *Biological foundations of language.* New York: Wiley.

Lerdahl, F. & Jackendoff, R. (1983). *A generative theory of tonal music.* Cambridge, MA: MIT Press.

Lester, B. M. & Boukydis, C. F. (1992). No language but a cry. In Papousek, Jürgens & Papousek (1992).

Lewin, R. (1993). *The origin of modern humans.* New York: Scientific American Library.

Li, C. N. & Thompson, S. A. (1976). Subject and topic: a new typology of language. In C. N. Li (ed.), *Subject and topic.* New York: Academic Press.

Liberman, A. M., Harris, K. S., Hoffman, H. S. & Griffith, B. C. (1957). The discrimination of speech sounds within and across phoneme boundaries. *Journal of Experimental Psychology*, 54, 358–68.

Lieberman, P. (1984). *The biology and evolution of language.* Cambridge, MA: Harvard University Press.

(1991). *Uniquely human: The evolution of speech, thought and selfless behavior.* Cambridge, MA: Harvard University Press.

(1992). On the evolution of human language. In Hawkins & Gell-Mann (1992).

Liem, K. F. (1988). Form and function of lungs: the evolution of air breathing mechanisms. *American Zoologist*, 28, 739–59.

Lindblom, B., MacNeilage, P. F. & Studdert-Kennedy, M. (1984). Self-organizing processes and the explanation of phonological universals. In Butterworth, Comrie & Dahl (1984).

Locke, J. (1690/1975). *An essay concerning human understanding* (ed. P. H. Nidditch). Oxford: Clarendon Press.

Locke, J. L. (1993). *The child's path to spoken language.* Cambridge, MA: Harvard University Press.

(1995). Development of the capacity for spoken language. In P. Fletcher & B. MacWhinney (eds.), *The handbook of child language.* Oxford: Blackwell.

Lorenz, K. (1950/1977). *Man meets dog* (Trans. Marjorie Kerr Wilson). London: Methuen. (Originally published as *So kam der Mensch auf den Hund*, Wien: Borotha-Schoeler. This translation first published 1954.)

Lyons, J. (1977). *Semantics* (vol. II). Cambridge University Press.

(1988). Origins of language. In A. C. Fabian (ed.), *Origins*. Cambridge University Press.

(1989). Semantic ascent. In Arnold et al. (1989).

Mackay, A. L. (ed.). (1991). *A dictionary of scientific quotations*. Bristol: IOP Publishing.

MacNeilage, P. F. (1991). The 'postural origins' theory of primate neurobiological asymmetries. In Krasnegor et al. (1991).

MacNeilage, P. F., Studdert-Kennedy, M. G. & Lindblom, B. (1987). Primate handedness reconsidered. *Behavioral and Brain Sciences*, 10, 247–303.

Maddieson, I. (1984). *Patterns of sounds*. Cambridge University Press.

Malinowski, B. (1935). *The language and magic of gardening*. London: Allen & Unwin.

Mallinson, G. & Blake, B. J. (1981). *Language typology*. Amsterdam: North Holland.

Marantz, A. (1982). Re reduplication. *Linguistic Inquiry*, 13, 483–545.

Maratsos, M. (1992). Constraints, modules, and domain specificity: an introduction. In M. R. Gunnar & M. Maratsos (eds.), *Modularity and constraints in language and cognition*. The Minnesota Symposia on Child Psychology: 25. Hillsdale, NJ: Lawrence Erlbaum.

Marler, P. (1976). Social organization, communication and graded signals: the chimpanzee and the gorilla. In P. P. G. Bateson & R. A. Hinde (eds.), *Growing points in ethology*. Cambridge University Press.

(1991a). Differences in behavioural development in closely related species: birdsong. In P. Bateson (ed.), *The development and integration of behaviour*. Cambridge University Press.

(1991b). The instinct to learn. In Carey & Gelman (1991).

Marler, P., Evans, C. S. & Hauser, M. D. (1992). Animal signals: motivational, referential or both? In Papousek, Jürgens & Papousek (1992).

Marshall, J. C. (1987). Review of Savage-Rumbaugh (1986). *Nature*, 325, 310.

Marslen-Wilson, W. D. (1989). Access and integration: projecting sound on to meaning. In W. D. Marslen-Wilson (ed.), *Lexical representation and process*. Cambridge, MA: MIT Press.

Matthews, J. (ed.). (1994). *Linguistic aspects of familial language impairment*. McGill Working Papers in Linguistics: 10. Montreal: McGill University.

Mayr, E. (1991/1993). *One long argument: Charles Darwin and the genesis of modern evolutionary thought.* London: Penguin.

McDonald, J. L., Bock, J. K. & Kelly, M. H. (1993). Word and world order: semantic, phonological and metrical determinants of serial position. *Cognitive Psychology*, 25, 188–230.

McShane, J. (1980). *Learning to talk.* Cambridge University Press.

Medin, D. L., Ahn, W.-K., Bettger, J., Florian, J., Goldstone, R., Lassaline, M., Markman, A., Rubinstein, J. & Wisniewski, E. (1990). Safe takeoffs - soft landings. *Cognitive Science*, 14, 169–78.

Mehler, J., Jusczyk, P., Lambertz, G., Halsted, N., Bertoncini, J. & Amiel-Tison, C. (1988). A precursor of language acquisition in young infants. *Cognition*, 29, 143–78.

Meillet, A. (1912/1948). *Linguistique historique et linguistique générale.* Paris: Champion.

Mellars, P. (1993). Archaeology and modern human origins in Europe. *Proceedings of the British Academy*, 82, 1–35.

Merton, D. V., Morris, R. B. & Atkinson, I. A. E. (1984). Lek behavior in a parrot – the kakapo strigops-habroptilus of New Zealand. *Ibis*, 126, 277.

Mihalic, F. (1971). *The Jacaranda dictionary and grammar of Melanesian pidgin.* Milton, Queensland, Australia: The Jacaranda Press.

Miller, G. A. & Fellbaum, C. (1991). Semantic networks of English. *Cognition*, 41, 197–229.

Miller, J. & Jusczyk, P. W. (1990). Seeking the neurobiological basis of speech perception. In P. D. Eimas & A. M. Galaburda (eds.), *Neurobiology of cognition.* Cambridge, MA: MIT Press. (Originally published 1989 in *Cognition* 33, 111–37)

Milroy, J. & Milroy, L. (1991). *Authority in language: Investigating language prescription and standardization* (2nd edn). London: Routledge.

Mithun, M. (1984). The evolution of noun incorporation. *Language*, 60, 847–94.

   (1988). Lexical categories and the evolution of number marking. In M. Hammond & M. Noonan (eds.), *Theoretical morphology: Approaches to modern linguistics.* New York: Academic Press.

   (1992). Is basic word order universal? In D. L. Payne (ed.), *Pragmatics of word order flexibility.* Amsterdam: John Benjamins.

   (1995). The legacy of recycled aspect. Paper presented at the International Congress of Historical Linguistics, University of Manchester, August 1995.

Mithun, M. & Chafe, W. L. (1979). Recapturing the Mohawk language.

In T. Shopen (ed.), *Languages and their status*. Cambridge, MA: Winthrop.

Molfese, D. L. & Morse, P. A. (1991). Developmental changes in nonhuman primate patterns of brain lateralization for the perception of speech cues: neuroelectrical correlates. In Krasnegor et al. (1991).

Morelli, R. & Brown, M. (1992). Computational models of cognition. In R. Morelli, W. M. Brown, D. Anselmi, K. Haberlandt & D. Lloyd (eds.), *Minds, brains and computers*. Norwood, NJ: Ablex.

Morris, D. (1967). *The naked ape*. London: Jonathan Cape.

Mühlhäusler, P. (1979). *Growth and structure of the lexicon of New Guinea Pidgin*. Pacific Linguistics: C-52. Canberra: Australian National University.

(1985). Syntax of Tok Pisin. In S. A. Wurm & P. Mühlhäusler (eds.), *Handbook of Tok Pisin (New Guinea Pidgin)* Pacific Linguistics: C-70. Canberra: Australian National University.

(1986). *Pidgin and creole linguistics*. Oxford: Basil Blackwell.

Muysken, P. (1981). Creole tense/mood/aspect systems: the unmarked case? In P. Muysken (ed.), *Generative studies on creole languages*. Dordrecht: Foris.

Nei, M. & Roychoudhury, A. K. (1993). Evolutionary relationships of human populations on a global scale. *Molecular Biology and Evolution*, 10, 927–43.

Nerlich, B. (1990). *Change in language: Whitney, Bréal and Wegener*. London: Routledge.

Newmeyer, F. J. (1991). Functional explanations in linguistics and the origins of language. *Language and Communication*, 11, 3–28.

(1992). Iconicity and generative grammar. *Language*, 68, 756–96.

Newport, E. (1990). Maturational constraints on language learning. *Cognitive Science*, 14, 11–28.

(1991). Contrasting conceptions of the critical period for language. In Carey & Gelman (1991).

Nichols, J. (1986). Head-marking and dependent-marking grammar. *Language*, 62, 56–119.

(1990). Linguistic diversity and the first settlement of the New World. *Language*, 66, 475–521.

(1992). *Linguistic diversity in space and time*. University of Chicago Press.

Noonan, M. (1988). Review of Tomlin (1986). *Language*, 64, 196–7.

Nottebohm, F. (1975). A zoologist's view of some language phenomena with particular emphasis on vocal learning. In E. H. Lenneberg &

E. Lenneberg (eds.), *Foundations of language development* (vol. I). New York: Academic Press.

Ortony, A. (ed.) (1993). *Metaphor and thought* (2nd edn). Cambridge University Press.

Orwell, G. (1946/1962). Politics and the English language. In G. Orwell, *Inside the whale and other essays*. Harmondsworth: Penguin.

Owren, M. J., Seyfarth, R. M. & Hopp, S. L. (1992). Categorical verbal signaling in nonhuman primates. In Papousek, Jürgens & Papousek (1992).

Palmer, F. (1994). *Grammatical roles and relations*. Cambridge University Press.

Papousek, H., Jürgens, U. & Papousek, M. (eds.). (1992). *Nonverbal vocal communication: Comparative and developmental approaches*. Cambridge University Press.

Passingham, R. E. (1982). *The human primate*. San Francisco, CA: Freeman.

Payne, D. L. (1992a). Introduction. In Payne (1992b).

  (ed.). (1992b). *Pragmatics of word order flexibility*. Amsterdam: John Benjamins.

Petersen, M. R. (1982). The perception of species-specific vocalization in primates: a conceptual framework. In Snowdon, Brown & Petersen (1982).

Petitto, L. A. & Marentette, P. F. (1991). Babbling in the manual mode: evidence for the ontogeny of language. *Science*, 251, 1493–6.

Piatelli-Palmarini, M. (1989). Evolution, selection and cognition: from 'learning' to parameter setting in biology and in the study of language. *Cognition*, 31, 1–44.

Pinker, S. (1994). *The language instinct: The new science of language and mind*. London: Penguin; New York: Morrow.

Pinker, S. & Bloom, P. (1990). Natural language and natural selection. *Behavioral and Brain Sciences*, 13, 707–84. (Includes peer commentary.)

Pinker, S. (1994). *The language instinct*. New York: Morrow, London: Penguin.

Ploog, D. W. (1992). The evolution of vocal communication. In Papousek, Jürgens & Papousek (1992).

Plunkett, K. (1995). Connectionist approaches to language acquisition. In P. Fletcher & B. MacWhinney (eds.), *The handbook of child language*. Cambridge University Press.

Posner, M. I. & Raichle, M. E. (1994). *Images of mind*. New York: Scientific American Library.

Pullum, G. K. (1991). *The great Eskimo vocabulary hoax and other irreverent essays on the study of language.* University of Chicago Press.

Radford, A. (1988). *Transformational grammar: A first course.* Cambridge University Press.

Raj, K. S. (1990). Application of Grice's maxims in Kannada: a note. *CIEFL Occasional Papers in Linguistics,* 2, 92–9.

Rapoport, J. (1990). *The boy who couldn't stop washing: The experience and treatment of obsessive–compulsive disorder.* London: Fontana/Collins.

Rée, J. (1999). *I see a voice: A philosophical history of language, deafness and the senses.* London: HarperCollins.

Rhodes, R. (1994). Aural images. In Hinton, Nichols & Ohala (1994b).

Ridley, M. (1993). *Evolution.* Oxford: Blackwell Scientific.

Rizzi, L. (1986). Null objects in Italian and the theory of *pro. Linguistic Inquiry,* 17, 501–57.

Robins, R. H. (1952). Noun and verb in universal grammar. *Language,* 28, 289–98.

Romaine, S. (1988). *Pidgin and creole languages.* London: Longman.

Rosner, B. S. (1995). Musical intervals, scales of pitch, and vowel phonetics. Ms., Phonetics Laboratory, University of Oxford.

Ross, P. E. (1991). Hard words. *Scientific American,* 264(4), 70–9.

Rousseau, J. J. (1852/1966). On the origin of languages. In J. H. Moran & A. Gode (Eds.), *On the origin of language* (essays by Rousseau and Herder, translated, with afterwords, by John H. Moran and Alexander Gode). Chicago and London: University of Chicago Press.

Ruhlen, M. (1987). *A guide to the world's languages* (vol. I: *Classification*). Stanford University Press.

  (1992). An overview of genetic classification. In Hawkins & Gell-Mann (1992).

  (1994). *On the origin of languages: Studies in linguistic taxonomy.* Stanford University Press.

Rymer, R. (1993). *Genie: Escape from a silent childhood.* London: Michael Joseph.

Sacks, O. (1989/1991). *Seeing voices.* London: Picador. (First published by University of California Press, Berkeley)

  (1995). *An anthropologist on Mars.* London: Picador.

Salmons, J. (1992). A look at the data for a global etymology: **tik* 'finger'. In G. W. Davis & G. K. Iverson (eds.), *Explanation in historical linguistics.* Amsterdam and Philadelphia: John Benjamins.

Sapir, E. (1921). *Language.* New York: Harcourt, Brace and World.

(1929/1949). *Selected writings in language, culture and personality* (ed. D. G. Mandelbaum). Berkeley: University of California Press.

Savage-Rumbaugh, E. S. & Lewin, R. (1994). *Kanzi: The ape at the brink of the human mind.* New York: Doubleday.

Savage-Rumbaugh, E. S., Murphy, J., Sevcik, R. A., Brakke, K. E., Williams, S. L. & Rumbaugh, D. M. (1993). *Language comprehension in ape and child.* (With commentary by Elizabeth Bates and a reply by E. Sue Savage-Rumbaugh.) Monographs of the Society for Research in Child Development: 58.

Schachter, P. (1985). Parts-of-speech systems. In T. Shopen (1985a).

Scherer, K. R. (1992). Vocal affect expression as symptom, symbol and appeal. In Papousek, Jürgens & Papousek (1992).

Sebeok, T. A. (1965). Animal communication. *Science*, 147, 1006–14.

Seyfarth, R. M. & Cheney, D. L. (1986). Vocal development in vervet monkeys. *Animal Behaviour*, 34, 1640–58.

Seyfarth, R. M., Cheney, D. L. & Marler, P. (1980a). Monkey responses to three different alarm calls: evidence for predator classification and semantic communication. *Science*, 210, 801–3.

(1980b). Vervet monkey alarm calls: semantic communication in a free-ranging primate. *Animal Behavior*, 28, 1070–94.

Shallice, T. (1984). More functionally isolable subsystems, but fewer modules. *Cognition*, 17, 243–52.

(1988). *From neuropsychology to mental structure.* Cambridge University Press.

Shettleworth, S. J. (1975). Reinforcement and the organisation of behavior in golden hamsters: hunger, environment and food reinforcement. *Journal of Experimental Psychology: Animal Behavior Processes*, 1, 56–87.

Shopen, T. (ed.). (1985a, b, c). *Language typology and syntactic description* (vol. I: *Clause structure*, vol. II: *Complex constructions*, vol. III: *Grammatical categories and the lexicon*). Cambridge University Press.

Simon, J. (1981). *Paradigms lost.* London: Chatto & Windus.

Singler, J. V. (ed.) (1990). *Pidgin and creole tense–mood–aspect systems.* Amsterdam: John Benjamins.

Slaughter, M. M. (1982). *Universal languages and scientific taxonomy in the seventeenth century.* Cambridge University Press.

Slobin, D. I. (1985). Crosslinguistic evidence for the language-making capacity. In D. I. Slobin (ed.), *The crosslinguistic study of language acquisition.* Hillsdale, NJ: Lawrence Erlbaum.

Small, M. F. (1994). Ay up, a chimp wi' an accent. *New Scientist* (4 June), 33–7.

Smith, N. V. & Tsimpli, I. A. (1991). Linguistic modularity? A case study of a 'Savant' linguist. *Lingua*, 84, 315–51.

(1995). *The mind of a savant: Language learning and modularity*. Oxford: Blackwell.

Snowden, C. T., Brown, C. H. & Petersen, M. R. (eds.) (1982). *Primate communication*. Cambridge University Press.

Spock, B. (1968). *Baby and child care revised*. New York: Pocket Books.

Springer, S. P. & Deutsch, G. (1993). *Left brain, right brain* (4th edn). New York: W. H. Freeman.

Studdert-Kennedy, M. (1991). Language development from an evolutionary perspective. In Krasnegor et al. (1991).

Sussman, H. M. (1989). Neural coding of relational invariance in speech: human language analogs to the barn owl. *Psychological Review*, 96, 631–42.

Sutton, D. (1979). Mechanisms underlying learned vocal control in primates. In H. D. Steklis & M. J. Raleigh (eds.), *Neurobiology of social control in primates: An evolutionary perspective*. New York: Academic Press.

Swadesh, M. (1939). Nootka internal syntax. *International Journal of American Linguistics*, 9, 77–102.

Sweetser, E. E. (1990). *From etymology to pragmatics: Metaphorical and cultural aspects of semantic structure*. Cambridge University Press.

Swift, J. (1726–1952). *Gulliver's travels*. London: Dent.

Symmes, D. & Biben, M. (1992). Vocal development in nonhuman primates. In Papousek, Jürgens & Papousek (1992).

Tannen, D. (1989). *Talking voices: Repetition, dialogue and imagery in conversational discourse*. Cambridge University Press.

Tennant, N. (1984). Intentionality and the evolution of language. In C. Hookuray (ed.), *Minds, machines and evolution*. Cambridge University Press.

Terrace, H. S. (1979). *Nim*. New York: Knopf.

Thelen, E. (1991). Motor aspects of emergent speech: a dynamic approach. In Krasnegor et al. (1991).

Thomason, S. G. & Kaufman, T. (1988). *Language contact, creolization and genetic linguistics*. Berkeley: University of California Press.

Thorne, A. G. & Wolpoff, M. H. (1992). The multiregional evolution of humans. *Scientific American*, 266(4), 28–33.

Todd, P. & Aitchison, J. (1980). Learning language the hard way. *First Language*, 1, 122–40.

Tomlin, R. S. (1986). *Basic word order: Functional principles*. London: Croom Helm.

Traugott, E. C. & Heine, B. (1991). *Approaches to grammaticalization* (vol. I). Amsterdam: John Benjamins.

van Cleve, J. V. (ed.) (1987). *Gallaudet encyclopaedia of deaf people and deafness.* New York: McGraw Hill.

Vargha-Khadem, F., Watkins, K., Alcock, K., Fletcher, P. & Passingham, R. (1995). Praxic and nonverbal cognitive deficits in a large family with a genetically transmitted speech and language disorder. *Proceedings of the National Academy of Science USA,* 92, 930–3.

Vincent, N. (1993). Head- versus dependent-marking: the case of the clause. In G. G. Corbett, N. M. Fraser & S. McGlashan (eds.), *Heads in grammatical theory.* Cambridge University Press.

Wallman, J. (1992). *Aping language.* Cambridge University Press.

Wang, W. S. Y. (1982). *Explorations in language evolution. Osmania Papers in Linguistics:* 8 (Supplement). Hyderabad: Osmania University Department of Linguistics.

Wavell, S. (1995). The almighty muddle from 4m years BC. *Sunday Times,* 20 August 1995.

Weiner, J. (1994). *The beak of the finch.* London: Cape.

Weizenbaum, J. (1976/1984). *Computer power and human reason.* London: Pelican. (First published by Freeman, New York)

Wells, G. A. (1987). *The origin of language: Aspects of the discussion from Condillac to Wundt.* La Salle, IL: Open Court.

Wesson, W. (1991). *Beyond natural selection.* Cambridge, MA: MIT Press.

White, R. (1985). Thoughts on social relationships and language in hominid evolution. *Journal of Social and Personal Relationships,* 2, 95–115.

White, T. D., Suwa, G. & Asfaw, B. (1994). *Australopithecus ramidus,* a new species of early hominid from Aramis, Ethiopia. *Nature,* 371, 306–12.

Whitney, W. D. (1893). *Oriental and linguistic studies* (vol. I). New York: Charles Scribner's Sons.

Whorf, B. L. (1956). *Language, thought and reality: Selected writings of Benjamin Lee Whorf* (ed. J. B. Carroll). Cambridge, MA: MIT Press.

Wilson, A. C. & Cann, R. L. (1992). The recent African genesis of humans. *Scientific American,* 266(4), 22–7.

Wind, J. (1983). Primate evolution and the emergence of speech. In E. de Grolier, A. Lock, C. R. Peters & J. Wind (eds.), *Glossogenetics: The origin and evolution of language.* Chur: Harwood.

Wittgenstein, L. (1958). *Philosophical investigations* (2nd edn, trans. G. E. M. Anscombe). Oxford: Blackwell.

Woolford, E. (1979). The developing complementizer system in Tok Pisin. In K. C. Hill (ed.), *The genesis of language*. Ann Arbor: Karoma.

Wurm, S. A. & Mühlhäusler, P. (eds.) (1985). *Handbook of Tok Pisin (New Guinea Pidgin)*. Pacific Linguistics: C-70. Canberra: Australian National University.

Wynn, K. & Bloom, P. (1992). The origins of psychological axioms of arithmetic and geometry. *Language and Mind, 7*, 409–16.

Yaguello, M. (1984/1991). *Lunatic lovers of language: Imaginary languages and their inventors*. London: Athlone. (Originally *Les fous du langage: des langues imaginaires et de leurs inventeurs*. Paris: Editions du Seuil.

Yamada, J. L. (1990). *Laura: A case for the modularity of language*. Cambridge, MA: MIT Press.

Index

men v. women, 218ff
Menozzi, P., 239n
Merrifield, W. R., 242n
Merton, D. V., 224n
metaphor, 124ff, 236n
Mihalic, F., 236n, 238n
Miller, G. A., 235n
Miller, J., 231n
Milligan, Spike, 223n
Milne, A. A., 240n, 241n
Milroy, J., 226n
Milroy, L., 226n
Minch, E., 239n
mind, theory of, 69, 229n
mindblindness, 69
mind-set, human, 118ff, 123, 128, 218
Miskito Coast Creole English, 134
Miskitu Indians, 161
Mithun, M., 226n, 236n, 239n, 240n
mitochondrial DNA, 58, 163
modularity, 43ff, 201, 227n
Mohawk, 26
Molfese, D. L., 231n
Monboddo, James Burnett Lord, 4
Mongolian, 168
monkeys
  chinchilla, 79
  macaque, 79ff
  rhesus, 79, 88
  squirrel, 79, 96
  vervet, 79, 96
mood, 136, 139f, 237n
Morelli, R., 243n
Morey, R., 235n
Moriarty, J., 229n
morphology, 203, 207
Morris, D., 225n, 226n, 229n
Morris, R. B., 224n
Morse, P. A., 231n

mosaic view of evolution, 14
Mountain, J., 239n
Mühlhäusler, P., 224n, 237n, 238n
Müller, F. Max, 17, 99, 234n, 224n
Murphy, J., 231n
music and language, 234n
Muysken, P., 224n, 237n

naming insight, 94ff, 109, 215
nasals, 183
natural selection, 53, 212
nature/nurture debate, 31
Neandertal (Neanderthal), 163, 238n
negatives, 206
Nei, M., 239n
neoteny, 91, 232n
Nerlich, B., 224n, 225n
Neurath, Otto, 237n
Newmeyer, F. J., 243n
Newnham, D., 233n
Newport, E., 234n
Newspeak, 29
Nichols, Johanna, 164, 169, 171ff, 234n, 238n, 239n, 241n
Niger-Kordofanian, 169
Nilo-Saharan, 169
Nim Chimpsky, 113ff
Nodier, Charles, 93, 233n
Noonan, M., 236n
Nootka, 112, 177ff
Nostratic, 168
Nottebohm, F., 223n, 224n
noun incorporation, 120
noun phrase accessibility, 196
nouns, 109, 111, 132ff, 177
number, 194

obsessive–compulsive disorder, 29